What a remarkable example of a determined father who bravely resisted the forces of anarchy while fighting the legal battles to assure equal treatment for all his fellow citizens, as seen through the eyes of his precious daughters!

—ALBERT P. BREWER
Former Governor of Alabama

Various people including me have written of the everlasting landmark civil rights cases fought and won by Arthur Shores. This new book reveals, ever so poignantly, the tolls that those victories often exacted on him and his family. Friends of civil rights across the nation are indebted to the daughters of Mr. Shores for having shared these sometimes awesome, sometimes delightful, experiences with us in *The Gentle Giant of Dynamite Hill*. It is a "must read" for those committed to the cause.

—U. W. CLEMSON, Civil rights lawyer
and Alabama's first black Federal Judge

I have seldom read a book that left me both so deeply pessimistic and so hopeful. Depressed because a provoked, repressed minority sometimes jettisoned the Sermon on the Mount for a gospel of vengeance and retaliation. Depressed because an oppressive majority that proclaimed their city to be the nation's "Sunday School Capital" and who vowed that their favorite pastime was reading the Bible so obviously learned little about Christ from either source. Depressed because a white Christian society produced a small cadre of violent terrorists and a huge silent majority that tolerated their excesses.

And hopeful because one man steered both his family and his community toward righteousness, forgiveness, and nonviolence by his fervent Christian faith and his incredible personal courage.

—WAYNE FLYNT
Distinguished University Professor
of History Emeritus, Auburn University

Attorney Arthur Shores used the law to change the segregation practices of Birmingham and Alabama. This book is a family memoir as well as a history of a turbulent time and growing up in a segregated city. It will be of interest to lawyers, social historians, and general readers. In essence, it is a fitting tribute to Arthur Shores, the authors' Daddy, who was "a strong and brave advocate, a gentleman at the law, but a lawyer who got results for his clients." He helped to change Alabama for the better.

—SAMUEL A. RUMORE, JR.
Former President, Alabama State Bar
Chairman, Alabama Lawyers' Hall of Fame

Arthur Shores was a lawyer's lawyer. When I was indicted by the Montgomery County Grand Jury in 1956, Shores was one of the attorneys who represented me and caused the indictment to be dismissed. His daughters and Denise George have done an excellent job of telling not only the life and work of their father, but also how his life affected their lives and many others, including me. I highly recommend this book.

—FRED D. GRAY, Attorney

I knew Mr. Arthur D. Shores all of my life. I first met him as a child attending Sunday school at the First Congregational Church. Mr. Shores was a member of the Trustee Board and taught the adult Sunday school class. He was a dynamic lawyer and a great person. He had attended Talladega College at the same time as my mother. Mr. Shores was one of my mentors and a great person to emulate.

The book is a very accurate and in-depth portrayal of the life of Arthur Davis Shores. It will make a great study for any high school or college student thinking about careers in the practice of law.

—J. MASON DAVIS, JR.
Senior Partner, Sirote and Permutt, P.C.,
Birmingham

THE GENTLE GIANT OF DYNAMITE HILL

THE UNTOLD STORY OF ARTHUR SHORES AND HIS FAMILY'S FIGHT FOR CIVIL RIGHTS

HELEN SHORES LEE & BARBARA S. SHORES
WITH DENISE GEORGE

ZONDERVAN.com/
AUTHORTRACKER
follow your favorite authors

ZONDERVAN

The Gentle Giant of Dynamite Hill
Copyright © 2012 by Helen Shores Lee and Barbara S. Shores

This title is also available as a Zondervan ebook. Visit www.zondervan.com/ebooks.

This title is also available in a Zondervan audio edition. Visit www.zondervan.fm.

Requests for information should be addressed to:

Zondervan, *Grand Rapids, Michigan 49530*

Library of Congress Cataloging-in-Publication Data

Lee, Helen Shores, 1941-
    The gentle giant of Dynamite Hill : the untold story of Arthur Shores
and his family's fight for civil rights / Helen Shores Lee and Barbara S. Shores ;
with Denise George.
      p. cm.
    ISBN 978-0-310-33620-4
    1. Shores, Arthur D. (Arthur Davis), 1904-1996. 2. African American lawyers
—Alabama—Birmingham—Biography. 3. Civil rights workers—Alabama—Birmingham
—Biography. 4. Civil rights movements—Alabama—Birmingham—History—20th
century. 5. African Americans—Civil rights—Alabama—Birmingham—History—20th
century. 6. Birmingham (Ala.)—Race relations—History—20th century. 7. Birmingham
(Ala.)—Biography. I. Shores, Barbara, 1945- II. George, Denise. III. Title.
F334.B653.S465   2012
323.092—dc23
[B]   2012010595

Published in association with the literary agency of WordServe Literary Group, Ltd.,
10152 S. Knoll Circle, Highlands Ranch, CO 80130.

Cover design: James Hall
Cover photography: © Bettmann / Corbis / AP Images / Graphic Mania
Interior design: Beth Shagene
Interior photography: provided by author unless otherwise noted
Interior photography background: James Hall / Graphic Mania

Printed in the United States of America

12 13 14 15 16 17 18 /DCI/ 22 21 20 19 18 17 16 15 14 13 12 11 10 9 8 7 6 5 4 3 2 1

For Mummee and Daddy,
and our children and grandchildren

Contents

Foreword

They called Stephen Douglas, who famously debated Abraham Lincoln, the "Little Giant," but that sobriquet is better suited to Arthur Davis Shores, who stared down Jim Crow segregation in his native Alabama and won a great victory for his nation. His story is at last and lovingly told by his daughters, Helen Shores Lee and Barbara Sylvia Shores. The story they tell is accurate and balanced, but it has the added value of firsthand memory of the man and his times. It is also the story of their "Mummee," Theodora Helen Warren Shores, his life mate, who endured the bomb blasts and kept her eyes on the prize her husband worked so hard to win. So it is the story of a family that both encouraged and experienced the greatest social transformation in American history.

Arthur Shores could be called the "Little Giant" for the same reason as was Douglas: he was short of stature but long on accomplishment. He was a handsome man, and as I once described him, a darker version of Errol Flynn, complete with a pencil moustache. Although he took on the most vexing cases of civil rights in a state determined to maintain white supremacy at any cost, he was forever calm, the eye of the storm of change. In what many called the most segregated state in America, he was the architect of the legal challenge to segregation: from "equity pay" for teachers (meaning African American teachers should earn the same as whites), to voting rights, and finally to equal public accommodations.

His greatest triumph came with the desegregation of the University of Alabama. On that June day in 1963, Alabama became the last state to maintain a vestige of legal segregation, although it was the first state ordered to desegregate under *Brown v. Board of Education*. It was Arthur Shores, aided by Thurgood Marshall and Constance Mobley of the NAACP Legal Defense Fund, who won the right for Autherine Lucy and her friend Pollie Anne Myers to become the first African American students at the University of Alabama. Although their rights were denied by violence at the university and intransigence by the university's trustees, Shores would ultimately win out when Vivian Malone and James Hood walked past George Wallace at the schoolhouse door. It was Shores's most gratifying victory.

But Shores's aim was always to win, not conquer. While he enjoyed watching white lawyers squirm as they tried to fit constitutional equality into the procrustean bed of racial politics, Shores remained composed. He knew he would win if the law were constitutionally applied, and increasingly it was. Shores could get along with anyone, even George Wallace, the state's and the nation's chief champion of segregation. Described in this book is a scene where Wallace, as a judge before becoming governor, invites Shores to have lunch with him in chambers because Jim Crow facilities made it impossible for the Little Giant to eat elsewhere. Shores understood the changeable side of the white South, even of George Wallace; and when it was all over, Wallace spent the rest of his days asking for forgiveness, which black Alabamians gave in full measure even if they could not forget.

Shores would go on in 1968 to become the first black city councilman in the South's most segregated city, Birmingham, thus fulfilling another political dream. He would serve until 1978, when he took a much-deserved retirement from paying civic rent. He would also earn an honorary doctorate from the University of Alabama in 1975, and this writer, in the early 1990s, had the honor of commissioning a portrait of him for the university's main library, where today he smiles down on a grandson, Damien Larkin, who is completing a doctorate.

What the daughters have accomplished in this book is the portrait of a Giant, no qualifiers needed.

E. CULPEPPER CLARK, Dean
Henry W. Grady School of Journalism and
Mass Communication, University of Georgia

To Daddy

There's joy in our hearts, Daddy, knowing you set a fine example as you patiently taught us your lessons of life.

You taught us to be strong enough to cope with disappointments and hard times, and strong enough to live with any weakness we may have.

You taught us courage—to be brave enough to do what we believe is right—to know that fear is natural, but not to let it stop us from doing what we must.

You taught us the value of knowledge so that we would be prepared to make decisions, big and small—so that when we made mistakes, we would try to learn from them and then go on from there.

But most of all, you taught us about love by setting an example with your own gentleness and openness and warmth.

You enriched our lives forever with your lessons and your love ...

And we thank you from the bottom of our hearts. Helen and Barbara

> (Written by Helen Shores Lee and Barbara Sylvia Shores on Friday, December 20, 1996, on the Obituary Order of Service of Arthur Davis Shores)

The LORD is my light and my salvation—
whom shall I fear?
The LORD is the stronghold of my life—
of whom shall I be afraid?

(PSALM 27:1)

Acknowledgments

Writing and publishing a book take a team of people. We want to offer our sincere gratitude to the people who helped us in so many ways with this exciting project. Our deepest appreciation to the skilled team at Zondervan, including John Sloan, Jim Ruark, Londa Alderink, Kim Tanner, Don Gates, Joyce Ondersma, Sarah Johnson, Beth Shagene, and Elizabeth Yoder. You have made working on this book a delight and joy for us!

Thank you to our book agent, Greg Johnson, with the Word Serve Literary Agency. You have offered us much helpful advice and teamed us with a great publisher.

For support and practical help, thank you to Yvonne Hill (Judge Lee's secretary), Sandy Brinson (Beeson Divinity School), Voncille C. Williams (*Birmingham News*), Laura Anderson (Birmingham's *Civil Rights Institute*), and Jim Baggett (*Birmingham Public Library*).

For those who granted us personal interviews, a special thank you to Richard Pizitz, Bishop Calvin Woods, and Karl Friedman, Esq.

To all those wonderful people who encouraged us and prayed for us during the entire length of this project, our great appreciation.

And to all our family members who helped and supported us in so many ways, we offer our deepest gratitude and love.

CHAPTER 1

"Why, Daddy?"

1953, at our home on Birmingham's
Center Street on "Dynamite Hill"

(Helen remembers.)

Daddy, why is it legal for someone to harass us,
but *not* legal for us to respond back to them?
—HELEN SHORES LEE, 12,
Birmingham, Alabama, 1953

I can still recall the *pinging* sound bullets made when someone in a passing car shot the window in our recreation room. The thick glass usually prevented the window from shattering, but the bullets would pierce through and lodge in our interior walls. Each bullet made its mark—a small hole through the glass—and each bullet brought our mother fresh new fear.

In 1953 I was twelve years old, living with my father, mother, and younger sister, Barbara, in Birmingham, Alabama, an old steel-producing city and the hotbed of racial injustice and violence in the United States. Shortly after World War II, the invisible line that supposedly divided black homeowners from white homeowners began to blur. Black residents built their homes a little too close to the white community, and the white-sheeted Ku Klux Klan tried to scare black residents from the area by bombing their homes. Our neighborhood had had so many unsolved, Klan-related bombings that people dubbed our street "Dynamite Hill," yet none of these bombers ever faced arrest or punishment.

Our ranch-style brick house had a good-sized grassy front yard, a fenced-in backyard for Barbara's beloved dogs, and a large thick picture window in our living room and recreation room facing Center Street. In the evenings my dad, mother, sister, and I often sat in the recreation room together and watched television. If it was a Saturday night, together we enjoyed my dad's favorite meal, hot dogs with mustard and fresh-squeezed lemonade. *Every* Saturday night!

On this particular night, however, our family sat outside on the front porch. It was unusually quiet, except for the sounds of crickets and a few cars passing by every now and then. Then the roar of an engine cut through the night air as a car filled with angry white youth raced down the hill toward our house.

A Legal Pioneer

For years, our mother, whom we lovingly called "Mummee," had begged Daddy to move us far away from Alabama and its unjust Jim Crow laws that segregated black and white people, away from white officials who responded with physical violence when anyone challenged their humiliating laws. But our dad, born and reared in Alabama, was committed to stay and help the state's black people in spite of the Klan's constant threats of violence to him. In all their years together, my mom lost only one major argument to my dad, whom she affectionately called "Shores," and that was refusing to move our family to Michigan as she requested.

Our father, Arthur Davis Shores, had studied hard and passed the Alabama Bar exam in 1937. He was not the first black man to pass the Alabama Bar Exam, but for a long time, he was the only *practicing* black attorney in the state of Alabama.* As one author

---

*Preceding our dad were Alabama black attorneys Moses Wenslydale Moore (1871), James Thomas Rapier (1872), Roderick B. Thomas (1876), Samuel R. Lowry (1875), John Henry Ballou (1891), P. L. M. Watkins (1881) and others, including William Hooper Councill, Thomas A. Harris, William Francis Crockett, Wilford Horace Smith, Luther Chambliss, Edward Austin Brown, and Nathan B. Young. Many were threatened, arrested, assaulted, and "run out of town." Following our father's admittance to the Alabama Bar in 1937 was Arthur H. Madison in 1938. "The filing of civil rights cases by black lawyers in Alabama was still a dangerous activity at that time, and for a good amount of time since," according to J. Clay Smith Jr., *Emancipation: The Making of the Black Lawyer 1844–1944* (Philadelphia: University of Pennsylvania Press, 1999), 271–75.

described the situation in those days, "Between 1925 and 1937, the need for black lawyers in Alabama was so great that 'hundreds of poor colored people are hard labor prisoners today, because they did not have a lawyer to represent them.'"[1]

Daddy was a pioneer who dared to step into the white man's court and defend the unjustly accused black man and woman. He had bravely represented and won civil rights cases in Alabama for some twenty-five years before Dr. Martin Luther King, Jr. arrived in Birmingham in 1963 with the Southern Christian Leadership Conference (SCLC). The Klan made life difficult for my family, and especially for my dad, a quiet, soft-spoken gentleman and a man of deep Christian faith. Known as a civil rights lawyer, he believed that "by continually representing Negroes in cases that resulted in changing the *status quo*, I became known as an enemy to the good people of Birmingham."[2]

On the Defensive

For our family's protection, our dad kept several guns in our house. One was a small Smith & Wesson he wore in a leather holster strapped to his shoulder under his suit coat every time he left the house. The other was an old Colt .45 he kept loaded in a dresser drawer in the guest bedroom. He never shot anybody and only reached for the gun once, when he felt our family was threatened. But loaded guns gave us, as well as many other black families on Dynamite Hill, some needed protection and a sense of security against repeated Klan threats and violence.

I loved and admired my dad, but it was not easy being his daughter. When our dad represented Autherine Lucy in the early to mid-1950s and got involved in the integration of the University of Alabama, things really heated up. Miss Lucy, the first black student admitted, caused an uproar when she wanted to enroll and study at the all-white state university. We kept the loaded guns close to us that year. Some men in our neighborhood took turns guarding our house, just in case Klan members decided to plant a bomb and blow it up. Our neighbors worked as volunteer security guards, and they would jump anybody who even looked like a threat to our dad or to our family. Once they tackled and pinned down to the ground a Western Union messenger who was simply trying to deliver a telegram to us. In those days, no one was above suspicion.

Life on "Dynamite Hill"

That year, 1953, we had moved from our home on First Street to Dynamite Hill's Center Street, only five blocks away to the neighborhood known as Smithfield — squarely in the middle of Birmingham's racial zoning conflict. Whenever our mother learned what new cases our father was taking on, she would exclaim with a look of fear in her face, "Lord, have mercy! What is your father doing now?!"

But each evening our dad knelt and prayed for safety and for change. And each morning he woke up early, determined to tackle the unfair status quo for African Americans in Alabama and in the South. Surely, our Dad's faith in God and His protection proved strong and sure, for he stood up and fought fearlessly for what he believed. Fortunately, nobody in our house ever got shot, but our window was shot so many times that our dad hired a permanent contractor to replace it — over and over again.

After each incident, our dad reminded us anew of the "family drill": "When someone fires into the house," he told us, "immediately hit the floor, put your head down, and crawl quickly to a safe place."

One time, early on in our life on Dynamite Hill, we called the police after a bullet blazed through our front window. During those days all of Birmingham's police officers were white, and when we told the white officer what had happened, he seemed disinterested. In fact, he didn't write down a word we said. Barbara found the bullet's casing on the ground by our house and pointed it out to him. The policeman took his foot, kicked the casing out of sight, and said, "That's nothing." We quickly learned that reporting the gun "pings" did little good.

Another time we heard a loud *bang* as something huge slammed into our picture window. A car had driven by and thrown a six-foot-tall object at our house. It was homemade, heavy, and looked like the "Tin Man" from *The Wizard of Oz*. Fortunately, the window held, and the Tin Man hit the ground without damaging our home.

A Front Row Seat to History

At that time, I didn't appreciate the fact that I had a front row seat to "history in the making" as Daddy met with and represented such civil rights leaders as Dr. Martin Luther King, Jr. in the Montgomery Bus Boycott trial. What I did know was that the threats of violence against my family meant I couldn't walk to and from school each day. I had to be driven. During those frightening years on Dynamite Hill, only a few relatives and very close friends would come to visit us, and Barbara and I were forbidden to give out our telephone number. I couldn't even give my phone number to my boyfriends—and I had lots of boyfriends! Regardless, every three or four days, because of all the threatening phone calls that somehow managed to seep through our personal home phone line, we had to change the number to yet another new unlisted one.

As a child, I felt so afraid of the Klan that I slept with the old Colt .45 under my pillow so that I'd be ready in case someone broke into the house in the middle of a dark night. Each evening, I'd sneak it from the guest bedroom's dresser drawer before I went to bed, place it under my pillow, and hide it from my parents. Barbara and I would lie awake at night and talk (I did most of the talking) about what we'd do to someone if they tried to "get us" in the middle of the night. It was a real possibility, and we both knew it.

My Uncle Rob often took me up to North Alabama to Uncle Farney's farm to hunt, and it was there that I learned to shoot, so a loaded gun within my reach at night made me sleep better. Had any intruders slipped into our bedroom, I would have shot them—no doubt about that! Early every morning, I'd tiptoe to the guest bedroom and place the gun quietly back in the dresser drawer. Fortunately, my parents never found out. Only my little sister, Barbara, knew.

A gentler soul, Barbara kept her majorette baton under her pillow at night. I knew that meek, quiet, animal-loving Barbara would never hit anyone with that baton. She worried more about the safety of her pet dogs than about her own safety, and she was too tender-hearted to hurt anybody, even if they threatened her life.

In that sense, Barbara and I were complete opposites. She was a peacemaker who lived with an inner fear, while I was a fighter, living with an inner volcano of rage burning inside at what I saw taking place around me and the restraints it placed on my freedom to move about at will.

Looking back as an adult, I understand my parents' strict safety precautions. They proved necessary, even if they did mess up my budding social life. But at the time, I resented the precautions and rules with a passion. They caused my fellow classmates to think I was "stuck up." They saw me as a girl who wouldn't give them her phone number and who got delivered by car to school every morning and picked up every afternoon. At the time I simply wanted to walk home with my friends from school, flirt with the boys, and stop for an after-school sandwich at Palmer's Barbecue like everybody else did. I saw only the restrictions placed on me. Only later did I appreciate the firsthand opportunities I had in that time and place in history.

The Shooting

As our family sat on our front porch on that tranquil night in 1953, the car of angry youths slowed down almost to a stop in front of our house, and someone in the car shone a spotlight in our faces.

We put up our hands to shield our eyes from the blinding light and to protect us from any flying objects that might be directed at our heads. Shouting hateful racial obscenities at us, the boys gunned the car's engine and sped away into the dark. I yelled names back at them.

"Chickadee," said our father, always placid and self-contained, "just ignore them."

But I burned with anger. I wanted to shout back. To be honest, I wanted to hurt them, because they called us such ugly names! I argued with my dad, but he insisted that I ignore the incident. For the next few minutes, we had a spell of quiet.

Then we heard the car engine roar once again as it raced toward our home. Stopping at our front porch and shining the bright light in our faces, they called us more horrible names. Then, like before, they sped away.

"Chickadee," Dad said to me again, "just ignore them."

How dare you insult my family and call us those ugly names! I fumed under my breath.

When I heard the loud gunning sound of their car engine a third time as it raced down the hill toward our home, I just couldn't sit still any longer. I jumped up from my porch seat and disappeared inside the house. I ran to the guest bedroom, opened the dresser drawer, and grabbed the loaded Colt .45. *Just you wait!* I thought. I hid it behind my back and walked to the front porch.

I didn't have to wait long. The car sped down the hill again. "Niggers, go home!" they shouted. I jerked the Colt .45 from behind my back, aimed it at the youths' hate-twisted faces, and pulled the trigger.

But something happened in the split second before the gun fired. Our dad caught sight of the raised gun, my finger squeezing the trigger. He thrust out his hand hard and quick, and he hit my arm. The bullet burst from the gun, firing high into the air and missing the car. Daddy snatched the gun out of my hand.

"Helen," Daddy said sternly, "You know you'd go to jail if you hit one of those boys! There would be nothing I could do to keep you from going to jail probably for *the rest of your life!*"

I wiped tears from my face as I felt the impact of his words. "It's not fair," I told him. "We were just sitting on our front porch, minding our own business."

Then I asked our father a question that had lived inside my mind for a long time: "Daddy, why is it legal for someone to harass us, but *not* legal for us to respond back to them?!"

He didn't answer.

I felt the fury of my anger, indignation, hurt, and fear, all burning deep within the pit of my stomach. That night was the beginning of a series of many racial incidents that would test and mold my youth and finally drive me far away from Birmingham, Alabama, for thirteen long years.

Looking back, I now see that I stayed angry for a long time. Anger became the fabric of my life and being. Even at that young age, I wanted to leave the ugliness of segregated Birmingham and never look back.

CHAPTER 2

The Bomb Blast

August 8, 2003,
in Judge Helen Shores Lee's Jefferson County,
Birmingham, Alabama, courtroom

(Helen remembers.)

The bomb blasted away her shins, destroyed her left eye,
severely damaged her right eye, and riddled her entire
body with nails and shrapnel.

—JUDGE HELEN SHORES LEE
describing bombing victim Emily Lyons

I moved far from Alabama and stayed away for a long time. But
half a century later, my anger had subsided. I had finally returned
home to Birmingham to sit on the bench as the first African
American woman judge in the civil division of the circuit court of
Jefferson County in Birmingham, Alabama. When I was young,
I never had any intention of living my life in Birmingham or following in our father's legal footsteps. But I've learned since never
to say "never."

I now saw the city through different eyes. I had a husband,
children, and grandchildren. I accepted with delight those things
that had changed for the better in the city and state—no more
"coloreds only" signs above nasty public water fountains and dirty
toilets, no more rules that forced black people to sit in the back
of city buses, and no more Klan intimidation when black people
lined up to register to vote.

As an attorney and as a judge, I was determined to serve as an
agent of further change for the good of Birmingham's populace.

Our father's fierce love for and dedication to this hurtful and wounded city had taken deep root in my own heart.

Forty Years Later, Another Bombing

As a freshly appointed circuit court judge, I hadn't been on the bench a full year when, on August 8, 2003, I listened to former nurse Emily Lyons tell the court how convicted bomber Eric Robert Rudolph had permanently disfigured her body and altered her life.

I had followed the newspaper accounts when Rudolph's home-made "dirty" bomb exploded on January 29, 1998, in a Birmingham abortion clinic. The explosion at the New Woman All Women Health Care Clinic killed off-duty policeman Robert Sanderson, a friend of my son, Arthur Shores Lee. Nurse Emily Lyons, the mother of two children, was working at the clinic that day, and when the bomb exploded, it blasted away her shins, destroyed her left eye, severely damaged her right eye, and riddled her entire body with nails and shrapnel.

Rudolph's hatred was not racially motivated. Instead, the bomb that spewed nails and other bone-penetrating debris into Emily's face, chest, and legs came as a result of a moral disagreement—Rudolph hated abortion and took violent action against those who worked in that particular clinic. He had planted bombs before, bombs that had exploded in Atlanta, Georgia, killing and injuring innocent people.

After the deadly clinic blast, a witness saw Rudolph calmly walk away from the clinic while others ran around in frightened chaos. When Rudolph got into his truck and drove off, the witness followed him and wrote down the North Carolina license plate number. Police found incriminating traces of the explosive used in the bombing in Rudolph's North Carolina trailer as well as in the truck he drove. But before he could be arrested, Eric Rudolph simply vanished.

A massive manhunt ensued, and for the next five years, Rudolph stayed in hiding, surviving in the rugged North Carolina mountains as a fugitive, dodging police. During those years, he ate wild game, acorns, and lizards to stay alive. Living exposed in the thick wooded mountains, he built campfires to stay warm.

One day, as a hungry Rudolph searched through a Murphy, North Carolina, supermarket's garbage can for food, policeman Jeff Postell discovered him. The rookie officer arrested him and took him to jail.

Rudolph initially pleaded innocent to the bombings. Later, to escape the certain death penalty and receive a prison sentence instead, he pleaded guilty. The plea deal called for four consecutive life sentences without the possibility of parole. As part of the plea deal, Rudolph provided the location of the dynamite he had planted in North Carolina.

The Victim of Bomber Eric Rudolph

Emily Lyons and her husband, Jeff, filed a complaint against the defendant, Eric Robert Rudolph, alleging "assault, battery, wantonness, and negligence." It ended up in my Jefferson County courtroom, and Rudolph, locked up in the Jefferson County jail just across the street from the courthouse, did not attend the hearing.

The Lyons alleged that Rudolph "wantonly and/or negligently caused a bomb or incendiary device to be detonated and explode with the expectation and intent that such detonation would cause serious bodily harm and physical injury to individuals, including the Plaintiff, whom were working at or near the clinic."

Emily Lyons limped to the witness stand. She claimed "extreme physical pain and mental anguish, physical disfigurement, permanent disabilities, loss of wages from employment, loss of future earning capacity, and loss of consortium."

After the bombing, Emily had spent eight weeks in the hospital. She endured numerous surgeries to repair her face and flesh —a body broken and mutilated by the abortion clinic blast some

five years before. The explosion had peppered her face with fragments of the bomb's debris, and she could only partially see out
of one eye. Scars covered her face. The shrapnel embedded in
Emily's body caused her agonizing pain. I could feel with my hand
and see the bomb's fragments still buried beneath the skin of her
legs, yet doctors told her that removing the deeply buried shrapnel
might cause more damage to her body than leaving it inside her.

Her husband, Jeff, also took the stand. He became tearful and
very emotional as he described caring for his wife and the suffering she had endured trying to recover her health. The couple also
brought photos of Emily that showed her injuries right after the
blast. Doctors' bills, hospital fees, and needed therapy and care-
taking expenses had all mounted up. Yet Emily faced even more
surgery and therapy.

Reflecting on a Painful Past

As I sat in my chambers after the trial that day, I reflected back to
the first time our family home on Birmingham's "Dynamite Hill"
was bombed on August 20, 1963—the *same month of August but
exactly forty years earlier than the Rudolph bombing*, I thought. I
recalled the second time the Klan bombed our Birmingham home
only two weeks after the first bombing, causing our mother a
brain concussion and hospitalization.

*I feel so thankful that our mother fully recovered from her injury
and lived to the ripe old age of 101!* I remember thinking.

I thought about our mother's long life, free from pain, and
all the fun times she shared with her family and grandchildren.
Then I thought about Emily Lyons and her permanent injuries,
how she would never fully recover and how the rest of her life
would be filled with surgeries and therapies. We all knew that Eric
Rudolph's hate had permanently altered Emily's life and the lives
of those who loved her.

Will the hatred and violence ever end? I asked myself.

CHAPTER 3

When Lightning Strikes

Tuesday evening, August 20, 1963,
at our home on "Dynamite Hill"

(Barbara remembers.)

It is time for all citizens both white and Negro to join
together in larger numbers to demand equal opportunities and equal protection of the laws. No citizen can be
safe until all citizens are safe.

— THE REVEREND FRED SHUTTLESWORTH

Daddy had been fighting for equal rights in Alabama for more
than two and a half decades when racial tension and violence
in Birmingham, Alabama, peaked during the spring, summer,
and fall of 1963. For years, the Ku Klux Klan had Daddy and our
family in its crosshairs. Death threats became commonplace as
Daddy, in his quiet but powerful work, represented court cases
that upset the status quo of Alabama's white population. My sister Helen and I lived our childhood in unexpressed fear, always
waiting for violence to erupt. Fortunately, we simultaneously felt
loved and protected by our parents, friends, and extended family.

At certain times in our childhood and youth, we sensed a
greater risk of Klan violence toward our family than at other times
— for example, in the early and mid-1950s, when Daddy, Thurgood Marshall, and Constance Motley, with the help of the NAACP,
represented Autherine Lucy, a young black woman who wanted to
enroll in the all-white student body at the University of Alabama.
The case lasted three years, and during that time the threat of violence and hostility toward us was high. So when the case finally
ended in 1955, our family drew a collective deep breath.

"We can relax now," Daddy told us. "If the Klan was going to bomb our home, it would certainly have been during this Lucy case."

A Dangerous Reputation

And so our family let down our guard a bit. The neighbors, who had sacrificially organized a twenty-four-hour protective watch around our house during the trial, disbanded. But Daddy still strapped the holstered Smith & Wesson to his shoulder every morning before he left home, and Helen still secretly slept with the loaded old Colt .45 under her pillow. We didn't worry quite as much about bombs, however, as we did during the heat of the Lucy trial.

Since the late 1930s, in his dignified way, Daddy had stood and fought boldly for equal rights for Southern blacks, and by 1963, he had earned a national reputation in the South's civil rights movement. As regional counsel with the National Association for the Advancement of Colored People (NAACP), he argued cases dealing with black voter registration, racial union conflicts, fair housing, segregated public transportation, equal salaries for black teachers, and the desegregation of Alabama schools. He aggressively pursued these cases, and he usually won. But his highly publicized work made him and our family direct and hated targets of the strong Alabama Klan.

That year, 1963, the Reverend Fred Shuttlesworth asked Dr. Martin Luther King, Jr., and the SCLC to come help him in Birmingham. Earlier, in January of that year, white racist George Wallace, in his inaugural speech as the new governor of Alabama, had promised the white people of Alabama "segregation today, segregation tomorrow, segregation forever!" And so, early that spring, Dr. King stepped right in the middle of Birmingham's racial hotbed of violence, and on April 3 "Project C" ("Confrontation") began.

On May 2–3, 1963, civil rights leaders enlisted thousands of the city's school children and youth to march peacefully through the streets of downtown Birmingham. But as they walked toward the Sixteenth Street Baptist Church, singing "freedom songs," Birmingham's Commissioner for Public Safety, "Bull" Connor, met the children with fire hoses, German Shepherds, and white army tanks. Violence ensued, and Connor arrested thousands of children during those two days of peaceful protests, some of them as young as four years old. He locked them in the Birmingham jail, and when the jails were filled to capacity, he locked the youngsters in the state fairground's open animal pens. As a local attorney, Daddy worked tirelessly to get each child released and back home safely.

Connor jailed some children for as long as two weeks and interrogated each one before he or she could be released — an arrest record that stayed on each child's record until 2009! Needless to say, Connor's war-strategy antics against Birmingham's black children got him ousted from his public position.

That year our father was also one of the attorneys who represented Vivian Malone and James Hood when they sought enrollment at the all-white University of Alabama in Tuscaloosa. On June 11, 1963, Governor George Wallace stood in front of the entrance door to the university blocking Malone and Hood from entry. It took the United States government to make Wallace stand aside and let the students in. That evening, an angry President John F. Kennedy addressed the nation on live television and delivered his memorable "Civil Rights Address."

That year, 1963, Birmingham, Alabama, was an open, stinking wound of racism. It was time for things to finally come to a head — and our father stood right in the middle of it.

The First Bombing

By the summer of 1963, I had finished one year of college, taken a trip to Europe, and come home to live while I got ready to return to Talladega College for the fall semester. Helen had married the year before, and she and her new husband, Bob, lived in California. I still had several weeks before school started, and our mother and I wanted to enjoy the time together. Mummee was recuperating from surgery for a blocked intestine, so we decided to do something that wouldn't physically tax her.

"Let's go see the new movie *Whatever Happened to Baby Jane,*" she suggested.

Before we left the house that Tuesday evening, August 20, 1963, I walked to the fence where my dogs, Tasso and Rex, wagged their tails and sadly watched me leave.

Rex was a mixed breed; we called him an "All American" dog. He often got into neighborhood dog fights, and would come home with cuts and scratches. He'd stand perfectly still, all the while watching me with his big trusting eyes, while I doctored his wounds.

Tasso, a lovable, gentle Cocker Spaniel that I had personally raised from a pup, was my favorite of the two. When Tasso broke his leg, I wrapped and massaged it after the cast came off until his leg healed. Once when Tasso got sick, I secretly gave him my own vitamins, and he got better. Even Mummee, who didn't care much for animals, loved Tasso.

That evening as we left, I rubbed them under their chins as I always did. "Mama will be back," I told them. I looked at Tasso and felt my heart melt at the look in his big brown eyes. *I love you little dog!* I thought as I helped Mummee into my car and we drove off to the theater to watch the movie.

The psychological thriller starred Bette Davis and Joan Crawford as sisters, Blanche and "Baby" Jane Hudson, two faded actresses who lived together. We watched, spellbound, as Baby Jane planned creative and devious ways to torment her sister, poor crippled Blanche.

Then, in the middle of the movie, someone tapped Mummee on her shoulder. She turned and saw our neighbor, Mr. Kress, standing behind her.

"Mrs. Shores," he whispered to Mummee. "Something's happened at your house. You'd better come home."

Mummee's body stiffened with fear.

"Come on, and I'll drive you home," Mr. Kress said.

"I've got my car," I told him. "I can drive us."

"No, Barbara," he responded. "I'll drive you."

I felt a strange sensation in the pit of my stomach. *Something bad has happened!* I thought. *I just know it!*

Our mother got into the front seat of Mr. Kress's car, and I climbed into the back. I leaned forward and put my arms around the front seat and Mummee. I held her as tight as I could.

"Mrs. Shores," Mr. Kress said. "Your husband's all right. But your house has been bombed."

Several seconds of dead silence passed while we tried to absorb the horrifying news. *What does "all right" mean?* I asked myself. *Is he hurt?*

Then Mummee cried out, "Where was Shores? Was he at the house?"

"Yes, Mr. Shores was in the house when the bomb exploded, but he's safe," Mr. Kress told her.

"Are you sure he's all right?" she asked Mr. Kress over and over again. "Are you sure he's all right?!"

She broke down and cried. Then her cries turned to loud wails.

"They finally did it!" she said between wails. "They finally did it! We knew this was going to happen. And it finally happened."

Chaos on Center Street

"I need to tell you something else," Mr. Kress said.

I tightened my arms around my mother. *What else could he possibly tell us?* I thought. I still worried about our father. *Is Daddy okay?* I wondered. I also thought about my dogs, Tasso and Rex. *Dear God, please let them be in the back yard, fenced in, and safe!*

"There's a lot of rioting and angry people all around the neighborhood," Mr. Kress warned us.

Why did this happen to us? I mumbled under my breath. *Daddy didn't deserve this! Our family didn't deserve this! Daddy has never done anything to hurt anyone!* I felt an unexpected and rare flush of anger flare up inside me.

I leaned forward and looked at Mummee's face. It looked drawn, and I saw fear in her eyes. Under them, her fair skin had grown red and swollen. She cried so hard, her whole body trembled.

Please Mummee, calm down. I'm worried about you, I thought.

Mr. Kress turned the car onto Eighth Avenue and Center Street. Even though he had tried to warn us about what to expect, it didn't prepare us for what we saw next. Outside the car thousands of angry, shouting people filled up Center Street all the way to our house. When Mummee looked out the car window and saw the violence, I thought she would faint. People screamed and pushed, and threw bricks and rocks at police. They carried sharp, broken bottles in their hands and pushed each other. For as far as I could see, people were shouting, screaming, and fighting. I felt scared for our lives, but I tried hard not to show my fear to Mummee.

I've never seen so many people in our neighborhood! I thought. *Where did they all come from?!*

A white police officer, holding a shotgun, stopped our car about two blocks from our home. "Can't go any further," he shouted at us. "It's too dangerous!" Then he cursed. "You can't take that car anywhere!"

"I have the Shores family in my car," Mr. Kress tried to explain to the officer, but he wouldn't listen.

Again, the police cursed us. "Get this *damned* car out of here! I don't care who you got in that *damned* car! Get it outta here!"

Mr. Kress pulled the car into the nearby housing project and turned off the engine. He rushed around to the passenger's door and helped Mummee out of the car. Her legs were like spaghetti. Mr. Kress put his arm around her waist on one side, and I supported her on the other side. I thought she might fall as we tried to walk through the violent crowds and up the hill to our home.

The rioting terrified me. Police struggled to get control of the mayhem. Broken bottles and glass covered the street and sidewalk. Men threw bricks at police cars, lashing out in uncontrolled anger. We tried to hold Mummee up while we walked, but we could barely move through the mob of angry people. She was frozen with fear, and I heard her struggle to breathe. Somehow we held her up and pushed our way through the brawling crowds and the flying bottles that barely missed our heads.

When we came to the edge of our driveway, we saw policemen standing in front of our house with shotguns raised and aimed at the mad, screaming people. Every now and then, they fired their guns into the air, over the demonstrators' heads, trying in vain to control the violence.

Losing Tasso

The crumpled roof of our home had collapsed and hung near the ground. The garage doors had blown wide open, and inside I could see Mummee's car crushed. The shattered glass from the house's windows lay all over the front lawn. The front side of our home had been demolished. We pushed our way past the armed police and went inside to find our father.

"Daddy!" I screamed when I found him. "What happened?! Are you okay?!" Our father's face looked different. He was visibly shaken. Maybe even a little scared. Daddy told me he had been sitting in the chair in the living room, reading the paper, when the bomb exploded.

After checking on Daddy, and finding him unhurt, I ran to the back door and called my dogs. "Tasso!" I hollered. "Come here, Tasso!"

I expected my dog to run to me, wag his tail, and express his canine delight to see me home. When Tasso didn't come, or even bark, I called for Rex.

"Rex!" I called. "Come here, Rex!" I clapped my hands. But neither dog responded.

I tore out into the backyard looking for Tasso. But though I called him again and again, I couldn't find him. Then I saw one of our neighbors placing a towel over something. It was Tasso, his little body blown to bits by the Klansmen's bomb. As I looked around, I saw bloody pieces of Tasso all over our back yard. I ran back into the house and straight into Daddy's arms.

"Daddy! They killed Tasso!" I screamed.

Daddy held me in his arms.

"I hate those men! I hate them!" I cried.

Daddy walked Mummee and me to the bedroom.

"Let's pray," he said softly.

Daddy believed in prayer, and he trusted God and His Word in everything he did. More than anything, our father passed down to me a deep trust in God and a dependence on prayer. He taught me that God always hears and answers my prayers—not always in *my* time, but always in *His* time.

We sat together on the bed, held hands, and above the noisy turmoil and chaos outside the bedroom window, Daddy began praying.

"Lord," Daddy said. "Thank you, God, for protecting us from injury."

Then Daddy prayed for the men who planted the bomb.

"We pray, dear God, that you will forgive the men who did this terrible thing. And please give us the strength to endure whatever else may happen. Help us to be strong."

Losing my little dog created a huge hole in my heart. More than fifty years later, I still can't call his name or talk about him without crying. We never did find Rex, dead or alive. We think that when the bomb exploded, poor Rex just took off running and never came back.

I guess I can't blame him.

CHAPTER 4

The Public Reacts to the Bombing

The morning of August 21, 1963

(Barbara remembers.)

The bombing of Attorney Shores' home is more evidence that Birmingham, Alabama, has a long way to go to develop adequate human relationship.

—THE REVEREND FRED SHUTTLESWORTH

On Thursday, August 22, the *Chicago Tribune* published a large photograph of Daddy standing in the living room, looking outside to the front yard through our shattered picture window. Other newspapers around the country, including the *New York Times*, published similar photos and articles about the bombing. When Klan member Robert Chandliss, known in Birmingham as "Dynamite Bob," heard about the bombing of our home, he said, speaking about our father, "I hope it killed him."[1]

The bombing of our home on Center Street enraged black people in Birmingham. Responding to their anger in a news release, the Reverend Fred Shuttlesworth, president of the Alabama Christian Movement for Human Rights, wrote,

Negroes have long been victims of violence of all types; for violence has for a long time been the trademark of Birmingham, Alabama. But violence will not stop the efforts for freedom and first-class citizenship in this city.

The popular pastor addressed the entire city:

It is time for all citizens both white and Negro to join together

in larger numbers to demand equal opportunities and equal
protection of the laws. No citizen can be safe until all citizens
are safe.

Shuttlesworth urged

all citizens and especially Negro citizens to abstain from all
forms of violence in any manner. Negroes know how to be
calm in the face of stress and persecution. Let us not retaliate
against those who would seek to do us harm and further damage the image of this city which is now trying to improve itself
in the eyes of the world.

He closed his appeal with these words:

We have come thus far by faith, we must continue to have faith
that Birmingham can become one of America's greatest cities.[2]

Not only did black leaders like Shuttlesworth ask for help, but
the 26th Biennial Convention of the National Alliance of Postal
Employees called upon President John F. Kennedy and Attorney General Robert Kennedy to quickly bring the bombers of
the home of Arthur Shores of Birmingham, Alabama, to justice.
"Hailing Attorney Shores for his vigorous civil rights leadership
and courage," wrote the *Birmingham World*, the postal employees
told the President and the Attorney General in a telegraphed message that they were "insisting upon the full activation of federal
power to protect the rights and property of all citizens." They
noted the more than "thirty-five bombings of homes of Negro citizens for which no penalty has been enacted."

The violence and the injustices against Negro citizens had
gone on long enough. Finally, people were stepping up and draw-
ing the boundary lines for justice. It was time.

Letters of Support ... and Opposition

In the days following the blast, letters poured into Daddy's law
office from around the United States and some foreign countries.
Most of them were positive.

"My Dear Friend," one encouraging letter from Indiana began. "I am most pleased that you and your family are safe and that the cowardly bombing did limited property damage. Congratulations on your vigilant fight — keep up the good work with faith and courage."

Another letter from New York said, "I was terribly distressed to read about the bombing of your home. The people who are fighting us and want to hold us in slavery forever are willing to go to any lengths and will stop at nothing, particularly in Alabama, Mississippi, and a few other places."

"My dear Mr. Shores," a letter from Vicksburg, Mississippi, began, "my sister and I were terribly shocked to hear ... about your home. We sent up a prayer of thanksgiving for you and your family's safety. This incident shows the depravity of some people, for to me you have exemplified in all of your dealings a magnanimity, restraint and dignity that cannot be excelled."

"Just a note to tell you our prayers are with you for your safety and that of your family and for courage in these dreadful days," wrote someone from West Hazleton, Pennsylvania. "When this fight for justice is won, as it must be, if we are to deserve to exist as a democratic nation, the contribution you have made will be considerable."

Letters from friends, associates, civil rights leaders, ordinary citizens, and strangers all encouraged us in spite of our loss and fear. One storeowner in Ottawa wrote on stationary advertising "Lawn mowers, washing machines, dryers, stoves, refrigerators, wheelbarrows, cement mixers." "Dear Mr. Shores," he said, "I must say I am ashamed that my skin is white." He invited Daddy and our family to vacation with him at his family home in Canada and advised, "Do not plan to make this trip in the winter unless you like snow."

Some of the letters weren't at all positive, however, but instead were downright hateful. One letter came addressed to "That Nigger Lawyer." "Sorry we missed you," it said. "Maybe next time we'll get you." Other letters contained signs of Ku Klux Klan adornment, including daggers, crosses, stick figures with dripping blood, etc. I think Daddy kept them all.

One letter written to Daddy might have been humorous, had it not been written in such earnestness. "Have you taken a Schofield Bible, read, traced and studied Noah's Children, the Noahic Covenant, Noah and Ham's sins and the curse?" it asked. "The races which stemmed from Noah's children? The curses put on them? God never breaks a Covenant. Also, take the same Bible and study Revelation—the Anti-Christ, 666. He is in the world today, in Alabama. He is a Jew. I know him personally—believe it or not. He owns Phillips 66 Service Station, is a millionaire, and is causing all your trouble—'Angel of Light,' Devil. Jews and Catholics ... are causing all the trouble—Communism. Jews are Anti-Christ —Catholics believe in the Church running the Government."

At the end of her long, handwritten ramblings, the white woman signed the letter, "Your Friend, A Baptist Missionary," and suggested: "Quietly go to Governor Wallace and solicit his cooperation for equal opportunities, and separate, segregated opportunities and representation. You certainly should enjoy the parks," she noted. "No wonder so much crime and delinquency is done by Negros and the poor people in general. I am for your up-building —work without malice—to better yourselves." The writer also sent a carbon copy of the letter to Governor George Wallace, the "House Un-American Activities Committee," Birmingham Mayor Albert Boutwell, and the Reverend Billy Graham!

The Damage Done

Early one morning shortly after the bombing, I walked past the yellow tape that the police had used to section off our front yard and went alone into the recreation room of our home.

The windows had been blown out, and the drapes were shredded, hanging halfway in and halfway out of the glassless window frames. When the bomb exploded, pressure from the blast shattered the window and sent shards of sharp glass flying through the air. They had firmly embedded themselves deep into the wall. Someone later told us that if anyone had been in that room at the time of the blast, they would've thought they had been shot with a machine gun. They would never have survived the flying glass! Daddy asked the contractors to cover the glass-gouged, forest green walls with wood paneling. One of these days, I want to pull back the paneling from the walls and see if the glass chips are still embedded there.

I don't remember my friends coming to see me after that horrible night. Maybe they were too busy getting ready to go back to college, or maybe they were afraid to be in our home on Dynamite Hill. But I do remember feeling quite lonely and isolated during those long days after the bombing.

I never saw the end of that movie starring Joan Crawford and Bette Davis. A half-century has passed by, and I still don't know what happened to "Baby Jane"!

"Well, they've finally done it," Daddy told Mummee and me some two weeks later after house repairs had been made, things had settled down, and our lives had returned somewhat to normal. The bombing had disgusted Mummee, and she took to her bed to continue recuperating from her previous abdominal surgery.

"They've bombed our home. They've been waiting a long time to do this, and they have done it," he added. "Now we won't have anything else to worry about."

CHAPTER 5

Lightning Strikes Twice

The evening of September 4, 1963,
in our home on "Dynamite Hill"

(Barbara remembers.)

The governor [George Wallace] is continuing to fight this integration of the school system of Alabama and he is continuing to fight the overpowering forces of the Federal government because he thinks it's destroying liberty and freedom in this country.[1]

—GOVERNOR GEORGE WALLACE'S
press secretary, Bill Jones

On the night of the August 20 bombing, Daddy telephoned Helen in California. "Chickadee," he said, "I want to tell you something before you hear it on the news."

"What is it, Daddy?" Helen asked.

"Our house has been bombed, but everybody's all right."

"Do you want me to come home, Daddy?"

"No, Chickadee, everything is okay. Stay there."

During the following two weeks, Mummee stayed in bed. Our housekeeper, Augusta, came every day to help with the cooking and house cleaning. My mother's sister, Aunt Teddy, who lived up the street, walked down almost every afternoon to check on Mummee, and to help us wash clothes and shop for groceries.

I helped with the work, but mainly I just wanted to be with Mummee. I sat at the foot of her bed most days, and we'd talk about how she was feeling. She slept a lot, and often complained of sharp pains in her stomach. She still had a lot of healing to do from her surgery.

I had made up my mind not to go back to Talladega College when the new semester started that September. I was afraid for my mother's safety, and I felt I needed to be with her at home. "Mummee," I told her. "I'm not going back to college next month. I want to stay here with you."

She looked me in the eye and said firmly, "You *are going* back to college, Barbara! You *are going* to finish your education!"

When I told Daddy my decision to stay home from college, he refused to even talk about it. "No!" he told me. "You're going back! I'll take good care of your mother!"

I knew I had no choice but to return to Talladega. So I started pulling my clothes together and packing to leave for school the following week.

One night I heard Mummee crying, begging and arguing with Daddy to move us far away from Alabama. She wanted to move to Michigan where one of her sisters had moved years before.

But Daddy's answer remained firm. "No," he said. "We are going to stay right here in Birmingham."

"But what if they bomb our house again?" she asked.

"They've wanted to do this for a long time," he said. "Now they've finally done it. It's over! Anyway, I'm not as actively involved anymore in civil rights cases like I used to be. I've turned that over to the younger attorneys. I've paved the way. Now it's their turn to take over."

Recovering From the First Blast

During those two weeks after the bombing, Daddy's contractors repaired our damaged home. The police filed the necessary reports. Newspapers all over the country published the house-bombing story. We received a lot of weird phone calls from people who issued new threats to our family. Others called to warn us: "You Shores just better watch out!"

During those tense days, we devised a sort of code to distinguish our family and friends' phone calls from the other calls we received. "Ring one time and then hang up," we told them. "Then call back immediately, and we'll know it's safe to answer."

But even more trouble was brewing in Birmingham. The public schools were scheduled to open that first week in September 1963, for the first time allowing black students to enroll into some of Birmingham's all-white schools. People braced themselves for more violence.

A week before the city's public schools opened, Alabama's Governor Wallace loudly denounced "mixed schools" and initiated a petition to stop integration. More than 30,000 white Alabamians signed the petition, giving George Wallace an "army" of civilian supporters.

Back in 1957 World War II veteran James Armstrong, a Birmingham barber, had joined with eight other black parents in filing a class action lawsuit against the Birmingham Board of Education. The black parents wanted their children to have the same good education that Birmingham's white children enjoyed. But *Armstrong v. Birmingham Board of Education* moved slowly through the courts. Finally, in the summer of 1963, the U.S. Fifth Circuit Court of Appeals demanded that Birmingham integrate their public schools. They chose three schools: Graymont Elementary School, Ramsay High School, and West End High School, and ordered their doors opened for the first time to register black students.

On August 19, 1963, one day before the Klan had bombed our home, a federal judge in Birmingham had approved the school board's desegregation plan. I guess the Klan thought Daddy was involved in that case. He had argued other cases in the past that dealt with Alabama school integration. But this wasn't one of them.

Integration Violence

When the schools opened their doors for new student registration on the morning of September 4, 1963, riot police stood ready and armed at each school's campus. Police and city leaders expected trouble—and they got it. Crowds of enraged people gathered on the front steps of each of the three chosen schools. Many carried Klan-related protest signs, shouted racial slurs, and threatened violence.

James Armstrong and his two sons, Floyd and Dwight, ten and eleven years old, slipped through a side door of the Graymont Elementary School, which was located just a few blocks from our home. Somehow they avoided being seen by the crowd, picked up their registration forms, and left undetected through the same side door.

In the *Birmingham Post-Herald,* reporter Lillian Foscue described the scene at one school: "Whites milled about at the front of the school, picketing, fighting, shouting, jeering, and even crying." Foscue quoted one young white girl who stood and watched the school demonstration: "I haven't seen this much excitement since the Freedom Riders," she shouted, as she "hopped up and down with glee as police scuffled with Confederate flag-waving National States' Rights Party demonstrators."

Mothers of white students carried protest signs that read "Keep Alabama White" and "Close Mixed Schools." Helmeted policemen forced back demonstrators who broke through police lines. "In contrast to the five or six older children who took part in the protest demonstration, smaller children trembled and wept as their parents walked them through pickets and hordes of newsmen and photographers," the reporter also noted.[2] All three schools stayed under twenty-four-hour police guard.

From his office in Montgomery, Alabama, Governor George Wallace vehemently and verbally opposed public school integration. He was determined to resist the efforts to take over the schools. "I am aware of the situation," Wallace said. "We will win regardless of how long the fight takes. It will be a fight of dignity in keeping with the tradition of Alabama."

In Washington, D.C., Attorney General Robert Kennedy held numerous strategy conferences in his office as he received updated reports from his assistant in Birmingham. He stood ready to use troops if necessary "to force compliance with the Federal court orders to desegregate the schools" in Birmingham.

The entire city, as well as the whole nation, felt on edge. The problem had come to a head. We waited to see what would happen.

The Second Home Bombing

We didn't have to wait long. That night, September 4, 1963, around 9:40 p.m., Mummee lay in bed, listening to the radio. Daddy sat in the living room chair reading the paper. I stood by the kitchen sink making a ham sandwich when....

Boom! Windows shattered hard on the floor around me, and the strong, pungent odor of dynamite shot up my nose, hurting like needles. Smoke enveloped the room, and I found I couldn't breathe. My knees buckled, and I fell to the kitchen floor.

I screamed out to Daddy. "Daddy! Daddy! Are you okay?"

No answer came.

"Mummee?! Please answer me, Mummee! Are you okay?!"

Again, no answer.

I lowered my head and crawled. I felt my heart beating wildly, and I began to panic. I kept calling our father and mother as loudly as I could. Still no answer.

Did they hurt or kill Mummee and Daddy?!

I could hardly see where I was going, but I kept crawling as fast as I could to the different rooms in search of them.

When I reached the front hallway, I saw Daddy struggling to open the mangled front door. The bomb had blown the door partially inside the house, and it was stuck in the door frame, blocking the exit. Houston Brown, our neighbor from across the street, stood outside helping Daddy by pushing against the jammed front door, trying to dislodge it.

When I saw that Daddy wasn't hurt, I stood up and ran to my mother's bedroom.

"Mummee!" I screamed as I ran. But she didn't answer.

The explosion had knocked our mother out of her bed, and she lay on the floor unconscious. *Mummee's dead,* I thought. I knelt and wrapped my arms around her. *No, she's alive! She's still breathing!*

We later learned that she had slammed her head on the nightstand when the explosion threw her out of bed. The blast had also damaged the large glass chandelier above the bed, and a huge glass ball had fallen and hit her head.

Daddy ran into the bedroom and saw Mummee lying on the floor.

"Damn it!" he exclaimed. "I can't believe they did this again!"

That's the only time I ever heard our father swear.

I feel like cursing too, Daddy, I thought. Out of respect for our father, I kept my mouth shut. But in my mind and heart, I uttered some choice words! I wanted to scream out, but I didn't because I wanted to appear strong and in control of my emotions.

I heard mobs of angry people gathering outside our home. They shouted, swore, and threatened. Soon thousands of people lined the neighborhood's streets. They held broken bottles, and threw bricks and rocks at policemen and their cars. Police fired shotguns into the night sky in an attempt to control the violence.

Daddy called our doctor, who came to our house and checked on Mummee. After about twenty minutes, she came to and opened her eyes.

Our mother was usually one who called on the Lord whenever she felt afraid, or faced a Klan threat, or worried about my dad's safety. But this time she wasn't herself.

"Just give me a gun!" the ordinarily soft-spoken, gentle woman I knew screamed. "Give me a gun! I'm going to shoot them all!"

The doctor examined Mummee and then told Daddy, "She's going to be okay, but we need to take her to the hospital tomorrow just to make sure. I'll send an ambulance in the morning to get her."

A Deadly Response

Newspaper and television reporters surrounded the house as the violent mobs of angry people grew larger and larger. The Reverend A. D. King (Martin Luther King's brother) and civil rights activist Tommy Wren climbed atop a parked car, and shouted to the crowds with a megaphone.

"Go home!" they begged. "Go home! Don't do violence! Just go home!"

But the mob shouted them down. Others tried to calm the crowd, but they wouldn't listen. Police fired automatic weapons —carbines, shotguns, and sub-machine guns—over the heads of the rioting people in an effort to disperse them.

Before the night was over, police ended up shooting 20-year-old John L. Coley in the back of the neck, killing the young black man. Others were stabbed and seriously injured. We later found out that University Hospital had to call in a full medical staff and order all off-duty personnel to come help with the emergency.

Concerned neighbors poured into our house during the chaos and violence outside. Our neighbor, Mrs. Wesley, pushed her way through the crowd and slipped inside to make sure we were all okay. Her only daughter, young Cynthia, would be killed ten days later when a Klan-planted bomb exploded on Sunday morning at Birmingham's Sixteenth Street Baptist Church.

When a light-skinned friend of Mummee's, Naomi Patton, drove toward the house and tried to check on us, black rioters —thinking she was a white woman—attacked her car, rocking it back and forth. Mrs. Patton put her hands to her head and screamed. Uncle Hollins ran to the car, gently helped her out, and shielded her from the mob. Then he brought her inside our house.

For an hour and a half outside our home that night, we could hear angry people shouting, shooting guns, and fighting in the streets. Our neighborhood had transformed into a war zone. Walls of people stood shoulder to shoulder rioting, throwing bricks, and stabbing each other. It took more than a hundred helmeted, riot-trained police to disperse the crowd and bring some order to the ranting mob.

It seemed like an eternity before the neighborhood became quiet again. I was trying to be brave, but deep down I was trembling. I kept thinking how blessed we were to have lived through the ordeal. That night the Reverend Harold Long and the Reverend Oliver came to pray with us.

Inside our house, I heard our neighbor, Houston Brown, tell Daddy, "Mr. Shores, when I heard the blast, I ran out of my house. I saw a police car parked in my driveway. Other police cars had already blocked off the street."

That night, after the chaos calmed and people went home, Daddy, Mummee, and I spent the night at Aunt Teddy's house nearby. The next morning, things were quiet in our neighborhood. In the daylight, we saw that our neighbors' windows had also shattered when the bomb exploded. Broken glass lay all over the lawns and street. Houston, whose parents were having some repairs done on their house during the week before the blast, later told us, "You know that pile of bricks we had in our yard to level the foundation of our house? There's not a one of them left!"

The doctor sent two ambulances later that morning. One parked in front of our house—a decoy, I guess, in case of more trouble from rioters. The other ambulance rolled up quietly to our side door, and we helped Mummee inside it.

The *Birmingham News* shocked the entire world when they published the story of this second bombing. The large, front-page headline read "Night of Violence Rocks City." The newspaper published a full page of photos of police pointing shotguns at angry jeering demonstrators, smoke rising into the night air, cars damaged by flying bricks, jagged glass from broken windows and street lamps scattered everywhere. They also reported the large number of injuries and the shooting death of the young black man.

When Helen, in California, heard about the bombing, she telephoned us immediately. Aunt Teddy answered the phone.

"I think you need to come home, Helen," Aunt Teddy said. She began crying into the phone. "Your mother's been hurt. You need to be here."

Helen caught the next plane and flew home to Birmingham.

The Aftermath

Our insurance company called Daddy and canceled our house insurance. We called every insurance company in Birmingham looking for a company to insure our home, but because we were still living on Dynamite Hill after two Klan bombings, no one wanted to insure it. I guess I can't blame them. Somebody even suggested we call Lloyds of London. We were amazed to see black families sitting in our front lawn, eating lunch and having a picnic, watching the contractors repair our house. Finally, the local Alexander Insurance Company came to our rescue and offered us house insurance.

One day, shortly after the bombing, I answered the telephone's ring and heard a woman say, "Attorney General Robert Kennedy to speak with Arthur Shores. Would you please have him available. I will call back."

I found Daddy and told him about the telephone call.

"Daddy," I asked. "I want to hear Robert Kennedy's voice! When the operator calls back, can I answer the telephone?"

Daddy agreed. I waited by the telephone, and when it rang, I picked up the receiver and heard Mr. Kennedy ask in his Boston accent, "May I speak to attorney Arthur D. Shores?"

I steadied my trembling hand and said as politely as I could, "Wait just a moment, please."

I handed the telephone to Daddy and stood close by to listen to their conversation.

"Mr. Shores," Kennedy asked. "I heard about the bombing of your home. How is your family?"

"My wife was injured. My daughter and I are fine," Daddy told him. "In fact, that was my daughter, Barbara, who answered the telephone."

"What is the atmosphere in Birmingham?" Kennedy asked.

Daddy and Robert Kennedy talked about six or seven minutes. Daddy explained the situation in Birmingham, thanked him for his concern, and then they ended the conversation.

Helen Comes Home

Helen arrived from California to be with the family and spent the next nine days with us. During that time, our family never sat down and talked about the two bombings, or what had happened to our house, or to Mummee, or to Tasso and Rex. We talked about other things. But not *those* things. Daddy was enraged the night of the bombing, particularly because Mummee was injured. But I never heard him express any feelings of hatred toward the Klan. He didn't have to. My sister, Helen—who was so angry all she wanted to do was retaliate—expressed enough to go around!

I still worried that someone might bomb the house a third time, so I didn't want to go back to college, but my parents insisted. It seemed that things had calmed down somewhat at home so, on Sunday morning, September 15, 1963, Helen caught a plane out of Birmingham and headed back to her home and husband in Los Angeles.

CHAPTER 6

The Bombing of the
Sixteenth Street Baptist Church

10:22 a.m. Sunday,
September 15, 1963

(Helen remembers.)

Our dad never appeared to be angry over the bombing of
our home. At least, he didn't allow his anger to show. But
I know he felt angry and frustrated—angry because our
mother had been hurt, and frustrated because the house
had been bombed a second time. But he never allowed
his anger to spill over into other parts of his life. God
knows I had enough anger for both myself and my dad.

—JUDGE HELEN SHORES LEE

Daddy drove me (Helen) to the Birmingham airport on Sunday
morning, September 15, 1963. I had flown to Birmingham after
the second bombing of my family home to be with our mother,
who had spent five days in the hospital with a brain concussion
due to the blast.

After my mother's injury, my anger intensified. I wanted to lash
out and hurt somebody—mainly the people who had bombed
our home and hurt my mother. I spent every waking minute with
her after she came home from the hospital; I didn't want to go
anywhere. During those days in Birmingham, I nursed my anger,
looking for somebody to say something out of place. I remember using some very ugly words to express my feelings. When
my anger flared, our dad tried to calm me down, but it didn't do
much good.

Heading Back to California

I stayed with our mother as long as I could. I had only been married nine months, and I missed my husband in California. Those days in Birmingham proved especially tense, with the court-ordered desegregation of schools, riots in the streets, and protests getting more and more ugly and violent. Though I worried about a third bombing of our house on Dynamite Hill, I decided to head home.

After we arrived at the airport, I checked in, waved goodbye at the gate, and boarded the Eastern Airlines plane. I sat down in my reserved aisle seat and buckled my seatbelt. The plane took off about 11:00 a.m.

Beside me, in the seat next to the window, sat a tall, slender, white man wearing a plaid jacket. His light brownish hair was cut in the popular and stylish crew cut.

To my surprise, the man looked me directly in the eyes and said, "You know there's been a bombing in Birmingham!" I expected the tone of his voice to show some surprise and sadness. But it didn't. He spoke loudly and with a sense of excitement.

I tried to avoid his gaze. "No," I replied softly. "I haven't heard anything about a bombing."

Even though bombings in Birmingham were frequent, I had heard nothing about a bombing that morning—not on the radio news during my drive with our dad to the airport, and not from anyone inside the crowded terminal. At first I wondered if he was making up the news to scare me.

"A *church* has been bombed in Birmingham!" he said in a sort of bragging way.

Then he said something that made my hands grip my seat.

"People were probably killed in that bombing!" he said.

Only ten days had passed since a bomb exploded in our house for the second time. *If someone bombed a Birmingham church,* I thought, *they might have bombed my parent's home again too!* I felt so scared, I could hardly think straight.

"Somebody planted the bomb on the side of the church, out-side the building," he continued. "When it exploded—this very morning—it blew a huge hole in the church."

Fear paralyzed my body. I sat frozen, unable to move, my heart pounding against my rib cage.

I'm sure he noticed my fear, but that didn't stop him. In fact, with an even louder voice, and with greater animation, he contin-ued to describe the details of the bombing.

"The blast broke the church's windows," he told me. "Did a whole lot of damage to the building too."

I couldn't speak.

"People were probably killed in that bombing!" he told me again. "I'm sure people died!"

I stared straight ahead at the back of the seat in front of me. *You know far too many details about this bombing,* I thought to myself, *not to be somehow involved with it!*

He never stopped talking, bragging, and excitedly repeating descriptive details about the bomb, the building, and the shatter-ing windows. I couldn't believe he was telling me all this. *How do you know all of this?* I wanted to ask, but at twenty-two years old, I felt too afraid.

He talked nonstop about the bombing until the plane landed in Dallas, Texas. I could hardly wait to reach Los Angeles, call my dad, and find out what had happened. I prayed that my family was safe. When my plane finally landed in L.A., I got off quickly, found a pay phone, and immediately called home.

Four Sunday School Girls Killed

"Daddy! A man on the plane told me a church in Birmingham has been bombed! Are you and Mummee and Barbara okay?!"

"Yes, Chickadee," Daddy said. He exhaled a long, deep breath. "Somebody planted a bomb outside the Sixteenth Street Baptist Church. It exploded right before the morning worship service began."

"Was anyone hurt?" I asked, concerned because some of our good friends and neighbors belonged to that church.

"Yes," Daddy said with great sadness in his voice. "Four little girls were killed."

The words spoken by the man on the plane suddenly came to mind and haunted me. "People were probably killed in that bombing!" he had said. *How in the world did he know that!* I wondered.

"Who were they, Daddy?"

Silence.

"Daddy! Who were they?!"

"Cynthia, the Wesleys' daughter, was one of them," he told me.

My heart broke. Her parents, Claude and Gertrude Wesley, had been our family's dear friends for as long as I could remember and lived just a block from us on Dynamite Hill. In the silent seconds that followed my dad's news about Cynthia's death, I thought about Mrs. Wesley. Our mother and "Gert," as my mom called Mrs. Wesley, got together often in each other's homes to sew. The spring before, they had made Barbara a green Easter dress with a matching cape. They had also sewed the beautiful tablecloths I used at my wedding just nine months before. I had always been so impressed with Mrs. Wesley and her fashionable clothes. In fact, I never saw her go outside her home without a lovely outfit, a colorful scarf around her neck, dress shoes, and gloves. I loved to be around Gertrude Wesley with her bubbly personality.

Cynthia was the Wesley's only child. *How awful for them,* I thought, *to lose their only daughter.* I wondered how Mrs. Wesley was taking the news. Our mother had told me that when the second bomb blew up in our own house, Mrs. Wesley had made her way through the dangerous crowds of brick-throwing rioters into the devastated house to calm my mother, whom she lovingly called "Dodie." I could envision my mother, getting out of her sickbed, driving up the hill to comfort her good friend, just as Gert had comforted Dodie ten days before.

"Buster and Diane's little sister, Carole, was also killed," he told me. I knew Carole Robertson, but not well. She was much younger than me. But her older brother, Buster, was close to my age, and we had some of the same friends. Carole's older sister, Diane, was roughly Barbara's age, and the two of them spent time together. Our mother was good friends with Mrs. Robertson, who lived in Smithfield too, less than a mile away from us.

"The McNairs' daughter, Denise, also died in the explosion," Daddy said. "And another child, Addie Collins, was killed."

"I'm so sorry, Daddy!" I cried. Then I told him about the white man with the crew cut who sat beside me on the plane and told me all about the bombing before anyone else seemed to know about it.

"He knew so much about it," I said, "I believe he might have been involved." Later that week, someone from the United States Justice Department telephoned me and asked about the man on the plane. I reported my conversation with him, but I never heard anything else about it.

I went home to my husband in Los Angeles, and that evening we listened to the television news anchor as he reported that two black youth had also been killed in Birmingham that day. Over the following days, we learned the horrible details of the Birmingham church bombing. The bomb, planted outside the building, had exploded at 10:22 that morning. Church people had just left their Sunday school classes and headed upstairs to the sanctuary to hear the pastor preach a sermon titled "A Love That Forgives."

As far as we know, Pastor Cross never got to preach that sermon. We also learned that most of the church windows had shattered when the bomb exploded. The blast blew a huge hole in the outside of the building, and on the inside, in the girls' restroom, four children were killed from the blast. They were in the downstairs restroom preparing to take part in the youth service upstairs in the sanctuary later that morning. We also learned that many people inside the church had been injured.

Later, Barbara told me that when my parents told her the news of the church bombing and the deaths of her friends, Cynthia,

Carol, and Denise, and also little Addie, she cried uncontrollably and felt sick to her stomach.

As I listened to the horrifying news, I felt glad to be far away from the violent city of my birth, but I worried about my parents' and my sister's safety. That year, 1963, had been a defiant, dangerous, and deadly year in Birmingham, Alabama. And now this.

Almost Fifty Years Later

Almost fifty years have passed since that September Sunday in 1963 when a bomb exploded at the Sixteenth Street Baptist Church and killed the four girls. I mourned inside for a long time about the violent deaths of those children. I have no way to prove it, but I still believe the white man with the crew cut who sat beside me on the plane that morning was somehow involved in that bombing.

I'll never know for sure.

CHAPTER 7

Our Father's Early Years

September 25, 1904, to 1927,
in Trevellick, Alabama

(Barbara remembers.)

One year before our dad was born, W.E.B.
DuBois wrote that the single greatest issue
of the twentieth century would be the "color
line." He was right.

—BARBARA SYLVIA SHORES

Our father, Arthur Davis Shores, was born on Sunday, September 25, 1904, the oldest of seven siblings born to Pauline Ray of Birmingham and Richard Shores of Montgomery, Alabama. At the time, an economic recession gripped the nation, and at least one-eighth of its people lived in poverty. Life expectancy for white males and females was about 47 years, and for African Americans only 33 years. The average worker made less than $13.00 a week, and that was based on a 59-hour work week.

The early 1900s was a harrowing and dangerous time to be a child or a person of color in the South. The United States had no child labor laws to protect children, white or black, from long hours of hard work in unsafe conditions. Many children received no education at that time, and the education of black students certainly didn't rank high among Alabama's priorities.

This was the environment Daddy was born into, and the injustices toward Negroes, the violence, and the poverty would shape his early years of growing up.

Humble Beginnings

Times during Daddy's childhood were very hard economically, and his mother, Pauline, a stay-at-home mom, treated him cruelly. Our mother once told us that Pauline had purposely burned Daddy's hand with a red-hot iron, creating a scar he carried his whole life. As children, whenever we asked Daddy about the scar, he always blamed it on "some kind of chemical burn or something." Yet we never heard Daddy say an unkind word about his birth mother, Pauline. But Mummee remembered her, and she told us about Pauline's abusive ways.

In 1910, when our dad was six years old, his parents separated. Our dad's father, whom we called "Papa Shores," worked as a contractor at the time in Montgomery, Alabama, so he asked his married sister-in-law, Sylvia Davis, if she'd take the young boy. Sylvia had no children of her own, so she agreed and took Daddy to live with her and her husband in Trevellick, a small community just a few miles southwest of Birmingham. Even though money was tight, Sylvia welcomed our father with open arms and loved him and cared for him like her very own child.

Sylvia's husband, William, worked for the popular Tennessee Coal, Iron & Railroad Company (TCI). The growing iron and steel industry in Birmingham had taken shape in the 1870s, hiring thousands of workers, and turning the steel-producing city into a "Little Pittsburgh." The huge TCI had moved its operation to Birmingham from Tennessee in 1895. TCI owned 76,000 acres of coal land, 460 coke ovens, two blast furnaces, and another 13,000 acres that included Birmingham's Red Mountain iron ore seam. The company produced iron, steel, and tin, as well as other related products, and played a significant role in Birmingham's steel industry.

TCI also gave thousands of employees a job when unemployment was high and everyone was struggling to keep food on the table. In order to educate the children of its thousands of black and white employees, TCI opened and operated a top-notch school. Papa Shores knew Daddy would get a better education at the TCI school than in the city of Birmingham, with its strictly segregated school system. So Aunt Sylvia signed him up to attend the TCI school, where he stayed enrolled until the seventh grade.

Most white Southerners at the turn of the century held the same viewpoint on educating black children as Mississippi's Governor James K. Vardaman. In June of 1899, before becoming governor in 1903 and while still editor of the Greenwood *Commonwealth*, Vardaman wrote an editorial that reflected the commonly held ideology of his times:

> In educating the Negro we implant in him all manner of aspirations and ambitions which we then refuse to allow him to gratify.... Yet people talk about elevating the race by education! It is not only folly, but it comes pretty nearly being criminal folly. The Negro isn't permitted to advance and their education only spoils a good field hand and makes a shyster lawyer or a fourth-rate teacher. It is money thrown away.[1]

Aunt Sylvia's Guidance

I (Barbara) received my middle name from my Aunt Sylvia, whom I remember as very tall and very strict, and a woman who believed wholeheartedly in education. When Daddy came home from the TCI school in the afternoons, she met him at the door, demanding that he work on his school lessons before supper. She allowed no "buts" or "lesson-postponing excuses." She proved a firm and unflappable taskmaster when it came to Daddy's studies.

After he finished his homework, Aunt Sylvia taught him lessons from the Bible, reading it to him before he learned to read and studying it together as our father grew from a child to a man. From that regular study of the Scriptures, she taught our dad how to live and what to believe. She grounded him firmly in the Christian faith, instilling a love for Christ in his young heart. It was this faith in God that sustained him throughout his life and gave him the courage to face the constant Ku Klux Klan threats of violence.

Aunt Sylvia also taught our dad to work hard, to set high goals in life, and then to follow through to reach those goals. She also made sure our father learned to cook, sew, polish his shoes, and clean house. Little did Aunt Sylvia know then how these lessons in domesticity would benefit him later in life. Her firmness about Daddy's education, Christian upbringing, and domestic duties proved an invaluable gift to him.

As a boy, Daddy often played with the children who lived around the neighborhood. They were all poor, and both black and white. They hung a rope swing in a tree and took turns swinging on it. They splashed and swam together in the muddy creek. Aunt Sylvia learned much later in Daddy's life that he had played with the white boys whose parents worked at TCI—something she probably would have forbade had she known about it. Black and white children didn't play together in those days in Alabama. It was simply too dangerous.

The Ku Klux Klan had become quite strong in Alabama during Daddy's youth and college years. Covered with white hoods and robes, the Klan used intimidation and violence against anyone who threatened what they called "traditional American values." But our dad thought nothing about socializing with white boys in the TCI community. Alabama's racism, unequal laws of society, and segregation confused him.

"The black boys and white boys got together, played, and had a great time!" Daddy later told Helen and me. "We were just boys, and all of us poor, and color didn't make a bit of difference. We just wanted to play together and have fun. When we got to know each other, we really didn't care what color our skin was." And more than once when he told us the story, he looked us in the eye and added, "And that's the way it should be!"

Daddy also received an important part of his education from an elderly relative named William Gayles. During Daddy's childhood years, while World War I raged, Gayles visited Aunt Sylvia's house often. He told our dad eyewitness accounts and stories about slavery and the nation's Civil War. Those personal and historical recollections and the strict school lessons and Scriptural life applications taught him by a kind, selfless aunt, stayed with our dad his whole life.

Educational Challenges

Around 1916, during the Great War (World War I), when Daddy was in the seventh grade at the TCI school, the company officials made a discovery. The manager called William into his office.

"Mr. Davis," he said. "We've discovered that Arthur is your *nephew*, not your *son*. We have learned that his father works in Montgomery as a building contractor."

"That's right. His mother and father separated, and Arthur lives here with us now."

"Well, I'm sorry to inform you," the manager said. "But the boy's not eligible to go to our school since his *father* isn't an employee of TCI."

That evening, William told Sylvia and Daddy the bad news.

"You'll have to drop out of the TCI school, Arthur," he said.

They decided to enroll Daddy into Birmingham's black Industrial High School. But they discovered that Daddy needed a Birmingham home address to enter the high school, so they simply made up an address. Daddy started school there in the eighth grade, and graduated from the twelfth grade in 1922 — and school officials never found out that he lived in Trevellick, not Birmingham!

After graduation, our father applied to Talladega College, a totally black school about sixty miles east of Birmingham. They accepted his application, and in September 1923 he started his college classes.

Talladega College had such a poor academic opinion of Birmingham's Industrial High School that the Dean made the school's graduates take remedial classes before they could begin their freshman year. Daddy later told us that Talledega's remedial classes — which he took with his friends from Industrial

High School, Richard Campbell and E. Paul Jones—just repeated everything he had learned in his senior year of high school.

Daddy's Dream

While Daddy worked hard on his teaching degree, he made some new friends at the College: Albert White, "Dump" Campbell, and his roommate, Noah Wills, who all proved to be lifetime friends. They often sat on the front steps of the College and talked about their goals and dreams for the future.

Alabama had a few black attorneys at that time, but no black trial lawyers practicing law before the state's all-white judges, all-white attorneys, and all-white jury courtrooms. The Klan was strong and used violence to keep black people in what they considered "their place." Daddy's friends, like everyone else in Alabama, knew that only *white* attorneys argued cases in Alabama courtrooms. In fact, of Birmingham's 32,000 registered white voters, around 18,000 of them were Klan members. They enforced the rules with threatened and actual violence.

"I want to be a lawyer here in Alabama," Daddy told his buddies.

"You're crazy, Arthur!" they joked. "You're a colored man. You can't practice law in Alabama! Anyway, no law school in this state will even admit a colored student."

"Well, I want to practice law here in Alabama just like white lawyers!" he told them.

They just shook their heads in disbelief. But Daddy had made up his mind. He felt determined to practice law in Alabama's white man's courts.

Money for School Runs Out

Aunt Sylvia and her husband, William, struggled to help pay for Daddy's first year of college—and then the funds ran out altogether. The Dean of Talladega College called Daddy into his office.

"Arthur," he said. "We can't offer you any scholarships. If you can't pay your tuition, you'll have to drop out of college. I'm sorry, but times are hard for everybody right now."

"Sir," Daddy pleaded. "Will you just give me some time to earn my tuition money?"

"Be realistic, Arthur," the Dean answered. "Jobs are rare these days. I doubt you can make enough money to stay in school."

"Please, sir," Daddy begged. "I know I can make enough money."

The Dean must have noticed the look of determination in Daddy's face, so he finally agreed.

The Hard Work Begins

That very afternoon, Daddy went to work. He asked fellow students if he could clean and polish their shoes, or wash and iron their white shirts. When a student gained or lost weight, or tore a jacket, Daddy took a needle and thread and made alterations. He trimmed and cut students' hair, and he catalogued books at the college library. He worked hard and non-stop during his college years to earn enough money to pay for his tuition and books. His shoe-shining business grew so large that he hired other impoverished students to work for him. This gave those students needed money for tuition so they too could stay in school. Aunt Sylvia had taught Daddy well.

Ultimately, Daddy made enough money to stay in school. One day, however, the Dean at Talladega called him back into his office.

"Arthur," he said, smiling. "Let me ask you a question. I see you working all the time all over the campus. Are you here at Talladega College to work or to go to school?!"

Daddy kept his grades up, became a member of the fraternity Alpha Phi Alpha, and even found the time and energy to play football. His teammates called him the "Eagle" because, they said, "Shores is short and fast and can fly like an eagle with the ball!"

Before Daddy finally graduated, the Dean of Talladega College offered him a scholarship to help with his expenses. Daddy accepted and appreciated the scholarship help, but he continued working his income-producing odd jobs.

After he graduated from Talladega College in 1927, two years before the 1929 stock market crashed and the Great Depression struck the nation, Daddy moved back to Aunt Sylvia's house in Trevellick. To make an income, he worked at the local funeral home and at a cement plant. The U.S. unemployment rate was starting to rise, and few schools or companies were hiring new workers. But when a teaching position opened up at Dunbar High School in nearby Bessemer, Alabama, Daddy interviewed for it and got the job. For several years he taught biology and English at Dunbar, working hard and proving his abilities, before the school asked him to become Dunbar's principal. During those years as Dunbar's principal, Daddy also enrolled into Chicago's LaSalle University extension courses and worked toward a law degree.

The Beautiful Young Woman at Dunbar High

It was there at Dunbar High School that Daddy met a beautiful young woman with smooth light skin and light green eyes—the woman who would become our mother, Theodora Helen Warren. Mother was at least six years older (some add a few more years to Mummee's age) than Daddy. She was from Alabama and was one of five daughters and seven sons born to Robert Warren and his wife, Ida Lovelady.

Several times Daddy asked her father for her "hand in marriage." But he refused. Our mother and several of her sisters had good jobs, and our grandfather, a Christian Methodist Episcopal (CME) minister, and our grandmother depended on the money they earned. In those days, only single women could teach school. When a woman married, she gained a husband but lost her teaching job. Grandpapa Warren held the opinion that if his daughters lived at his house and ate his food, they would also give him their weekly paychecks.

Daddy wanted to marry the lovely Theodora, whom he called "Dodie," but he could do nothing about it. Our mom and dad fell in love and secretly "courted" for more than thirteen years. The culture of that day gave fathers complete control over their unmarried daughters, including permission to marry. To keep Daddy interested in her and away from all the other women who greatly admired him—the "dapper dresser"—Mummee enlisted her sister Iola, a good cook, to bake cakes for him.

At least once a week, Mummee brought Daddy a freshly baked cake at Dunbar, where they both taught, but she never told Daddy that it was Iola who had baked the cakes. He just assumed his beloved "Dodie" had baked them.

Mummee got caught, however, in her deceptive cake-baking scheme. She tried to bake one of the cakes herself, but her "experiment in baking" proved disastrous. She took the cake to Daddy anyway. He took a bite of the cake, struggled to swallow it, and then said, "Dodie, this doesn't taste quite as good as your other cakes."

"I know," Mummee told him, and then quickly added, "Iola baked this cake."

Later, Daddy told Iola she ought to take some cake-baking lessons from Dodie. The secret came out!

During the years of my parent's long courtship, Mummee's older sister Minnie married and moved to Michigan. Then Mummee's younger sister Teddy met a man named W. H. Hollins and fell in love with him. She begged her father to let her marry, but he said no.

"I've already lost Minnie's check," he said. "I don't want to lose your check too!"

Daddy decided to approach the Reverend Warren one more time and ask for permission to marry Mummee. For some reason, after the thirteen-year courtship, he unexpectedly said yes.

When Teddy heard that her sister Dodie had permission to marry, she begged her father for permission to marry Hollins.

"Dodie and I can have a double wedding!" she suggested.

"No," said her father.

Yet one week after her sister's wedding, Teddy married W. H. Hollins, who would become good friends and business partners with Daddy in the years to come.

CHAPTER 8

The Early Practice

The 1930s in Birmingham, Alabama

(Helen and Barbara remember.)

> The great work of the Negro lawyer in the next genera-
> tion must be in the South, and the law schools must send
> their graduates there and stand squarely behind them as
> they wage their fight for true equality before the law.[1]
>
> —CHARLES HOUSTON
> in the *Journal of Negro Education*

In 1935, Daddy graduated from Chicago's LaSalle University with his law degree at age 31. In Alabama at that time, however, the state's law schools admitted only white students. So when white student lawyers graduated from Alabama law schools, the state did not require them to take the Alabama Bar exam in order to become a member and practice law. They were automatically admitted to the Bar associations. But *colored* students could not attend the state's law schools, and when they graduated from an out-of-state law school, they were required to pass the Alabama Bar exam before they were admitted to the Bar associations. Oftentimes, Bar examiners simply did not pass *colored* lawyers. The unfair restrictions meant that many black lawyers educated in other states could not return to their Alabama home to practice law. Daddy still needed to take and pass the Alabama Bar examination before he could practice law.

So in 1935, he took the Alabama Bar exam for the first time. To make sure his answers could be easily read, he hauled in his heavy old Smith Corona typewriter and typed them out. When the results came back, however, he was devastated. "I failed it," Daddy told Aunt Sylvia. Not one to give up easily, Daddy took the Alabama Bar exam the next year, 1936—and for the second time, he failed it. Another black man took the Bar exam that same year with Daddy. He failed it too.

The Help of Judge Walter Burgwyn Jones

Our dad inquired about taking classes to help him study in order to pass the Alabama Bar exam on his third attempt, but school officials told him those classes were "closed to coloreds." When Papa Shores, who still worked in Montgomery, heard that Daddy had been turned away from the classes, he talked with one of his white employers, Judge Walter Burgwyn Jones, for whom he had worked on a construction project.

Judge Walter B. Jones, based in Montgomery, was the son of attorney Thomas Goode Jones, a Civil War veteran-hero and a two-term Alabama governor (1890–94). President Theodore Roosevelt had appointed Thomas Goode Jones to serve as the U.S. District Judge for the Northern and Middle Districts of Alabama. Judge Walter B. Jones had founded a law school in Montgomery in 1928 and named it the Thomas Goode Jones School of Law after his father. (Faulkner University ultimately acquired the ABA-accredited Jones School of Law in 1983.)

"Richard," Judge Jones told Papa Shores. "You tell that boy of yours to come to Montgomery, and I will *personally* teach him what he needs to know to pass the Alabama Bar exam."

"Thank you, sir," Papa Shores responded.

"Tell him to come see me on the weekends, when he's off from working at Dunbar, and I'll personally tutor him."

Perhaps the sympathetic judge had seen more than one man fail the Bar exam due to black skin. Daddy felt elated. He traveled to Montgomery every weekend, and sat under Judge Jones's teachings until the judge felt confident that Daddy could pass the exam.

The Third Bar Exam

In 1937, Daddy took the Bar exam for the third time. He wrote his answers in long hand and answered each question in the same way he had done twice before. Sixty-two other lawyers took the Bar exam that day. When Daddy walked to the front of the classroom to turn in his paper, he slipped his finished exam in between the white men's tests instead of visibly placing it on top of the stack. He made certain that no one would connect his skin color with the paper he turned in.

Only nineteen lawyers passed the Bar exam that day, and Daddy was one of them. Later he learned from Judge Jones that he had made the highest score! When the newspapers learned that Daddy—a black man—had passed the Alabama Bar exam, they announced it to the world! One 1937 newspaper article read:

A. D. Shores, popular principal of the Dunbar high school, Bessemer, and widely known civic worker, received notice this week that he had been admitted to the Alabama Bar. Attorney Shores enjoys the distinction of being the first Negro to pass Alabama's Bar since about two decades. He was born and reared in Birmingham. He is a graduate of the Industrial High School, Talladega College, and LaSalle University of Chicago.

Attorney Shores is now serving as President of the Omicron Lambda Chapter of the Alpha Phi Alpha Fraternity, Board member of Bessemer Elks, Officer in Masonic Lodge and one of the founders and the citizenship director of the Jefferson County Negro Democratic Club. He has served as vice-president of the National Association of Teachers in colored schools and Secretary of the Alabama State Teachers Association.

When asked, "Where are you going to practice?" he replied: "Here in Birmingham. We have about 100,000 Negroes and only three lawyers to serve them." Attorney Shores and Attorney [Charles] Hendley, Grand Master of the Masons of Alabama, plan to establish a law firm with offices in the Masonic Temple.[2]

Accompanying the article was a photo of a happy, smiling young Arthur Shores. Daddy's dream of becoming an attorney had finally come true.

Setting Up the New Practice

After passing the Alabama Bar exam, Daddy set up his new law practice in the Masonic Temple with Mr. Hendley. Charles Hendley had passed the Alabama Bar examination in 1919, but did not go into the courtrooms. He was the attorney for the Masons, and that assumed much of his time and paid him well.

Our father, a brand new lawyer, couldn't yet afford to resign from his principal's job at Dunbar High School. He needed the income to support my mother, who could no longer teach because she had gotten married. So for extra money, Daddy worked lots of odd jobs during those first few years. He started a nightclub called the Congo Club in a large room over a gas station. And during the day, he closed the nightclub and ran a day care program for young children in that same room!

Attorney Hendley's law practice was quite successful, but not long after he and our dad set up their law office together, Mr. Hendley died. To fill Mr. Hendley's shoes, our dad had to work night and day to serve and assist Hendley's numerous clients. At the end of the summer of 1939, millionaire black businessman, Mr. A. G. Gaston, appointed our father the legal counsel of Gaston's company, the Smith & Gaston Funeral System. And a few weeks before Thanksgiving of that same year, the Jefferson County Negro Democratic Council elected our father chairman of the organization, the first chartered black organization in Birmingham and the second in the state. He was installed on November 16 of that year and headed the organization of more than 3,000 members.

Daddy's law practice grew so large, in fact, that by 1939 he was able to give up his position as principal of Dunbar High School to concentrate solely on his legal career.

Establishing a Precedent

In the late 1930s, white lawyers thought black lawyers were inferior to them. As a result, black attorneys were usually relegated to doing the background work for trial cases and then turning the cases over to white attorneys to argue in courts in front of all-white juries. But our father was determined to represent his own clients in Alabama's courtrooms, even though he believed "they just naturally resented a Negro practicing law."

"Many of my friends and associates were surprised," he told us, "that I would want to set up practice in Alabama ... mainly because they felt that Negro lawyers weren't allowed in court. But this wasn't the case. However, problems did arise in many cases involving juries."

People warned our father that arguing cases in white courts would be difficult for him, that he would encounter prejudices and possibly even threats on his life. Friends of the family asked questions such as, *Will the other attorneys treat you like a second-class citizen because you aren't white? Will they call you Mr. Shores, or Attorney Shores, or just Arthur?*

During the first three years of his law career, our father worked as the "Lone Ranger" black attorney in the state of Alabama. However, during the next twenty years of his law practice, he would practice all over the state of Alabama—from the Tennessee line to the Gulf of Mexico at Mobile Bay, and from the Mississippi borders to the Georgia limits. "Because of my extensive involvement in civil rights cases," our dad once said, "I was considered by most whites as a troublemaker out to create havoc just to change the status quo."

The Alabama "Lone Ranger" Lawyer

More than three decades later, our dad told his fascinating story of those early years of his law practice to the members of the Birmingham Bar Association:

Thirty-two years ago, when I began telling friends that I proposed to practice law in Alabama, they thought that I was some kind of a nut. There had been Negro lawyers, who practiced in Birmingham prior to my being admitted to the Bar. I knew the last three, lawyers Hendley, Chambliss, and Edgar A. Brown. Their practice had been confined, to a large extent, to office practice. Brown was considered an authority on titles. Since black lawyers had not been known, generally, to appear in court, the general feeling was that a Negro lawyer could not appear in court and actually try a case; that he would have to obtain the services of a white lawyer.

At any rate, I passed the Bar examination, one of the nineteen out of sixty-three who took the examination. This was October of 1937, and at a time when times were not too good. The greater portion of my practice was in the bankruptcy court.

Archie Mays, an assistant clerk in the United States District Court, would send clients to me, who would go to the court thinking that they could file their own cases. I would file on the average of five or more cases per week. I bought books on bankruptcy and studied them to understand more about the laws.

As to most other areas of the law, most Negroes still were a little apprehensive about my appearing in court. This was completely dispelled, however, about two years after I had been practicing.

A Black Lawyer in Alabama's White Courtrooms

White attorney Karl Friedman later told us about working with our father during the early days of his practice. "Arthur and I were friends," he said. "There was a little food service place in the [courtroom] deck, [but] Arthur couldn't go there. But there was a little machine room downstairs where you could put a quarter in and get a sandwich or soft drink. I'd walk down there and

Arthur and I would have lunch together standing up. I can't tell you how many dozens of people came there and remarked [how startled they were] to see a black man and white man eating lunch together in the courthouse."[3]

"Every Monday," Mr. Friedman also told us, "I took about 150 files to the Courthouse. I represented finance companies, department stores, banks, and retail collection consumers. I would sit with Judge Thrift and we'd go through the files together.

"One day Arthur came in. At the time, I was the only person in the court other than the judge. Arthur had only one case. 'Mr. Shores,' the judge stated. 'You sit right where you are. I'm going to be here a long time with Mr. Friedman. I'll see what I can do for you later.' That was such a hostile atmosphere for Arthur in those early days. The judges and most everybody in the courthouses were members of the Klan."

In his first few cases, the white judges made our father stand behind the railing at the front of the courtroom. They allowed only the white attorneys to stand up front near the bench and the all-white jury. White judges and other white attorneys also called him by his first name "Arthur," rather than by the customary and respectful title "Attorney Shores." One white judge even demeaned him by calling him "Arthur Boy" during a trial! Our father never rebelled against the system, the rules, or the disrespect directed at him.

"My client is what matters," he told us. "I'm there to win the case for my client."

CHAPTER 9

Standing Up to Be Counted

(Helen remembers.)

Attorney Shores has risen to national heights for his fearless and unprecedented move in the fight for the civil rights of these clients. Voting is one of the most sacred and precious rights known to an American citizen. Any nullification of this right strikes at a cancellation of the principle upon which democracy is built.

—*BIRMINGHAM WORLD*

Our father began his law career at a time when white society and community leaders kept most black people in the South from registering to vote in city and national elections. In order to register to vote in Alabama, for example, black adults had to pass unfair literacy tests and pay poll taxes. The law concerning white voter registrants was clear, but ignored: "Every person who prevents, hinders or intimidates another from exercising the right of suffrage, to whom that right is guaranteed by the Fifteenth Amendment to the Constitution, by means of bribery or threats or by depriving such persons of employment or occupation ... shall be punished...."[1] As a result, by 1940, only 3 percent of eligible African Americans in the South were registered to vote.

The Unfair Rules That Hindered Black Voter Registration

In those days, an adult had to register to vote in person and then receive a voter certificate in order to vote in an election. The Fifteenth Amendment, passed in 1870, gave former slaves, and adult males of any race, the right to vote in spite of race, color, or previous condition of servitude. In 1890, however, the state of Mississippi adopted a literacy test for both white and black men before they granted them a voting certificate. If a man couldn't read or write, he couldn't vote. Numerous other states—not just in the South—also established literacy tests before giving out voting certificates.

During the same period Florida, as well as other states, adopted a poll tax (1889). If a person couldn't pay the tax, he couldn't vote. The poll tax kept many men, both black and white, from casting their votes. Some of these taxes had been abolished by the 1940s, but amazingly, it was not until the ratification of the Twenty-fourth Amendment in 1964 that the government disallowed poll taxes as a prerequisite for voting in federal elections.

The literacy tests in the state of Alabama, however, were not only unfair to black voters but often were downright ridiculous! W. C. Patton, an Alabama civic leader who worked for voter registration among African Americans before and during the civil rights movement, described some of the tricks voter registrars used to keep black people from registering to vote. "They'd ask you to interpret the Constitution," he said, and "they'd ask questions like how many stars are there in the sky, how many bubbles in a bar of soap."[2]

Later in life, our dad shared an amusing but pathetic story of what happened in one Alabama voter registration office:

Fifty years ago, there were less than a thousand black voters in Jefferson County (Alabama). It was almost impossible for a black person to become a registered voter. After meeting the resident requirement [that a voter lived a certain length of time in the county/state], it was necessary to be able to read and write or own property with a minimum value of three hundred ($300) dollars.

Registrars, themselves, in many instances, were not too scholarly and often indulged themselves in asking questions which had no relevance to one's qualification.

A story is told of a group of blacks presenting themselves

for registration.... The first black, when asked how long he had resided in Alabama, replied: "Ten years." The chairman's response was: "That was too long." So the next one answered that he had been a resident for four years; the chairman replied: "That was not long enough." The next black decided that he would give as the number of years that he had been a resident, halfway between the other two, so he replied: "Five years." That satisfied the Board as to residency.

The next question asked was: "Can you recite the Constitution of the United States?" His reply was, "Sure, I can recite the Constitution of the United States," and he was requested to proceed. So he stated: "Fourscore and ten years ago, our Fathers brought forth on this continent a new nation, conceived in liberty and dedicated to the proposition that all men are created equal," and finally ended with the words: "And that nation of the people, for the people and by the people, shall not perish from the earth."

The chairman, who was chewing tobacco, spat over in the corner and remarked: "Well, I'll be damned, I didn't know that there was a nigger in the United States who could recite the Constitution!" So the applicant was registered.[3]

In 1942 black leader J. J. Green appeared before the Jefferson County legislative delegation at the courthouse. He stated that "only five out of one hundred Negro applicants are allowed to register to vote." He appealed "for impartial administration of registration laws to give Negroes the privilege of suffrage."

"There is nothing to fear in the Negro vote," he said, "but we must fear denial of the Negro voting."[4]

An Unfair Voting System

Working with the local NAACP, our dad filed the first suit in the history of the city of Birmingham on the rights of African Americans to register to vote. Seven school teachers charged the Jefferson County Board of Registrars with violation of the Fourteenth and Fifteenth Amendments. The registrars had denied them voter registration because, they said, they were "unqualified" to vote. The court ordered the seven plaintiffs to report at a special closed session of registrars, where they were quizzed on their knowledge of the U.S. Constitution, Alabama code, legal questions, property ownership, and other topics. However, the case never went to trial. After our father filed the suit, the registrars quickly mailed the plaintiffs the certificates that allowed them to vote.

Daddy once told a newspaper reporter that he had as many as twenty-six voter registration cases at one time in his early law career. "White citizens are registered forthwith," he told the *Birmingham Post* in the summer of 1939, "while the petitioners [the African Americans] have been refused registration because of their race." He also claimed that "these cases were particularly difficult … because my clients still had to pass those outlandish tests in order to qualify. They had to name various governmental agencies, their heads, members of Congress, read certain passages of the United States Constitution and interpret them, and all that. You almost had to be a Philadelphia lawyer to pass it."

According to an article in the *Birmingham World*, our dad officially began "his personal attack" on African American voting discrimination practices in Alabama on June 20, 1939. On that date, the paper announced:

> The petitions were filed by lawyer Arthur D. Shores and is the first step in the court fight attacking arbitrary procedure of the board of registrars in denying voting certificates to Negroes in violation of the state constitution and the Fourteenth and Fifteenth amendments to the United States Constitution.
>
> Attorney Shores said Saturday that the case will be appealed to circuit court and arguments presented before a jury which will determine the applicants' qualifications as electors. He said that the case will be taken to the Federal Supreme Court if victory is not won [in] the lower courts. Meanwhile cases were being prepared for filing in the Federal Courts.[5]

At one voter registration trial hearing, our dad told the court, "It is common knowledge that it is a policy of boards of registrars in this state to adopt whatever scheme, device or conspiracy necessary to keep Negroes from voting."[6] At another hearing, our father told the court, my "client [W. L. Patterson of Birmingham] passed every requirement for registration in this state and county, answered all questions correctly, filled out forms as requested, but still failed to qualify — while white registrants before and after him were not submitted to such inquiry, had their registration forms filled out by the officials, yet were registered as voters."[7]

Our father was determined to see that Alabama's white voting registrants stop charging African Americans a poll tax and demanding they pass complicated (and at times, ridiculous) literacy tests in order to receive a voter registration certificate. When he legally challenged the status quo and filed a petition to take the "cause" to court, white registrants began to send African Americans their certificates. It proved to be risky business stepping into the white man's courtroom, challenging the state's "traditions," and threatening lawsuits — but he did it. And he did it courageously, never backing down. Due to Daddy's dedication to equalize voting rights for all people, the tide of injustices that kept black people from voting was about to change.

The NAACP Takes Notice

The NAACP took notice of our father's fight to change unfair practices, and asked him to provide legal assistance when new voting applicants failed to hear from the Board of Registrars about receiving their voter certificates. The NAACP also *actively* sought out and addressed new voters, promising them legal help through our father.

Our dad not only argued cases in court for African American voter rights, but he also spoke at large rallies across the state and the South urging black people to register to vote. He addressed churches, schools, women's groups, and others.

We always knew our father as a quiet, soft-spoken man and can remember Daddy in the basement, typing out a speech on his old manual Smith Corona. Sometimes we pretended to be his audience and listened to him rehearse his speech. But when he addressed the crowds, he changed from a gentle "Clark Kent" to a "Superman." His speeches were persuasive and electrifying, and they got results!

We often traveled to the rallies as a family—Aunt Teddy and her husband, Hollins, our mother, and Helen, who was just a baby. The more our father addressed the concerns of African Americans and civil rights, however, the more the Klan issued threats against him and our family. Rumors about the NAACP siding with Birmingham's growing Communist Party heightened the risk of violence. Over time, as these threats grew in intensity, our mother decided she, her sister, Teddy, and baby Helen needed to stay home and not travel with Dad and Uncle Hollins. She thought it was just too risky and dangerous, so just Hollins, and sometimes Dad's friends, traveled together.

For months, Daddy had urged African Americans in Birmingham to open new businesses as a partial cure for their economic, social, and political ills. In 1923, African American businessman A. G. Gaston had opened the Booker T. Washington Insurance Company in Birmingham and had great success. In 1932, another African-American, T. M. Alexander, had opened an insurance company in Atlanta, Georgia, and had also succeeded. Other black Americans had also opened businesses and done well, so our father encouraged Birmingham's African Americans to go into businesses. When no one responded, he and Uncle Hollins made a special study of the real estate business and the insurance business. In the summer of 1939, in an office at the Masonic Temple in Birmingham, they opened a real estate and insurance office.

The Rally in Atlanta

In April of 1942, Daddy drove to Atlanta, Georgia, to speak to students invited to a meeting sponsored by the Eta Lambda Chapter of Alpha Phi Alpha. The event was held at Atlanta's Greater Wheat

Street Baptist Church. He spoke directly and powerfully to the young black people of voting age, telling them that the time had come to stop sitting idly by and allowing those things that were rightfully theirs to be snatched from them. He told them that as long as we make ourselves satisfied with conditions as they are, just so long will those conditions remain.

One person later described our father as "the militant young speaker, Arthur D. Shores," a description we would never have used to describe him. *Young,* yes! But *militant?* Never! We never saw that side of him.

Our father also told the students that day that they could get equal teachers' salaries, equal school facilities, street improvement, anything they wanted if they had the vote and used its power wisely. If Negroes voted in large numbers throughout the South, they could have an anti-lynching bill, they could do away with the poll tax, and gone would be the days of hearing Southern representatives get up in Congress and belittle the Negro. He closed his speech by telling the young people to cherish the privilege of the ballot as the greatest and most sacred thing in their lives.

The president of the Eta Lambda Chapter, Alonzo G. Moron, was so impressed with our father's message and the powerful results it brought that he sent him a letter of appreciation. In the letter he said:

> I am sure you would have been gratified if you had been with me Monday morning to see four lines of Negroes in the Court House, all day long, registering [to vote]. It created quite a commotion in the local political circles because we may have, for this election, the largest Negro registration in our history. Of course, we cannot take all the credit for this, but I am sure that we had no small part, since so many of the people I saw were young people registering for the first time....[8]

Our father's speeches not only got these kinds of results. They also captured the undivided attention of the Alabama Ku Klux Klan, the Birmingham police chief, and Alabama's FBI.

CHAPTER 10

The Communist "Red" Scare

The 1930s in Birmingham, Alabama

(Helen remembers.)

During the 1930s, the American Civil Liberties Union listed Birmingham as one of 11 "centers of repression," and anti-communist violence peaked during this period. Communists advocated for whites, blacks, the poor, and even women. These were truly revolutionary ideas for the time.... Communist ideas ran contrary to "business as usual" and big businesses, such as the Tennessee Coal, Iron and Railroad Company, felt threatened by their presence. These big corporations, which essentially dominated Birmingham economically, publically condemned communists and surreptitiously helped finance violence against them.

"FIGHT TO WIN!"
from the History Engine website

The Communist Party in Alabama

After the 1929 economic collapse, people went hungry, couldn't find jobs, and became angry and dissatisfied. These economic woes prompted various political groups to initiate reforms in Alabama. The Communist Party moved its regional headquarters to Birmingham in 1930. The International Labor Defense Fund, for example, was a community-front Communist organization that called for change among steel industry workers and coal miners. They spread their propaganda leaflets primarily in black communities where unemployment had soared.[1]

With the Communist Party headquartered in Birmingham during the 1930s, a witch hunt commenced in the South. Anyone who tried to change the white status quo—the "traditions" of Alabama—was called a "Communist."

Our father was not a Communist! He didn't believe or support the Communist Party's beliefs and policies. But in fact, the Communist Party in Birmingham, Alabama, was growing stronger as more and more African Americans joined their ranks and supported their cause.

Like offering a hungry man a piece of bread, the Communist Party knew that the time was ripe to make their move and recruit dissatisfied workers. The Party saw the black man's plight in Jim Crow Alabama and purposely and actively reached out to help them. They began to spread fliers throughout the state urging miners and steel workers to fight for higher wages. At the bottom of each flyer, they issued an invitation to all to join the Communist Party. Big businesses such as the Tennessee Coal, Iron & Railroad Company and other companies who dominated and controlled Birmingham's economy condemned the Communists publically and helped finance violence to stop them.

Communist organizers campaigned throughout the South to promote labor reform and interracial cooperation, often upsetting local authorities. Violent clashes became routine. Police frequently arrested and jailed radical labor organizers who, they said, "tried to incite insurrection." When arrested, the organizers could expect long prison sentences, if not the death sentence.

Some people claimed the NAACP had active associations with the Communist Party, so it's no wonder that on July 15, 1941, Birmingham's Chief of Police typed a letter to the FBI labeling our father a Communist! The police chief sent the letter to Mr. E. P. Guinane, the special agent in charge of Birmingham's Federal Bureau of Investigation. He began the letter: "RE: Arthur D. Shores, colored, Communist activities."

Dear Sir:
Referring to your letter of June 20, relative to the above

named subject, the following is a report of the investigation made by Detective Osborne: Arthur D. Shores, American Negro, age 36, 5'8" [*sic*]* tall, weighs 160 pounds, dark brown complexion, was born in Birmingham in 1904, day and month unknown. During the years of 1929 to 1939, this subject was employed as a teacher, and later a principal, by the City of Bessemer Board of Education, his last school being the Dunbar High School, Bessemer, Alabama, where he was the principal. Following his employment with the Board of Education at Bessemer, under the direction of Mr. J. C. Orr, Superintendent of Education at Bessemer, this subject tried several times to place himself on an equality basis with the white teachers on the faculty of the Board. There was a time when he was known to have petitioned the Board of Registrars of Jefferson County, Office Division, to force them to open the books to register Negroes.

At this time this subject resides at Bessemer, Alabama, R. F. D., No. 1, Box 755, with his wife, Theodora Shores. His occupation is that of an attorney, practicing law at 702 (Negro) Masonic Temple Building, 4th Avenue and 17th Street, Birmingham, Alabama.

Records reveal that this subject is a member of the Advisory Council for the Southern Conference for Human Welfare. It is known that he has communistic sympathies and affiliates himself *in trial cases of communists* or other suspects of being violators of the law that would point to the borderline of sedition and internal security with a well-known lawyer, Mr. Crampton Harris, an attorney in this city who is known to be the counsel of Robert F. Hall, Joseph S. Gelders and other well-known communists.

This subject has been recognized as an active head in the Communist Party's activities and other front organizations for the past five or six years, even while he was a teacher in the public school system in Bessemer, Alabama. As a matter of fact, the secretary of the school board told him to either con-

---

*Our dad was only 5'2" tall! People often perceived him taller than he actually was.

fine himself strictly to the teachings of the American ideoli-
gists [*sic*] or resign and practice his wishful ideas elsewhere.

The Chief of Police ended his letter with these words:

> Shores is tabbed by this department as being a "guiding
> light" with the Negro element and especially with the whites of
> the Communist Party in this city. He is tabbed as the "Number
> Two" Negro* in the activities above mentioned.

The Communist "tag" hounded our father for years—and
it would revisit him in 1948 during his legal representation of
Idaho's Senator Glen Taylor.

---

*We're not sure who the "Number One" Negro might have been.

CHAPTER 11

The Case That Changed Everything

The summer of 1939 in Birmingham, Alabama

(Helen and Barbara remember.)

Officers regularly beat black suspects in an exercise of authority to show who ruled the streets. If reported— a rare event—offending officers received a light reprimand, if any at all ... A prejudiced court system wherein judges called black defendants "niggers" concluded the dispensation of white man's law.

—GLENN T. ESKEW, *But for Birmingham*

In the summer of 1939, our dad took a court case that launched his legal career and forever changed his life. When he won it, his victory was a feat almost unheard of at that time. It put his name in newspaper headlines—and made him and our family an even greater target of the Ku Klux Klan.

In those days, the all-white Birmingham Police Department "had developed a well-deserved reputation for brutality, especially against African Americans."[1] Black Alabamians had few legal rights. The white officers knew they would receive neither criticism nor punishment for their cruel actions. Black victims simply did not win court cases involving the white police force, especially when the judges and juries were all white.

The Beating of Will Hall

On one occasion, a white police officer, George Williams, turned on a black prisoner, Will Hall, with a rubber hose, injuring him severely. The local branch of the NAACP heard about the crime and retained our dad to prosecute the white policeman before the personnel board. The NAACP had earlier responded to other cases of white police brutality against African Americans, but white officers had never received a guilty verdict.

Our dad took the case, argued Will Hall's rights in court, and to the amazement of everyone, the court found white officer George Williams guilty of the crime and suspended the white policeman from work for thirty days. The New York *Daily Worker* (a newspaper published by the American Communist Party) ran a story about the incredible victory case on July 29, 1939.

After the trial ended, our dad and some of his family and friends stood in the corridor of the courthouse. People came up to him to shake his hand and congratulate him on winning the case. During those few minutes, a black police informer named Monroe Conner approached our dad.

"Attorney Shores," he asked. "May I speak to you?"

Our father slipped out of the crowd of people and followed Mr. Conner to talk in relative private. But the moment Mr. Conner had our father cornered, he balled his hand into a tight fist, and with all the strength he could summon, he tried to plant it in the middle of our father's face.

In a split second, our dad saw the fist heading his way and somehow dodged it. Before Mr. Conner could strike again, our father's friends and family members came to his rescue. They saw Mr. Conner take a swing at him, and they quickly descended upon the black police informer, pinning him to the floor.

Fortunately no one was hurt. But the nearby city police heard the unexpected scuffle in the courtroom and arrested our father, his family, and all his friends—as well as Mr. Conner. They all ended up in the city jail.

The Newspapers Had a Field Day!

Newspaper reporters grabbed the headline story and ran with it— Attorney Arthur Shores had won the police brutality case in court, and then he and his family and friends spent the afternoon in jail, all of them arrested for disorderly conduct! Our mother drove to the jail and bailed them out. In order to keep our dad's story from being picked up and published by other newspapers, the judge decided to hold his "disorderly conduct" trial the very next day.

Attorney Crampton Harris, referred to as a "New Dealer and former partner of Supreme Court Justice Hugo Black," defended our dad in court, where he was pronounced not guilty. Our father's family and friends were fined $5.00 each and court costs. Mr. Conner, the attacker, had to pay a $10.00 fine and court costs.

That evening, July 28, 1939, the *Birmingham World* reported, "Lawyer Arthur D. Shores, charged along with three other citizens for disorderly conduct when the four were allegedly in an altercation in the Courthouse following the Wednesday trial of Officer George Williams, on Thursday was found 'not guilty by reason of self defense' in Judge Martin's court. The four Wednesday were placed in city jail and later released on bond."

Mr. Monroe Conner, who had attacked our dad, admitted later that he was paid to create a disturbance during the trial recess in an effort to stop the hearing. However, the incident in court proved a fortune in positive publicity for our father. Newspapers from Birmingham to New York City carried the story. From that day on, our dad became known by everyone as a "civil rights" lawyer and never lacked for clients. The NAACP was so impressed with his legal abilities that after that trial the organization made him an integral part of the civil rights work in the South. In fact, he became their regional council and the NAACP's most prolific attorney in the South.

CHAPTER 12

The Rape

1931 to the early 1940s, in Alabama

(Helen remembers.)

In those early days, black youth and men had no rights. When black men were accused of raping a white woman —whether it was true or not, the death sentence was almost always automatic.

—JUDGE HELEN SHORES LEE

On Friday, November 22, 1940, the day after Thanksgiving Day, a 12-year-old white girl and her 5-year-old brother walked the fields near their Pratt City, Alabama, home searching for their cow that had strayed. Everette Washington, a 16-year-old black youth, also from Pratt City, offered to help the children look for the family's farm animal. According to the police, Everette Washington attacked the girl, threatened her with a knife from his pocket, and raped her. The youth dropped the knife when he ran away, and the police connected the knife to Everette. When they arrested him, they said the youth admitted to the attack.

Our father represented the young man when the case went to court, and on February 27, 1941, after hearing only two testimonies (from the 12-year-old victim and the arresting police officer, Deputy J. L. Boggan), the jury deliberated for just two hours. They returned with a guilty verdict, and Everette Washington received the death sentence. He faced the electric chair. No one was surprised with the verdict.

The death sentence was routine for black men accused of raping white girls or women—even 16-year-old boys were sentenced to die from crimes of rape. With white judges and all-white juries, the jury deliberations lasted only a brief time before they would find defendants guilty and strap them in the electric chair.

Less than a decade before, and throughout the 1930s, the Scottsboro Boys case had made the headlines of every newspaper in the nation. Our dad knew about the Scottsboro Boys' trials, and he knew the predictable electric chair death sentence outcome for his young client, Everette Washington. Throughout the trial of Everette Washington in February of 1941, our father had begged the court to imprison the 16-year-old, due to his young age, instead of choosing his death by electric chair. But the jury had refused.

They demanded the death sentence.

But then our father made a startling discovery: nine of the twelve jurors testified that they "had no definite recollection of having been sworn in." When our father brought this illegal oversight to the attention of the court, a new hearing was scheduled for the youth. Our dad brought in another attorney, Crampton Harris, to help him represent Washington. On Friday, March 21, 1941, our dad again pleaded with the court to consider the offender's young age. Surprising everyone, the jury gave Everette Washington a life sentence in prison instead of the death sentence.

Everette's life sentence in prison was an unexpected victory for civil rights. It served as a sign that things were changing and had, in fact, already changed since the Scottsboro Boys' trials of the 1930s.

The Extracted Confession of James Erwin

Around the same time, the court case of James Erwin, a 38-year-old African American man, also brought our father newspaper headlines early in his legal career. James Erwin had argued with white store owner, Herbert Thomas, in Tarper City, Alabama, near Bessemer. Two days later, at midnight, the state contended, Erwin had gone to Thomas's store with a gun and shot him to death through a window.

Erwin testified that he was at home in bed asleep that night and was not responsible for Thomas's death. But somehow, in the early morning hours, after being questioned in a third-floor office at the Bessemer courthouse, Erwin confessed to the crime.

Chief Deputy Clyde Morris and Deputies W. W. Kilpatrick and Lacey Alexander testified that Erwin was not intimidated in the early-morning questioning but had made the confession of guilt freely and without threat. Erwin, however, told the court that the deputies had questioned him and beaten him with a length of rubber hose from dusk until 3 a.m. And Erwin still maintained his innocence.

Our father represented James Erwin at his Bessemer trial in November of 1940. He asked the court to strike the alleged confession from the records, claiming that the confession had been obtained after Erwin had been beaten by law enforcement officers for several hours. He also told the court that he had asked to see his client, James Erwin, three days after police arrested him—but police had denied him permission. Our father waited one week and then returned to the jail to see Erwin. Police finally allowed him to visit with his client, and our dad told the court that Erwin's face and back showed signs that he had been violently beaten.

Amazingly, the jury deliberated and found James Erwin not guilty of Herbert Thomas's murder.

During those early years, Daddy was the lone black lawyer who represented the NAACP at the local level. Author and historian Glenn T. Eskew later described our father in this way: "[Shores'] law practice, real estate interests, and directorship of a black-owned bank placed him among the elite of Birmingham's black middle class. Short and stocky, above the crisp suit and polished attire a warm face often smiled, slightly turning up the tips of a distinctive mustache. His controlled posture underscored a shrewd mind and determined will."[1]

Daddy had a will of steel, a deep faith in God, and a determination to right the wrongs of the South's racial injustices. And it kept him going strong even in the time of blatant discrimination.

CHAPTER 13

Family Life on First Street

The 1940s, at our home on First Street,
Birmingham, Alabama

(Barbara remembers.)

Attorney Shores was very calm, he thought very deep, and it was hard not to like him if you would just see him as a man. He stood for what was right, and in addition to that, he was also known as a good church man. Yes, he was very involved with his church and homeland ministries, very involved.... He was a chosen vessel by the Lord, he represented his people well. And in representing them, he was representing God, representing this city and through this state also.

—BISHOP CALVIN WOODS, a longtime civil rights
leader, in a personal interview with Judge Lee

During the beginning years of our dad's career, my sister, Helen, was born. She arrived on Saturday, May 3, 1941, some three years after my parents married and eight days before Mother's Day. Four years later, on November 23, 1945, the Friday after Thanksgiving, I was born.

On my third birthday, Mummee baked a beautiful birthday cake for me. But before the party, Helen sneaked into the dining room and bit chunks out of the cake. To cover up her mischief, she turned the cake's huge gap against the wall so Mummee could not see it from the kitchen. Then Helen went outside and hid under the house until Daddy got home. She knew Daddy would not let Mummee whip her.

During those days of my childhood, Papa Shores (Daddy's father) came around often to visit us. He always wore brown and white wing-tipped shoes and a red rose in his lapel. He smoked cigars, and would hand us silver dollars.

Daddy never spoke an unkind word about Papa Shores' first wife, his birth mother, Pauline. But Helen once told me that she was mean and that she never saw her smile. Daddy did whatever he could to help her as well as helping his half-brothers and sisters and especially Aunt Sylvia, who had raised him.

As Aunt Sylvia grew older, Daddy made sure to look after her. Sylvia came to live with us on First Street in Birmingham, and Mummee took care of her every need. Our house there on First Street had an abundance of rooms upstairs and downstairs, with one room serving as our playroom with nothing in it except toys. We had an enclosed back porch and a spacious backyard for all the stray cats and dogs I routinely brought home.

Aunt Sylvia never liked our mother much, even after she'd come to know her over the years. Before the wedding, she advised our dad not to marry the woman because "her skin is too light." "Marry someone else, Arthur, a woman with darker skin!" she told my dad. "Theodora looks like a white woman with that fair skin and those light green eyes!"

As Aunt Sylvia aged, her mind started to decline, and eventually dementia set in. Over time she became more and more difficult to live with, and soon she made Mummee's every day pretty miserable. Once she slapped 3-year-old Helen across the face. A few days later, Helen came down with the mumps. Helen always thought that Aunt Sylvia's slap gave her the mumps!

Another time, when our mother went shopping, Aunt Sylvia stayed home, took a sharp knife, and cut Mummee's beautiful lace wedding dress into pieces. It broke my mother's heart. At the end of her life, Aunt Sylvia became bed-ridden—but, as difficult as she was, Mummee faithfully took care of her until she died in 1949.

Fast Cars and Glove Compartment Guns

As a child, I often overheard our father tell stories about traveling to other towns to argue court cases. In one particular rural town, after Daddy had won the case and got in his car to drive home, he noticed angry white men in a car behind him and heard them shout obscenities. Fortunately, he outran them, driving as fast as he could along the narrow country roads. But after that incident, for his own safety, he decided he'd always drive a fast car—he liked the Cadillac—and carry a loaded gun in his glove compartment.

He only reached for that gun one time. As Daddy drove us in the family car to the beach one summer on one of our regular family vacations together, a car driven by a white man tried to run us off the road. The driver pulled in front of us and blocked our car. He jumped from his car, ran up to Daddy's rolled-down window, and began to verbally harass us.

He looked Daddy in the eye and shouted, "What are you doing in the car with that white woman and those *pickaninnies* in the back seat?!"

From the back seat where I sat, I watched our dad slowly move his hand toward the glove compartment where he kept the loaded gun. He opened it slightly, and reached inside. I don't know if he planned to shoot the man, or just scare him, but Mummee saw Daddy grasp the gun.

"It's not worth it, Shores," she said. "Just pull away." At the same time, she reached over and slammed the glove compartment shut on Daddy's hand. The white man ranted and raved for a while, but then returned to his car and sped away.

An Amazing Childhood

(Helen and Barbara remember.)

We didn't realize while we lived it that we enjoyed such an amazing and protected childhood. We lived in a nice home. Our dad always drove a late-model car. We enjoyed regular vacations together. Daddy never lacked for clients in his career or places to speak for civil rights.

Mummee dedicated herself to homemaking and to nurturing her two girls. On Sunday mornings we sat down at the kitchen table and ate the same wonderfully hearty breakfast: pork chops, drop biscuits, and grits. She also made sure we attended piano and dance lessons, and Daddy never missed our recitals. He made our family feel we were the most important people in his life.

Every evening at bedtime, Daddy read to us, or told us stories about his own childhood. We'll never forget his "Yellow Nellie" horse stories. We always imagined "Yellow Nellie" as a beautiful show horse, but we later found out that "Yellow Nellie" was actually a mule!

Then, before we went to sleep each night, Daddy always prayed with us. I remember him telling me (Barbara) that the grace of God protected us, individually and as a family. As a little girl, when I felt most afraid, I imagined an angel's arms around me and our family, protecting us against violence and threats and bombs. We loved our father and learned early in our lives that we could talk with him about anything that troubled us.

(Barbara remembers.)

Every night Daddy would read to us from God's Word. Then we'd get down on our knees, fold our hands, and pray together. Daddy prayed that God would forgive us and that He would also forgive the people who made our lives, and the lives of others, so difficult and so dangerous, and he always thanked God for the safety and blessings He provided our loved ones. Daddy personally asked his heavenly Father for strength to help make changes in the world. He asked God to open the eyes of the world's people to see what was just and fair.

Daddy taught us God's Word about love and forgiveness and kindness and respect for others. He quoted Scripture when he spoke to groups of people in schools and churches and rallies, but more than just quoting, he *lived* God's Word. I watched him practice a deep abiding faith and trust in God throughout his long life. In turn, Daddy taught me to trust God no matter how hard that sometimes proved to be. I regularly placed my fears and troubles on God and stepped out in faith, just like Daddy did.

Every morning Daddy drove us to school. He dressed in his suit, put on his hat, and strapped the loaded gun and holster to his shoulder. He said he wanted to spend that extra few minutes with us in the mornings, but looking back I now understand that, in the midst of controversial court cases and Klan threats, he also wanted to make sure that Helen and I got to school safely.

A Tight-Knit, Extended Community

Our neighborhood on First Street was a tight-knit community. Everyone watched out for all the children, and if we got out of line, the neighborhood parents told Mummee and Daddy, and we got spanked when we got home.

Our parents had many good friends and an active social life during the years of our childhood and beyond. They regularly gave dinner parties in our homes, both on First Street and on Center Street, for the other black professionals who lived around us. They formed a group of ten couples called the "Holiday Club," and each month they threw a dinner party at one of the couples' homes.

Later, when we lived on Center Street, Mummee had a large group of women friends that met together regularly. They discussed their community projects and their families, and genuinely enjoyed each other's company. Sometimes Mummee gave a "Come as You Are" party. Mummee, Helen, and our cousin, Bettye, would call the members of the group early in the morning and tell them to "come as you are." Often the women came in pajamas, with rollers in their hair, and beauty cream smeared on their faces. This became an annual affair during the Christmas holidays. None of the women knew what day the call would be made. Before long, however, they began to get more prepared for the "unexpected" early morning phone call, and dressed up in silky lounging pajamas, trying to outdo each other!

Playing Horsey with Thurgood Marshall

(Helen remembers.)

It was during our early years in the big house on First Street in the late 1940s and early 1950s that we met Constance Motley, former Federal District Judge in New York, and Thurgood Marshall, who later became the first African American Justice of the United States Supreme Court. They all spent a lot of time at our house working with Daddy on various civil rights cases.

About the time that Mr. Marshall became general counsel of the NAACP in New York, our dad had already established himself as a full-service lawyer in Birmingham. They became fast friends once Daddy became the Alabama lawyer handling NAACP cases, and Mr. Marshall became the director-counsel of the NAACP Legal Defense and Educational Fund.

Mr. Marshall and our dad often worked on cases together, and he became a much-loved member of our family. He made Barbara laugh by calling her by the nickname he'd come up with for her, "Sop." He kidded her about how she would "sop up" her syrupy breakfast pancakes.

As a child I loved to play cowboys and Indians, a popular trend in those days. My heroes were Johnny Mack Brown, Lash Larue, Hopalong Cassidy, and Gene Autry, and I spent many hours watching their movies. Daddy would take us to the local theatre every Saturday evening, and after we watched the film, he always bought us an ice cream cone. No matter where his work took him, he always came home each night, and he made sure the three of us saw a movie together every weekend.

I always liked Mr. Marshall because he took a lot of time playing cowboys with me. He was a big, tall man, so he made a particularly good horse! I'd jump on his back and pretend he was my pony. I'd shout "Giddy-up, horsey!" and slap him on the rear with my rope. And he'd gallop through the living room on his hands and knees with me on his back. He was a good sport about it all.

One time Mr. Marshall sent Barbara and me red-and-white cowboy bedspreads, which we used on our beds for years. When my son was born, I spread it on his bed. We still have those treasured bedspreads.

Mr. Marshall stayed at our house when he and Daddy worked together because it was too dangerous for him to stay at a motel. Besides, few motels in Birmingham allowed black people to stay there.

Mr. and Mrs. A. G. Gaston also lived in our neighborhood, and drove a new shiny black Cadillac. He owned the Smith and Gaston Funeral System in Birmingham, and also built the Gaston Hotel near the Sixteenth Street Baptist Church primarily for visiting black civil rights leaders to have a place to stay overnight and hold their meetings.

Moving onto Dynamite Hill

One day Daddy told us he wanted us to move away from our Smithfield house on First Street. When we asked him why, he told us the house was "just too big for such a small family." During that time, Daddy battled some unfair zoning laws in Smithfield, mainly on Center Street, the invisible property line that separated the white community on its west side from the black community on its east side. He decided he needed to move his family right in the middle of Smithfield's most controversial black/white zoning battle to an area the townspeople had dubbed "Dynamite Hill."

Mummee didn't like the idea. "I don't want to move up 'on the hill,'" she told him. "All those bombings up there. It will put our family in too much danger!"

But Daddy was determined, so within a few years, we would

leave our spacious and safe home on First Street and move just a few blocks away to our new brick house on Center Street in a neighborhood where we would learn firsthand what it meant to grow up in Birmingham's dangerous section of Smithfield, dubbed *Dynamite Hill.*

But before we moved there, Daddy would argue and win several high-profile cases, some of them landmark decisions that would change the course of history.

CHAPTER 14

The Fight to Equalize Salaries for Black Teachers

1942, in Birmingham, Alabama

(Helen remembers.)

You know these white folks are not going to pay you the
same money they make. You're a fool if you try to get
them to. You're gonna be out of a job....

—STATEMENT MADE TO BLACK TEACHERS
IN 1942 BY JOHN P. BURGESS, president of the
Teacher's Association, Orangeburg, South Carolina

In the spring of 1942, William J. Bolden, black principal of the
Leeds school in Leeds, Alabama, claimed that "Negro teachers
with the same qualifications as white teachers are paid lower salaries in the Jefferson County Schools." Bolden asked our father to
file a petition for him that sought to restrain the Jefferson County
Board of Education from making a distinction in payments of salaries because of race and/or color. Our father and attorney Thurgood Marshall, special counsel for the NAACP, agreed to represent
the plaintiff William Bolden.

Teaching school represented prestigious positions for African
American men and women in the South. But black teachers faced
low wages, a severe lack of teaching supplies, and poor school
facilities. In fact, a study made in 1939–1940 on the salaries of
white and black teachers in eleven Southern states showed that
the average white teachers in these states received a salary 80
percent greater than that of the average Negro teachers. The study
also noted that in order to bring the salaries of Negro teachers

up to the level of white teacher salaries, more than $25 million would have to be added to the salaries of Negro teachers. Black teachers in the South, according to the research, also shouldered much heavier workloads and had many more students to teach than white teachers.[1]

Bolden's case went to trial, and in May of 1945 Judge T. A. Murphee of the U.S. District Court in Birmingham declared that the salary differentials based on race were "unlawful and unconstitutional," winning Bolden the case. A decree was signed in Birmingham, Alabama, ordering the equalization of the salaries —based on individual qualifications, not color—of Birmingham's colored school teachers with those of white school teachers.

The superintendent of the Jefferson County public schools, Dr. John E. Bryan, the man our father had worked under as a principal and teacher in his early career, agreed with the decision, which was based on the Fourteenth Amendment to the Constitution. He said the decision was fair and that he would make no appeal. The court then demanded that the equalization begin with the start of the new school semester in September of 1945.

To bring about equalization of black and white teachers' salaries during the late 1930s and early to mid-1940s, the NAACP represented other black teachers who brought lawsuits in many states, including Virginia, Maryland, Texas, Mississippi, South Carolina, Florida, Arkansas, North Carolina, and Alabama. In fact, more than thirty cases were tried between 1936 and 1950, and the majority of them were decided in favor of the plaintiff. As a result of these lawsuits, the pay scale inequity changed drastically between 1940 and 1950, with the average annual salaries of black teachers increasing 82 percent in that decade![2]

The Firing of Ruby Jackson Gainer

In spite of the decision of Birmingham's U.S. District Court, their school boards were taking their own good time to equalize black teachers' paychecks, which led to the teacher-related case of Ruby Jackson Gainer. Mrs. Gainer was a black teacher in Jefferson County's public school system in Birmingham who served as president of the United Public Workers of America (UPW) as well as president of the Jefferson County Negro Teachers Association. Due to the slowness of Birmingham's school boards to obey the decision and equalize black teachers' pay, Ruby Jackson Gainer sued the city's school board for contempt of court in 1947. After Gainer and another black teacher, Maenetta Steele, testified in court, the Birmingham school district fired both women from their teaching positions.

The firings became quite public because Ruby Jackson Gainer's brother was Emory Jackson, a noted NAACP activist, an officer of the National Negro Publishers Association, and the editor of the *Birmingham World*. Needless to say, the NAACP and other black activist groups rallied to support the two teachers, and the black press published their stories in newspapers in Atlanta, New York, Chicago, and other cities. Emory Jackson started a campaign to raise money for the two terminated teachers. They then hired our father and Thurgood Marshall to file a new suit in the Birmingham Circuit Court that demanded their teaching jobs back.

Daddy actually became involved that very same month in another case related to this situation. He along with Crumpton Harris filed a contempt suit in the U.S. District Court.[3] The *Birmingham News* ran the following story on February 18, 1947: "Negro teachers filed suit in U.S. District Court yesterday to require the Jefferson County School Board and Dr. J. E. Bryan, superintendent of County School Board, to show cause why they should not be held in contempt of court for what they claim is non-compliance with the equal pay decree of April 29, 1945. The suit was filed by Arthur D. Shores, Negro attorney on behalf of Jefferson County Teachers Union, Local 683, United Public Workers of America."

It was two years before the Circuit Court made its decision, ordering the Board of Education to rehire Gainer and Steele. And that decision was prompted in part by much publicity brought about by Emory Jackson (and by Mrs. Gainer's numerous speaking engagements where she told her story). The *Pittsburg Courier*, reporting on the case, said,

> Last week when a Birmingham circuit judge ordered the Birmingham Board of Education to reinstate Mrs. Ruby Jackson Gainer, discharged teacher-leader of the equal salary fight, it was the culmination of another fight valiantly and sagaciously waged by the intrepid Mr. Shores. The *Courier* is pleased to recognize the consistently persevering service being rendered by Attorney Shores on the home grounds of prejudice and oppression, and takes pride in saluting him for his courageous and persistent fight against injustice, discrimination and oppression in the South. He is setting an example which is well worth emulation by all other Negroes in responsible positions in the South. The South needs more Negro leaders like Arthur D. Shores, champion of right and justice for his people.

Maenetta Steele returned to her teaching position in Fairfield and also received eighteen months of back pay. By that time, however, Mrs. Gainer had moved to Pensacola, Florida, and had taken another teaching position. Mrs. Gainer decided to keep her job in Florida and immediately resigned the Birmingham position after the School Board reinstated her. The State of Alabama surely lost a wonderful teacher and a hard-working woman!

Interestingly, it took the U.S. District Court eight years before it rendered its final opinion. It appears that U.S. District Judge Lynn had appointed a special master to investigate and recommend finding of fact and conclusions of law. Five years later the special master made his report. Three years after that, in 1955, Judge Lynn issued his decision.[4] The District Court found that differences in salaries paid white and Negro teachers represented arbitrary discrimination and that in final analysis, they were based solely on race or color. The court concluded that a case for civil contempt had been made. The plaintiffs had asked the court to access a fine in the amount of $2,970 for compensation for salaries they did not receive as a result of its disobedience of the injunction. The court denied their request.

In the State of Alabama, the decades of the 1930s, 1940s, and 1950s saw the organization of worker labor unions, worker strikes, and employer threats and intimidation; employee terminations and court-forced job reinstatements; Communist activities, committee hearings, and court cases; black activists battling for equal rights and justice, black resistance, and white violence, Jim Crow laws, bombings, and segregation. And yet Dr. Ruby Jackson Gainer, with the legal representation of our father, had won a key battle in the Alabama Supreme Court, setting the legal precedent for salary parity and tenure for black teachers.

CHAPTER 15

Working on the Railroad

1941–1944, railroad workers in Alabama

(Helen remembers.)

The reason that they have black firemen in the early days is 'cause that was the lousiest job you could have. You're stoking coal, and it was an ugly job, and it didn't pay too very much, but it—all of a sudden you get diesel engine. All a fireman has to do is pull this lever, pull this lever, and sit, sit and enjoy himself. Well, you can imagine what the whites—how quickly they went after those jobs. Well, Charlie Houston was a genius. He won a case called the Steele case [*Bester Steele v. L & N Railroad*], and where that was declared illegal for the white union to negotiate to give the jobs that the black firemen had to white firemen just 'cause they were now easy jobs.

—JOSEPH L. RAUH, Jr.,
railroad worker[1]

Established on March 5, 1850, the Louisville & Nashville Railroad was granted a charter by the Commonwealth of Kentucky "to build a railroad between Louisville, Kentucky, and the Tennessee state line in the direction of Nashville," and on August 25, 1855, their first train ran the rails carrying three hundred people a distance of eight miles at a blistering speed of fourteen miles per hour!

In 1861, the beginning of the Civil War, L&N trains served both Confederate and Union armies, because the railroad was located almost in the middle of the two opposing armies. Over the next thirty years, through construction and acquisition of existing railroads, the L&N extended its tracks to St. Louis, Missouri;

Cincinnati, Ohio; Birmingham and Mobile, Alabama; Pensacola, Florida; and New Orleans, Louisiana. Before the new century dawned, the L&N railroad had grown from a small local carrier into one of America's major railroad systems.[2]

William Bester Steele Demoted

William Bester Steele, an African American man, 53 years old, had been employed with Louisville & Nashville Railroad in Birmingham for thirty-one years. Since 1910, he had worked hard at his job as locomotive fireman, serving L&N faithfully.

When the railroad began additional expansion and growth, he worked his way up to the highly desirable "passenger pool," an enviable position given only to the most valuable senior firemen. He loved his work and the good hours, and he made more money than most of the other firemen working in such lower positions as freight or switcher positions.

The railroad continued to expand and grow over the years and bought its first diesel locomotive in 1939. The future of the L&N railroad looked bright as World War II began to take shape that year. In fact, L&N trains would transport more than 90 percent of the nation's military equipment and supplies and some 97 percent of all its troops during the war. In the early and mid-1940s, L&N traffic soared, increasing 80 percent in freight traffic and 300 percent in passenger traffic.

During those early years of the L&N railroad's history and after the Civil War, an organization was founded in December 1873 to provide mutual support for railroad firemen. They emphasized health insurance for the firemen, and later branched out into labor-management relations. This railroad union, the Brotherhood of Locomotive Firemen, was not affiliated with the American Federation of Labor, and only white men could join. African American workers were purposely excluded. In March of 1940, the white-dominated Brotherhood decided to ultimately exclude *all* Negro firemen from the service. "Only white firemen," they announced, "can be promoted to serve as engineers." The notice proposed that only "'promotable,' i.e., *white men* should be employed as firemen or assigned to new runs or jobs or permanent vacancies in established runs or jobs."

The next year, the Brotherhood decided that "not more than 50% of the firemen in each class of service in each seniority district of a carrier should be Negroes; that until such percentage should be reached all new runs and all vacancies should be filled by white men," and that "the agreement did not sanction the employment of Negroes in any seniority district in which they were not working." The agreement also reserved the right of the Brotherhood to negotiate for further restrictions on the employment of Negro firemen on the individual railroads.

Steele worked in the passenger pool with five black firemen and only one white fireman. In early April 1941, the Brotherhood and the L&N railroad, acting under the new agreement, suddenly and without warning, disqualified all the African American railway firemen and claimed their jobs as "vacant." They then hired (and replaced them with) four white men, all junior in seniority to Steele and the others, none more competent than Steele and the others, but all members of the Brotherhood.

For the next sixteen days, Steele had no work and no income. Then the railroad assigned Steele to a job in local freight service, a position much more arduous, with longer hours and less money. Not long after he had been demoted to the freight service job, they demoted him to a more difficult and lesser paying job on a switch engine. And again, they replaced Steele with a white man.[3]

Clear Discrimination

The Brotherhood had clearly discriminated against Steele in a hostile and disloyal way. Steele protested the two demotions and appealed to the L&N railroad and the Brotherhood, but they simply ignored him. Angry and frustrated, Steele turned to the Birmingham Chapter of the International Association of Railroad

Employees (IARE) and the Association of Colored Railroad Train-men (ACRT). Then Mr. Steele contacted our father, who filed suit on behalf of Bester William Steele in the Alabama court in August 1941, asking Charles H. Houston to work with him on the case. *The Pittsburg Courier* newspaper ran the following story on September 6, 1941:

> William Bester Steele, fireman on the L&N railroad, filed suit in the Circuit Court against the Brotherhood of Locomotive Firemen and Enginemen for $50,000, charging destruction of his seniority rights and job discrimination.... Steele has been a fireman on the L&N since 1910 with a brilliant service record. By virtue of his seniority he was assigned to the firemen's "pool" on the Southern and Northern Alabama division, which is the best assignment in the district.
>
> On April 7 the lily-white brotherhood, which bars Negroes from membership caused Steele to be taken out of the "pool" and replaced by a junior white fireman, member of *The Brotherhood*. The *International Association* held conferences with representatives of the L&N and *The Brotherhood*, but could get no results. Steele next filed the suit against the railroad and *The Brotherhood*, asking $50,000, restoration of his seniority rights and a permanent injunction to prevent *The Brotherhood* from representing Negro firemen. The case is in the legal hands of Attorneys Arthur D. Shores of Birmingham, J. T. Settle of Memphis, Joseph C. Waddy, and Charles H. Houston of Washington.[4]

A Slow Judicial System

Over the next three years the case made its way slowly through the judicial system. Steele and other black railroaders gained publicity when they testified before the federal Fair Employment Practice Committee hearings regarding discrimination in the railroad industry.

The case ultimately went to the Supreme Court of Alabama, but the Court sided with the Brotherhood and the L&N railroad.

It claimed the union had the right to decide on working conditions and pay scales for its workers and had no legal obligation or duty to protect the rights of minorities from discrimination or unfair treatment, however gross. It held that "neither *The Brotherhood* nor the Railroad violated any rights of petitioner [William Bester Steele] or his fellow Negro employees by negotiating the contracts discriminating against them."[5]

Our father, Charles Houston, and other NAACP attorneys then took Steele's case to the United States Supreme Court, arguing the case on November 14 and 15, 1944. The question raised was "whether the Railway Labor Act, 48 Stat. 1185, 45 U.S.C. §§ 151 *et seq.*, imposes on a labor organization, acting by authority of the statute as the exclusive bargaining representative of a craft or class of railway employees, the duty to represent all the employees in the craft without discrimination because of their race, and, if so, whether the courts have jurisdiction to protect the minority of the craft or class from the violation of such obligation."[6]

The United States Supreme Court's Decision

On December 18, 1944, the United States Supreme Court handed down its decision:

> 1) The fair interpretation of the statutory language is that the organization chosen to represent a craft is to represent all its members, the majority as well as the minority, and it is to act for and not against those whom it represents.... It is enough for present purposes to say that the statutory power to represent a craft and to make contracts as to wages, hours and working conditions does not include the authority to make among members of the craft discriminations not based on such relevant differences. Here the discriminations based on race alone are obviously irrelevant and invidious. Congress plainly did not undertake to authorize the bargaining representative to make such discriminations.
>
> 2) Further, ... [the Railway Labor Act] permits the national

labor organizations chosen by the majority of the crafts to 'prescribe the rules under which the labor members of the Adjustment Board shall be selected' and to 'select such members and designate the division on which each member shall serve,' the Negro firemen would be required to appear before a group which is in large part chosen by the respondents against whom their real complaint is made ... There is no administrative means by which the Negro firemen can secure separate representation for the purposes of collective bargaining ... In the absence of any available administrative remedy, the right here asserted, to a remedy for breach of the statutory duty of the bargaining representative to represent and act for the members of a craft, is of judicial cognizance.[7]

William Bester Steele had won his case! The U.S. Supreme Court reversed the judgment of the Alabama Supreme Court, ruling that a whites-only railroad union could not exclude African Americans from membership and then deny them better jobs because they were not union members. The case became a "landmark"* decision.

Steele proved to be a courageous individual in his stand against the L&N railroad. In those days, "victims of discrimination and oppression were often afraid to come forward to serve as plaintiffs—for it sometimes involved not simply a sacrifice of dignity, body integrity, loss of job—it sometimes called for the ultimate sacrifice of life."[8]

Over the years, other victims of workplace discrimination would follow Steele's example and file suit against unjust employers. Judges would inevitably point to the Supreme Court's 1944 ruling *Steele v. Louisville & Nashville Railroad* as a basis for their decisions.[9] Our father and Mr. Houston's landmark case would eventually help shape Title VII of the Civil Rights Act of 1964, a bill that would prohibit discrimination against an individual worker due to race, color, religion, sex, or national origin.

---

*A landmark case is a decision that sets a pattern and establishes a precedent on the way a law is interpreted in the future.

CHAPTER 16

The Continuing
Voting Rights Battle:
Mitchell v. Wright

1946, in Tuskegee, Macon County, Alabama

(Helen remembers.)

To some, the final insult to Negro pride is the appearance of the European refugee, *who is free to vote,* eat where he wishes, and attain full citizenship, while the native-born Negro, often of old U.S. stock, must remain a semi outcast."

—*TIME*, November 13, 1944

By 1945 our father's reputation as a civil rights attorney had been well established. The NAACP depended on him, as did Thurgood Marshall, Constance Motley, and others, for legal counsel and work. Daddy's legal cases were varied—housing ordinances, railroad and teachers' salaries and treatment, and labor unions, among others—but all involved Negroes whose civil rights had been violated.

However, our dad spent the majority of his early career working for Negroes' voting rights. He was tireless as he spoke to church and college groups, urging black voters to register and vote. He represented numerous Negroes who stood in long lines for hours to register and who, though they possessed the necessary qualifications and documents, were turned down by white registrars. Their refusal plainly violated the Fourteenth and Fifteenth Amendments of the U.S. Constitution, but Southern states seemed to get away with it time and time again.

The Voting Rights Battle

On July 5, 1945, William P. Mitchell, a well-respected black man, drove to the Macon County Court House to register to vote. Mr. Mitchell worked with the Tuskegee Civic Association as well as Tuskegee's VA hospital. Forty miles east of Montgomery, Tuskegee was the county seat of Macon County, Alabama. The majority of the population was African American, although the white populace controlled the city politically.

Mitchell waited in line a long time. When his turn came, he filled out the regular form for voter registration application. He produced two people to vouch for him. And he correctly answered all the questions posed to him by the white registrants, Mrs. George C. Wright and Mr. Virgil M. Guthrie. He did everything required in order to register to vote in future federal and state elections.

But Mrs. Wright and Mr. Guthrie refused to register Mr. Mitchell, though during the time Mitchell waited and filled out forms, he observed that white men and women endured no lines and no problems in registering to vote. Later, when testifying before U.S. District Judge C. B. Kennamer, the registrants said that Mr. Mitchell "did not comply with a requirement that would-be registrants have a 'voucher' sign their application papers." A "voucher" was a voter known to board members who would attest to the applicant's residence qualification papers.[1] Mitchell told the court that the white registrars refused him solely on account of his race, color, and previous condition of servitude. He also added that it has become the general habitual and systematic practice of the Macon County Board of Registrars, including Mrs. George C. Wright and Virgil M. Guthrie, and their predecessors in office, to refuse to register Negro residents of Macon County, including himself.

The United States District Court for the Middle District of Alabama dismissed the case. They said the plaintiff, Mr. Mitchell, "had not exhausted the administrative remedy of a state-court challenge to the registrars' rejection of his application."

Our father and Thurgood Marshall represented Mr. Mitchell on April 24, 1946, when the case went to the United States Court of Appeals, Fifth Circuit. The court document records this description of Mr. Mitchell and his case:

> Plaintiff, William P. Mitchell, is colored, a person of African descent and Negro blood, is over the age of twenty-one years. He is a taxpayer of the State of Alabama, and pays tax on real property with an assessed valuation in excess of three hundred dollars. Plaintiff alleges that he is able to read and write any passage of the United States Constitution, that he has never been adjudged guilty of felony or any crime and that he is not an idiot or insane. Plaintiff further alleges that by reason of the allegation herein above made, he was in all particulars on the 5th day of July, 1945, and still is possessed of the qualifications of an elector and as such was and is entitled to be registered as such elector.[2]

The U.S. Court of Appeals did not agree with the U.S. District Court's claim and reversed its decision, which had ruled in favor of the white registrars because they said that they saw "no evidence of racial discrimination." U.S. Court of Appeals said that "the federal courts could entertain the claim" and that a "state-court challenge was not administrative in nature, so the exhaustion doctrine was not applicable." However, when Mr. Mitchell appealed, a registrar unexpectedly produced a document that showed that Mr. Mitchell's application had already been approved several years before. Mitchell claimed no one had told him about it, and the court then "moved to dismiss the appeal as moot."[3]

The Strange Case of Charles G. Gomillion

More than ten years after the William P. Mitchell case, another Macon County voting registration case involving the Tuskegee Civic Association came our dad's way. The TCA had elected Charles G. Gomillion as its first president, and Mr. Gomillion had joined the Tuskegee Institute faculty in 1928. At that time they

called the school the "Tuskegee Normal and Industrial Institute."
With all the voter registration requirements, registering to vote in
Macon County took Mr. Gomillion five years.*

The black population in Macon County, Alabama, put a high
value on the right to vote, just as William Mitchell did. After World
War II, the growing black population threatened the city's white
political control. So in 1957, the Alabama Legislature decided to
change the shape of the municipality by altering the boundaries
of their city. As Professor of Law and Political Sciences at Case
Western Reserve University Jonathan Entin put it, they changed
"a square to an uncouth twenty-eight-sided figure." It was a move
that protected Tuskegee's six hundred white voters but removed
almost every African American voter from the city limits.[4]

In fighting this change of voting boundaries (Act 140), Mr.
Gomillion took his case all the way to the United States Supreme
Court. Our father and Attorneys Fred Gray and Robert L. Carter
represented Mr. Gomillion in the case *Gomillion v. Lightfoot*
(Mayor of Tuskegee) at a time when "civil rights lawyers ... risked
their own lives and the ongoing threat of being disbarred, or
charged with the crimes of *barratry* or *champerty*."[†] Attorney Gray
argued this court case before the U.S. Supreme Court, and Justice
Felix Frankfurter ultimately delivered the following opinion of
the Court:

> The essential inevitable effect of this redefinition of Tuskegee's
> boundaries is to remove from the city all save only four or five
> of its 400 Negro voters while not removing a single white voter
> or resident. The result of the Act is to deprive the Negro peti-
> tioners discriminatorily of the benefits of residence in Tuske-
> gee, including ... the right to vote in municipal elections.

---

*Mr. Gomillion came to our house frequently for Sunday dinners, and Mum-
mee always made a special dinner when he visited us.

†*Barratry* is the practice of bringing legal actions (that have little or no merit)
repeatedly in an attempt to harass. *Champerty* is illegal. A person with no previous
interest in a lawsuit will help finance the lawsuit in order to share in its bounty,
if the case is won.

These allegations, if proven, would abundantly establish that Act 140 was not an ordinary geographic redistricting measure even within familiar abuses of gerrymandering. If these allegations upon a trial remained un-contradicted or unqualified, the conclusion would be irresistible, tantamount for all practical purposes to a mathematical demonstration, that the legislation is solely concerned with segregating white and colored voters by fencing Negro citizens out of town so as to deprive them of their pre-existing municipal vote.[5]

In this landmark case, the U.S. Supreme Court had to decide whether or not an electoral district created to disenfranchise black voters violated the Constitution. On November 14, 1960, the Court decided that it did, indeed, violate the Fifteenth Amendment.

Mr. Gomillion's successful lawsuit against racially motivated gerrymandering* in Tuskegee was central to the eventual passing of the Voting Rights Act signed into law by President Johnson on August 6, 1965. The Act did away with literacy tests on a nationwide basis. It also allowed for the appointment of federal examiners to step in to a voting rights dispute and to monitor the nation's county polling places.

Did the 1965 Voting Rights Act stop voting discrimination? No. Gerrymandering, annexations, and other changes sought to prevent newly registered black voters from voting. Counties also discriminated against Hispanic, Asian, and Native American citizens regarding using the ballot. While the 1965 Voting Rights Act helped—and it was certainly a step in the right direction—other amendments (in 1970 and 1975) had to be added to provide further protections from voting discrimination for United States' citizens.

Gerrymandering is manipulating the boundaries of an electoral constituency so as to favor one party or class of people.

CHAPTER 17

Unfair Zoning Laws

1945, 1947, and 1949,
in Smithfield, Birmingham, Alabama

(Helen and Barbara remember.)

If you let Arthur Shores on that hill [Dynamite
Hill], niggers will be everywhere!
—EUGENE "BULL" CONNOR

For many years, the use of property in certain sections was restricted by race. Under Birmingham's zoning ordinances, Negroes were restricted to certain areas and whites were restricted to certain areas—yet such ordinances had been declared unconstitutional by the U.S. Supreme Court in 1910.

What began in the early 1900s as a good movement to control land use in U.S. cities became clouded by other motives. Instead of helping homeowners separate neighborhoods from spreading industry, land-control laws became a way to prevent African Americans and immigrants from living in certain areas of the cities. Southern cities, in particular, used these zoning laws to keep segregation alive and to separate and distance black and white residents.

The NAACP, founded in 1909, took action on behalf of the unfair treatment of African Americans in the area of housing, and in 1917 it won the early Supreme Court victory *Buchanan v. Warley*, "which barred municipal ordinances requiring racial segregation in housing."[1] Nevertheless, in 1925 the city of Birmingham enacted a modified racial zoning ordinance whose purpose was to protect the property holders against manufacturing plants and corner grocery stores *and to restrict the Negroes to certain districts.*

Smithfield's Unfair Zoning Laws

By 1926, Birmingham's zoning system became a "rigid racial separation of residential areas." The Birmingham City Commission used its power to give, refuse, or even revoke building permits to "construction of Negro housing contiguous to White neighborhoods." The city kept these racial zoning laws and residential development patterns from 1926 to 1949.

Smithfield, an area near downtown Birmingham, covered about six hundred acres. Around 1882, developers began to subdivide the old Southern plantation-farm into individual lots. A "color line" was drawn, and even though it was unconstitutional, black families and white families bought their lots and built their houses according to the imaginary racial boundaries. Birmingham paid no attention to the U.S. Supreme Court's 1910 ruling and strictly enforced the color line laws in their city. And whenever it best-suited Birmingham's city government, they voted at will to move old boundary lines and draw new ones.

By 1909, primarily black families had moved into the Smithfield community, which had become a thriving neighborhood. But in 1926, an unfair disruption came from the city government when they decided to revise the general zoning code into a *zoning ordinance*. The new city ordinance claimed that in certain areas of Smithfield, black families were now living in a newly zoned *white family* area. Black families, who had long since settled into their homes, schools, and neighborhood life, couldn't live there anymore! The city forbade them to live in their own homes because they had zoned it "white only."

Although the ordinance was unconstitutional to begin with, the ensuing battle lasted for decades. Eventually, the city reached a decision they hoped might end the housing "war." They drew an imaginary color line down the center of Smithfield, even naming the street "Center Street." Black families were ordered to live on the east side of Smithfield and could not move within one hundred feet of Center Street. White families were ordered to live on the west side of Smithfield. They too could not move within one hundred feet of Center Street.

On occasion, the city of Birmingham allowed black families to buy lots in restricted white areas and to build their homes. But then the city refused them a certificate of occupancy, so that black homeowners then had empty homes that they were forbidden to live in. Black families often challenged these unlawful housing zones and ordinances in Smithfield and moved too close to white residents. That's when the Ku Klux Klan and other white racists secretly planted bombs inside and beside these black families' homes and blew them up.

Most of the Klan-related dynamite blasts happened in Smithfield. In fact, the bombings that started in 1947 did not end until 1965. During those eighteen years some fifty Klan-planted bombs exploded in Smithfield, and the blasts both damaged and destroyed black houses.

During the early years, black residents of Smithfield called on the NAACP for help, and the NAACP looked to our dad to represent these clients and to put an end to racial zoning ordinances in Alabama. It was a difficult task, but our father stepped right into the middle of the controversy.

The Case of Alice P. Allen

One of these clients was Alice P. Allen, a black woman who purchased a home in Smithfield on November 8, 1945. Miss Allen had light skin and was often thought to be a white woman. She taught classes at Miles College, a school for African American students and looked forward to moving in and celebrating the Thanksgiving and Christmas holidays in her new Smithfield home.

But one week after Allen bought the house, the Birmingham City Commission, who had heard about the black woman's purchase, met and decided to rezone the land, changing her property's zone classification to "whites-only housing." Mrs. Allen owned a home she wasn't allowed to move into, so she hired our dad to file a federal suit against the City of Birmingham. When city leaders heard that our father would be representing Alice P. Allen and filing a suit against them, they backed off, quickly repealing the zoning change they had just made, and allowing Allen to live in her home.

The Case of Samuel and Essie Mae Matthews

Our father also represented Samuel and Essie Mae Matthews, an African American couple who purchased two lots a few blocks away from Center Street in 1945. The lots were located on 11th Court, between First and Second Streets on the west side of Center Street. They stood a half block from a thickly populated black settlement and three blocks from the nearest white residence. When they bought the lots, the Matthews said they thought their land was in the "black section" of Smithfield. But they were wrong. They had unintentionally built their new home in the "white section" of Smithfield!

The City had allowed the Matthews to buy the lots in the "whites only" zoned real estate. On February 25, 1946, the city even issued them a building permit to begin the construction of their home. Mr. Matthews, the son of a coal miner, built a sturdy, simple six-room frame house at the cost of $4,250—a lot of money in those days.

But white residents in that area complained about the Matthews' moving into their section of Smithfield. They feared a black family might hurt their property values, and they stirred up a ruckus that got the city leaders' attention. When the Matthews finished their house and prepared to move in, the City of Birmingham refused to give them the necessary certificate of occupancy. It seemed they could buy the land and build the house, but as a black family, they could not move into the house located in the "whites only" area of Smithfield.

The Matthews family was baffled, and they approached our father for help. He filed a petition on their behalf on October 30,

1946, and took the case to court. During the trial, our dad received several anonymous threatening phone calls.

At the end of the trial, Judge Clarence Mullins, of Birmingham, ruled that the ordinance supporting the segregation ban was unconstitutional and violated the Fourteenth Amendment. Our dad had won the Matthews' case!

The trial and its outcome made headlines around the country. The *Pittsburg Courier* picked up the story and ran it on Saturday, August 9, 1947, with the headline "Alabama Court Rules Zone Laws Illegal." Other newspapers claimed that this "was a very important victory for American Negroes" because housing segregation evidenced the worst menace confronting African-Americans in the nation. They noted that a legal precedent had now been set by the federal court, and that the ruling might help other cities battling the same unfair racial housing ordinances.

The Matthews family gathered their belongings and prepared to set up and settle into their new home. But on August 18, 1947, before they could move in, someone planted sticks of dynamite in the empty house during the night. It exploded—blowing out the walls, collapsing the roof, and crushing most of the house.* To make matters worse, the Matthews had no homeowners insurance.[2]

In response to all the violence, bombings, and court cases involving housing ordinances, Birmingham's Bull Connor issued an emergency zoning law in August of 1949, making it illegal (and a crime) for whites and blacks to move into areas zoned for the other race. Three days later, several more homes in Smithfield were bombed. The U.S. Supreme Court had long ago ruled against segregation in communities based on the Fourteenth Amendment to the Constitution, but Alabama didn't observe federal statutes. They just made up their own rules, and somehow they got away with it.

---

*The Matthews' house bombing marked the first of some fifty racial-related dynamite explosions between 1947 and 1965 in Birmingham, thus giving it the name "Bombingham."

The Case of Mary Means Monk

Our dad agreed to represent another Smithfield segregation case in December of 1949, when a black woman named Mary Means Monk contacted our father after she bought a vacant lot zoned for "whites only" on Center Street. She paid $2000 for the lot. She then hired a building contractor, H. E. Hagood, to build the house at the cost of $2000. But the city of Birmingham refused to give Mary Monk a building permit. Because she was black and the property was zoned exclusively for occupancy by members of the white race, the city forbade her to build her home. By Birmingham's city code, had Mary Monk moved into her new home on that particular lot, she would have committed a criminal offense — subject to both fine and imprisonment.

In a class action suit, Thurgood Marshall, Peter A. Hall, and David H. Hood Jr. assisted our father, who addressed the U.S. Court of Appeals Fifth Circuit in the case *City of Birmingham v. Monk.* They asked for "a declaration that ordinances prohibiting Negroes from residing in certain districts and persons of the white race from residing in certain other districts, were unconstitutional, and for injunctive relief."[3] In doing so, they brought this important question to the judge: "Whether or not the zoning laws and supplemental ordinance in question constitute a legitimate exercise of the police power of the State [of Alabama] ... or are unconstitutional and void as violative of the Fourteenth Amendment to the Constitution of the United States...."[4]

The court struck down Birmingham's zoning ordinance and declared it unconstitutional and in violation of the United States Fourteenth Amendment to the Constitution. Some white leaders weren't happy that our father, Marshall, Hall, and Hood won Mary Monk's class action case. The broker George B. Alexander defended Judge Mullins's ruling but blamed the problem on "people of the ilk and breed of the negro lawyer, Arthur Shores." Birmingham's Mrs. R. D. DeLaure wrote Mayor Green to say that the Ku Klux Klan "ought to get Shores."[5]

Several years after that trial, black Americans who lived on the east side of Smithfield's Center Street started building houses and moving into Smithfield's west side—the former "whites only" zone. One after another, black families moved across Center Street and set up residence on the west. In 1953, our father followed suit and had our house built in Smithfield's black section on the east side of Center Street.

CHAPTER 18

Living under Jim Crow Laws

Late 1940s and early 1950s,
in Birmingham, Alabama

(Helen remembers.)

I remember well the very day I first came face to face
with the Jim Crow laws of forced segregation. Birmingham's child-amusement park, KiddieLand, opened in the
summer of 1948. I was seven years old, and I couldn't go
because I didn't have "white" skin.

—JUDGE HELEN SHORES LEE

Rain or shine, winter or summer, our family never failed to take
our special Sunday afternoon family drive around Birmingham.
On one particular Sunday, we drove out toward Bessemer, a city
a few miles west of downtown Birmingham.

Kiddieland, a children's amusement park at the Alabama State
Fairgrounds, had just opened the week after Memorial Day that
year. From the car's backseat I saw the new park, lit up like some
kind of fairyland. The Ferris wheel whirled around, and the place
swarmed with children and their parents. I could smell the pop-
corn and cotton candy, and I could hear the loud, exciting music.

"Daddy," I begged. "Please take us there!" I wanted to go to
Kiddieland so badly I could hardly stand it.

"No, Chickadee," our father gently said. "We can't go there
now, because only white people can go to Kiddieland. But I promise you," he assured us, "one day we will be able to go."

I cried. Got mad. Pouted. "I wish I was white!" I shouted. I had
"fire in my bones" even at that young age!

That's when our father said to me, "Never wish to be white,
Chickadee. Just wish to go."

Our father had promised me that "someday things will be different in Birmingham and Alabama." And I believed him—he worked hard to keep his promise to me, fighting to change unfair laws, especially in the arena of public accommodations.

Growing Up with Segregation

As I got older, I naturally became more and more aware of segregation and its implications, especially in terms of what I could do and could not do. We never questioned certain practices. I suppose the "rules" had been around for such a long time that both blacks and whites saw them as "just the way things are." But I was in a constant tug of war over what I was told to do and what I wanted to do.

Because of my mother's light complexion, for example, she could easily pass as a white woman. Whenever Mummee took us downtown to shop with her, we usually stopped at the Kress "five and dime" store to buy freshly roasted peanuts. We could smell the peanuts before we entered the store. The white store clerk took one look at Mummee and routinely poured her peanuts into a white, wax-lined bag that protected the white customer from the oil of the peanuts that soaked through the skimpy, unlined, brown paper bags. The same clerk put our peanuts in the thin brown bag. I guess she thought we were the children of her black maid.

I also never questioned why we had to eat at a separate lunch counter in the basement of a downtown department store while white people ate in the beautifully decorated restaurant on the main floor. While the lunch counters went unchallenged, the separate water fountains posed a challenge. On one occasion our mother and I went to Loveman's department store in downtown Birmingham. Between the two bright brass elevator doors was a white porcelain water fountain. The sign over the fountain read "Whites Only." Around the corner from this fountain was a dirty, unkempt fountain with a sign that read "Colored Only." I was eight years old and determined to take a drink from that "Whites Only" water fountain. I stared at that fountain for a moment and then asked myself, *Why not?* As I was taking a long delicious drink of "Whites Only" water, a white man came up behind me. He jerked me away, shook me, and told me I knew better than to drink from *that* fountain. Mummee saw the commotion, grabbed me, and we left the store. Needless to say, when I got home I got a whipping. Our mother was furious with me, and I was sullen and defiant.

The Streetcar's Separating Wooden Sign

Another time our mother and I got on the streetcar headed for downtown Birmingham. When we boarded, we walked to the back, but we saw no place for blacks to sit. All of the seats midway to the front, however, were empty. Rather than sit down in the "Whites Only" section, the black people stood up in the back. A wooden board separated the white section up front from the black section in the back. The board was portable and could be moved forward or backward, depending on how crowded the streetcar was. The streetcar driver moved the sign to allow white passengers more seats when the front section filled up.

If white passengers boarded the streetcar and found no place to sit in the front section, bus drivers ordered black passengers to stand up and vacate their seats for the white passengers, or get off the streetcar.

When our mother and I boarded the streetcar and saw no empty seats in the "Colored Only" section, I simply decided to move the separating board myself and open up two seats so Mummee and I could sit down.

I sat down in the newly available seat, and I saw the look of horror on my mother's face. She froze, remained standing, and refused to sit down in the now-empty seat. Fortunately, nothing happened. Had I been a youth or an adult and been caught, I would have been arrested and jailed for moving the board. Needless to say, when I got home, I got another whipping.

Throughout my childhood, our mother scolded me time and

time again for my defiance of Jim Crow laws. I became even more defiant when I got older and discovered I was different only because I was black and not white. I also learned that as Arthur Shores' daughter, I had to behave myself or possibly face physical danger. All those feelings had come to a head by the time I shot a gun at the car filled with the racially bigoted white youth.

The Driver's License

My young life began to look up when I was finally old enough to go to high school and get my driver's license. As soon as I turned 16, our dad took me to get my license. Of course, I failed. Had Daddy been a white man, I'm sure I would have passed. I felt angry and disappointed. The next week I asked my mama to take me. Mummee looked like a white woman with her fair skin.

Mummee agreed, and I again took the driving test. Afterward, when we reached the main desk and waited to see if I had passed or failed, Mummee smiled at the white woman behind the desk.

"Your girl didn't do too good on the test," the woman told Mummee. "But I will go on and pass her because she works for you." (Again, it was assumed that Mummee had brought in a maid's child.)

Word got around about the incident, and family members came to Mummee and asked if she would take them to get their driver's licenses. Someone even put a maid's white apron and cap in the back seat, just in case they needed it. Mummee agreed to take them, and they all passed the test and got their licenses.

Still, I detested the city's Jim Crow laws and the mistreatment I received from white people in pre-1957 Alabama. I looked forward to graduating from Parker High School.

"I want to leave Birmingham and never come back!" I told everyone I knew. I decided to enroll at Fisk University to pursue my educational goals. For some reason, I thought Nashville would be different from Birmingham.

CHAPTER 19

Helen Leaves Birmingham

(Helen remembers.)

I want no part of this profession!
—JUDGE HELEN SHORES LEE

When I was ready to leave Birmingham to go to Fisk University, Mummee and Daddy helped me pack my things into the car. All ready to go, my parents and Barbara waited in the car for me to come out of the house. After a while, I finally came to the car. Tears streamed down my face. I wanted to leave Birmingham, but I had mixed feelings about leaving my family behind. Maybe I just didn't know what to expect in Nashville.

Daddy always stressed the importance of an education. "Education is your ticket to freedom," he told Barbara and me.

Become a Lawyer?! No, Thanks!

To the disappointment of our father, my career goal was to become a medical doctor. I wanted no part of becoming a lawyer. I had been with him in court, and I remembered the Autherine Lucy case. The opposing counsel, and especially the judge, were so disrespectful to Daddy. I wanted to stand up and shout, "You can't talk to my daddy that way!"

But I didn't. Our dad, in his mild mannered way, kept looking over his shoulder at me as if to say, "Chickadee, don't you dare say a word!"

I was so proud of him as I watched him. He kept his "cool" in spite of the disrespectful comments by the judge. Then and there I said to myself, *If this is the way I am going to be talked to in court as an attorney, I want no part of this profession!*

When I arrived at Fisk, I quickly learned that Nashville also had strict segregation laws. While at the school, I participated in the sit-ins of the department store lunch counters, demonstrations led by my classmate, civil rights activist Diane Nash. Students from Fisk University as well as from Tennessee State participated. We entered a store and immediately took our seats at the lunch counter. The store manager turned off the lights, dragged us outside, and then locked the doors. We then ran to another store and sat down at their lunch counter. Again the store manager put us out and locked the doors. Soon storeowners figured out we planned to come to their stores by the hundreds, and they simply locked their doors before we got there.

We were taught in frequent meetings how to behave. We kept the sit-in demonstrations orderly, but that didn't stop the police from arresting many of our group for "disorderly conduct." And the arrests didn't stop us from going back again and again. I must admit, I was afraid. The whites heckled us and pushed us during our demonstrations. Some of our group got punched in the face. But we remained calm and orderly.

During the 1960 sit-in demonstrations, protesters challenged Ben West, the mayor of Nashville (1951–63), to take a stand against segregation. He did. As a result, Nashville's business community desegregated department store lunch counters, making Nashville the first southern city to desegregate public facilities.

I was proud to have been a part of such a significant event, and when I called home to tell our Dad what I had done, I could tell he was proud of me. But he also warned me to be careful.

The Sunday Letters

On the day I left my home in Birmingham, Alabama, and enrolled into Fisk University, I began receiving our father's long, handwritten letters. The letters came every Sunday by special delivery and without fail, so I looked forward to Sundays. In page after page, he wrote about the family, his law practice, his travels, the city of Birmingham, his hopes and dreams, and many other things. Whenever I read the loving and informative letters, I felt like I had had a heart-to-heart conversation with our dad. I don't know where he found the time to pen such long notes, but I guess he wanted to make sure I knew I was loved and lovingly remembered.

When Barbara left home and enrolled in Talladega College, Daddy also wrote her long loving letters. Most of the letters he wrote late at home, after a hard day's work.

To my regret, those hundreds of letters have been lost. I kept them for a very long time, and then suddenly they were gone. Perhaps they were lost in a move from one city to another. I don't know, but I mourn their loss.

Recently I found one of his letters to me. It is probably the only letter that I still have, and it has become a treasure. He wrote it on a Monday evening shortly before Thanksgiving, in November 1962, about a month or so before my wedding on December 22, 1962. At the time I lived in California. I was a graduate student at UCLA and shared an apartment with my childhood friend, Norma Willis.

"Chickadee," he began the letter.

It has been some time since I talked with you. Each night last week I would plan to write, but after my work I would be too sleepy to write.

I spent last week in Talladega. I was in court during the day and at the college at night. I would also take my meals at the college. I would visit with Puchie [Daddy's nickname for Barbara, a student at Talladega College at the time] before and after lunch, and also before supper. We certainly enjoyed each other, and for me it was reliving my [college] memories at Talladega.

The case* has been recessed again until Feb. 4, 1963. At the rate we are moving in the trial of this case, it will take us until

---

*It is not known what case he was referring to here.

this time next year to complete it. We expect a favorable decision from the U.S. Supreme Court....

Friday of last week, I brought Puchie home for the weekend, and she brought three of her classmates as house guests. They really had some time. Friday night Mummee and I took them to see Miles College and Benedict College play [football]. Saturday we took them to see Ala State and Ala A & M play. Saturday night Mummee took them to the *Ebony* fashion show. By the way, we sent your name in on two of the tickets for subscription to *Ebony* [Magazine] for a year, and [to] *Jet* [Magazine] for 6 months.... You can have them send the magazines to your new address when you change.

I had to go to Montgomery again yesterday. Mummee and Puchie took the guests to church, and they went back to Talladega [College] about 6 p.m. They had left when I arrived from Montgomery about 7 p.m. Hollins went with me to Montgomery. As I journeyed to and back from Montgomery, my yester years came back to me, and I thought of yours and Barbara's youth when we would take our trips to Florida. It seems as if it were just a couple of years ago, and to think that now both of you are away, and our family will never be as it once was. It has come so quick, yet I knew it must come, and in time I must adjust to being without both of you. At any rate, I enjoyed Puchie and the kids she brought with her, and they really had a ball.

We were all quite concerned over the Cuban situation* last week. After the President [Kennedy] spoke and informed us how imminent it seems that we will have war, many of the children at Talladega [College] became frightened and called home. Puchie said there was a line waiting to use the phone.

Everything is simmering down now. Mummee and [Aunt] Teddy are in the recreation room working on some phase of the coming marriage [Helen's wedding planned for December 22, 1962]. Mummee's whole mind is on the wedding now. It really keeps her occupied.

I am going to Washington [D.C.], Thursday. Back [home]

---

*The Cuban Missile Crisis.

Saturday, I hope. Then to Talladega [College] for Founder's Day. [Then] I go to New York. I will stay in New York until Wednesday afternoon, and then will go to Pittsburg where I will remain until Sunday. I will stay at home then until Nov. 19, when I will go to New York again.

I have been talking about myself so much I forgot to congratulate you on making a B in your test. How did you come out in your other test? Did you drop the course you mentioned that you would [drop]? How is your job serving you? How is Bob doing on his job? Is Norma [Helen's roommate] still enjoying her work? Let me know the answers to my questions in your next letter.

Well, "Sweetie," I guess I will do a little reading now, then go to bed. I will close this letter tomorrow. Good night.

The next morning, while waiting for his secretary, Agnes Stoudmire, to come back to the office from lunch, he finished his love letter to me:

> *(Tuesday 1:30 p.m.)* "Sweetie," Agnes has not come in from lunch yet, so I thought I would complete my letter. I have been very busy today. I will be in court all day tomorrow. Business has been good with me. I certainly need it with this coming wedding … and you know Mummee! This wedding will be "the talk of the town" for years to come. I am enclosing a clipping from Sunday's paper. Well "Sweetie Pie," this is all for now. Give my regards to Bob and Norma. May God bless and keep you always, With Love Daddy.

Graduating from Fisk

After I graduated from Fisk in 1962 and moved to California to attend graduate school at UCLA, nobody knew who I was. I was just Helen Lee, and my husband, Bob, and I could walk freely down Hollywood Boulevard and not worry about being identified as the "black civil rights attorney's daughter." We were part of the "Hip, Cool, and Groovy" generation, the "Age of Aquarius," "Let the sunshine in," and all that!

I am often asked, Why did you return to Birmingham? I had vowed never to return to the South, especially Birmingham, Alabama, but I came back in 1971. Even though I was aware of the progress Birmingham had made, I never really wanted to move back. It was my husband's idea because we were driving home to Birmingham twice a year. My father would fly out to L.A. in May and bring his grandsons back to Birmingham where they would spend the summer. Then Bob and I would drive back every August to pick them up and bring them back to L.A.

On one occasion, after Kiddieland desegregated, my father called me and happily told me he had just taken the boys to Kiddieland Park and that they had a good time. I could tell he had a good time too.

My husband often talked about moving back, but I didn't take him seriously until I saw the different moving companies giving him estimates. I told him, "You can move back, but I'm staying right here!"

Well, we moved!

To my surprise, however, I found a different Birmingham than the one I had left in 1958. People, both white and black, worked together, played together, ate at the same restaurants — even across the table from each other. They also worshipped together in the city's churches. Slowly, my anger from the past began to subside.

It took time, but years later my anger had changed into a sort of appreciation and a much deeper understanding of the great racial strides Birmingham had finally made.

CHAPTER 20

Bull Connor Arrests
Senator Taylor

1948, in Birmingham, Alabama

(Helen remembers.)

Dear Friend: Thank you very much for the splendid job
you did at the hearing in Birmingham … I didn't have
the opportunity to thank you personally then, but I do
now and I congratulate you on the fight you are making
to bring equality and justice to the South.

—LETTER FROM U.S. SENATOR GLEN H. TAYLOR
to Arthur D. Shores

The trial of U.S. Senator Glen H. Taylor proved to be one of those
cases that heated up Birmingham's atmosphere, got the attention
of the Ku Klux Klan, and drew intense criticism from Alabama's
white citizens.

Born in 1904, the same year our dad was born, Glen Taylor
served as Idaho's Democratic senator from 1945 to 1951 and
was known as a successful businessman and country-western
singer. In 1948, Senator Taylor was running as the potential vice-
president with presidential hopeful Henry Wallace of Iowa on the
ticket of the United States Progressive Party, a leftwing political
party with a goal to end segregation, give full voting rights to
black citizens, and institute universal government health insurance. The American Communist Party supported the Wallace/
Taylor ticket. Henry Wallace had served as vice-president under
Franklin Delano Roosevelt (1941–45), though *Time* magazine has
since called Wallace "America's Worst Vice President." One writer

later termed his candidacy for president as "the closest the Soviet Union ever came to actually choosing a president of the United States." He also noted, "Not that Wallace posed much of a threat: he garnered zero electoral votes."

In the hysteria of the Communist "witch hunt" in the spring of 1948, the Southern Negro Youth Congress (SYNC) invited white Idaho Senator Glen H. Taylor to speak in Birmingham, Alabama, on May 1. Even though Taylor was busy and in the middle of his vice-presidential campaign, he agreed to come.

When the larger black churches, intimidated by the Klan's bomb threats, turned down the opportunity to host the event, the SNYC arranged to meet at the Alliance Gospel Tabernacle, a tiny African American church in Birmingham.

The "Bull's" Orders

When Birmingham's Commissioner of Public Safety, Eugene "Bull" Connor, heard that both black and white citizens planned to attend the function, he told Senator Taylor that, due to Alabama's segregation laws, he could not speak to a black and white audience meeting together in the same building. When backed into a corner, however, Connor consented to the mixed racial audience but ordered the church to have two separate entrances —one for whites and one for blacks.

A bevy of Birmingham's white police, as well as Klan members, stationed themselves around the small church. The atmosphere before the meeting was tense, ready to explode with violence. Perhaps playing to the newspaper reporters and trying to make a point about Alabama's unconstitutional segregation laws, Senator Taylor purposely entered the church through the door marked "Negroes" instead of the one marked "Whites Only." White police tried to block his way, and when he resisted, they scuffled. Birmingham police officers visibly and roughly arrested Taylor for "disorderly conduct." They took him to jail, searched him, and fingerprinted him.

The Resulting National Fury

The nation's newspapers ran the story, highlighting Birmingham's unkind treatment of the U.S. senator as well as its unjust segregation laws. Senator Taylor made a national radio broadcast explaining the unfair treatment and imprisonment he had received. Alabama's newspapers, as well as other Southern newspapers wrote editorials and fought back.

"It is well to recognize this maneuver of Senator Taylor for what it is," wrote a reporter from the *Huntsville Times*:

> It [entering through the door marked "Negro"] was meant to serve no useful purpose: it was made solely to use as political propaganda in the Wallace campaign. He [Taylor] and Mr. Wallace unquestionably plan to play upon Negro sympathies, to get Negro ballots in those states where there are large numbers of Negro voters....[1]

Another newspaper, the *Alabama Journal*, wrote of the incident,

> Senator Glen Taylor, circus performer, showman and banjo player, has put on one of his acts in Birmingham and got his name in all the papers, just as he planned. It is regrettable however to see even a United States senator, circus performer or not, deliberately defy laws, abuse policemen, play with dynamite. His conduct gives his *pinkish-ness* a very red aspect.[2]

Alabama's *Talladega Daily Home* wrote,

> Public Safety Commissioner Eugene Connor of Birmingham is a man of many fine qualities, not the least of which is his sincere desire to prevent the spread of Communism in the Magic City. The Commissioner can sit at his desk at the City Hall and smell a Communist at the farthest reaches of the city limits.[3]

It was in this tense racial atmosphere in Alabama that our dad and Birmingham's black attorney, George Traywick, as well as two white attorneys—the Progressive Party's attorney John J. Abt, from Washington, D.C., and Morel Montgomery, from Birmingham—began preparing for Senator Taylor's highly publicized trial.

Senator Taylor's Trial

In August of 1948, on United States Senate stationary, Senator Taylor wrote our dad and asked him to send him a copy of the Birmingham segregation ordinance. He sent it immediately. Then, on December 8, 1948, on Progressive Party stationary, Attorney Abt wrote our father:

> Dear Mr. Shores: Senator Taylor told me on the phone yesterday that he had received a letter from you indicating that the appeal in his case has been set for Jan. 17. I told the Senator that I would write you for additional information so that I might be in a position to discuss procedure with him.
>
> Am I correct in my recollection that the appeal in fact is a trial de novo in the Circuit Court before judge and jury, at which time we can raise the question of the constitutionality of the Birmingham ordinance as a defense to the charge of resisting an officer in the performance of his duty?
>
> As I recall, immediately after the original trial you secured statements from all of the necessary witnesses in preparation for a possible early hearing of the appeal. In that case, I take it that no extended preparation of the evidence will be necessary.
>
> I did not discuss with the Senator whether January 17 would be a convenient date for him. Before discussing this with him, I should like to find out from you whether there would be any problem in securing a continuance, in the event that the Senator prefers a later date, and, if so, how quickly we should move for such a continuance.
>
> I should very much appreciate it if you would advise me on these matters so that I might take them up with the Senator and come to a conclusion on how to proceed. I should also appreciate any thoughts of your own with reference both to

the legal and policy questions involved in the case. Sincerely yours, John J. Abt.[4]

Consequently, our dad asked Circuit Judge George Lewis Bailes for a continuance — or postponement — from the trial's original date of January 17, 1949. Judge Bailes granted the new date, scheduling the trial for March 16, 1949. By that time, Wallace and Taylor had lost the presidential and vice-presidential election in 1948.

The Senator's Trial

Senator Taylor flew to Birmingham that spring to stand trial on the charges of disorderly conduct, resisting arrest, and assault and battery. The *Birmingham Post* described Glen Taylor in a derogatory way as the senator arrived in Birmingham: "His neat homburg hat was cocked jauntily to one side as he stepped out of the twin-motored Eastern Air Lines plane at Municipal Airport. The Windsor knot, which he sported in his necktie when here almost a year ago, was present again. Gone was his Wallace button. Gone, also, was any advice as to where Public Safety Commissioner Eugene Connor could go...."[5]

Senator Glen Taylor received a 180-day jail sentence and was fined $50.00. (The jail sentence was later suspended and replaced with a six-month probation period.) The senator also received a fierce tongue lashing from police. After the trial, our dad received a letter from Senator Taylor along with an 8" x 10" photograph of himself. At the bottom of the photograph, the senator wrote, "A friend in need is a friend indeed."

Before Senator Taylor left Birmingham after his trial, he waved his hat and posed for photographers of the *Birmingham Post* under a large sign that said, "Welcome to Birmingham — The Magic City."

Why did our father take this case? It wasn't because he had any Communist sympathies. He did not. In fact, our father was a devoted Christian who chose to be politically conservative. It wasn't because our dad wanted, or needed, the newspaper headlines. Nor was it to gain the nation's attention. He always chose to work in the background, out of the limelight. He wanted to get unjust laws changed, not publicize himself.

We think our father took Taylor's case because the arrest of Glen Taylor, a World War II hero, a U.S. senator from Idaho, and a candidate running for the office of vice-president of the United States, showed the nation how unjust and unconstitutional Alabama's laws were concerning public accommodations. The nation took notice of how Alabama had made up its own laws regarding segregation, ignoring the Supreme Court's ruling based on the Fourteenth Amendment. The senator's arrest for simply entering a church through the door marked "Negroes" highlighted for the nation the unconstitutional horrors happening in Birmingham.

CHAPTER 21

The Problem with Segregated Schools:
Brown v. Board of Education

Early 1950s in the nation's schools

(Helen remembers.)

Discrimination in education is symbolic of all the
more drastic discriminations which Negroes suffer in
American life.... The equal protection clause of the
14th Amendment furnishes the key to ending separate
schools.

—ATTORNEY CHARLES H. HOUSTON

On June 7, 1892, in New Orleans, Louisiana, 30-year-old Homer
Plessy, an African American shoemaker, stepped aboard the East
Louisiana Railroad bound for Covington, Louisiana, into the car
marked "White."

Plessy had been born a free person, and he was seven-eighths
white and one-eighth black. Under a Louisiana law enacted in
1890, the state classified him as black and required him to ride
in the "Coloreds" rail car. While the "Whites" car stayed clean,
comfortable, and well-maintained, the "Coloreds" car was often
uncomfortable and dirty.

When asked by railroad officials to move to the black section,
Plessy refused. Police then arrested and jailed him.

Mr. Plessy took the matter to court, basing his case on the
question, *Does not this Louisiana state law violate the Thirteenth
and Fourteenth Amendments to the United States Constitution?*
The Thirteenth Amendment made slavery illegal in the United
States. The Fourteenth Amendment states that all people born in

the United States are citizens of the country as well as of the state of their birth—and no state can deny equal protection of the laws to a U.S. citizen.

Judge Ferguson decided that Plessy was guilty, and he lost the case. Mr. Plessy then took his case to the Louisiana Supreme Court. Again, he lost. In one last attempt to prove his innocence, Mr. Plessy went all the way to the U.S. Supreme Court in Washington, D.C.

The Supreme Court's Decision

On May 18, 1896, the United States Supreme Court rendered its verdict in *Plessy v. Ferguson:* "Yes. The states can constitutionally enact legislation requiring persons of different races to use 'separate but equal' segregated facilities."[1]

As a result, "separate but equal" became law for the next sixty-four years. The nation separated the two races by providing "Negro" and "White" railway cars. African Americans had to attend separate schools, eat at separate restaurants, sit in the back of public buses, drink from separate public water fountains, use separate toilets. "Separate but equal" was based on the argument that while blacks and whites were "politically equal" (they had the same political rights), they were "socially unequal" (blacks were not as socially advanced as whites.) Although the U.S. Supreme Court ruling kept the races separate, the facilities granted for black citizens proved to be far inferior to the facilities for the white populace.

Brown v. Board of Education of Topeka, Kansas

In the early 1950s, the "separate but equal" law meant that Linda Brown and her sister had to go to an all-black elementary school in their city of Topeka, Kansas. In order to catch the bus to the all-black school, the young girls had to walk through a dangerous railroad switchyard. Naturally, they wanted to avoid the hazardous commute and attend the school near their home. But that particular school accepted only white students.

The Brown family believed that the Topeka public school system violated the Fourteenth Amendment by not allowing their children to attend a school in their neighborhood. Linda's father, Mr. Oliver Brown, a minister, took the case to court. The Federal District Court decided that segregation in the public educational system was harmful to black children, but that black children had their own schools, and segregation was legal. The Browns then appealed their case to the Supreme Court. "While the facilities are similar," they argued, "segregated schools are not equal."[2]

Other parents in other states, including Delaware, the District of Columbia, South Carolina, and Virginia, were also challenging racial segregation in their own public school systems. With help from the NAACP lawyers, *Brown v. Board of Education* became the consolidated name for a group of five individual law suits happening around the country, which our dad worked on, along with Thurgood Marshall, in writing up the "Statement as to Jurisdiction."[3]

The Case of Mr. Harry Briggs

The children in the all-white public schools of Clarendon County's town of Summerton, South Carolina, had a fleet of buses to pick them up, deliver them to school, and bring them safely back home each day. The black children of Clarendon County, who attended all-black schools, however, had no buses. The county required them to walk great distances to school and back each day. Some of the children walked eight or nine miles one way!

With the help of the Rev. Joseph Armstrong DeLaine, principal of Silver School, located near Summerton, and a local parent, Modjeska Simpkins, Harry Briggs and his wife, Eliza, joined with nineteen other black families to request transportation help with the forty-six black children among them. Briggs, a service station attendant, and Eliza, a domestic maid, and the others, asked the

Clarendon County officials for just one bus to take their children to school. But the county officials said no. They told the black parents "since the African American community did not pay much in taxes, it would be unfair to expect white taxpayers to provide transportation for African American school children."[4]

The Rev. DeLaine launched a letter writing campaign, but it did no good. The African American parents decided to collect money within their community and buy a used school bus. But the old bus needed frequent repairs, and it proved to be too costly for the parents to maintain.

The School Bus and the Lawsuit

In 1947 Rev. DeLaine filed a lawsuit against the Clarendon County School officials demanding school bus transportation for the county's black children. But due to a technicality, the case was withdrawn two years later. Still, they didn't give up. In March 1949, DeLaine asked NAACP's Thurgood Marshall and his team of attorneys (which included our father) to represent them in a lawsuit.[5] The petitioners argued that the separate schools for African Americans were "inadequate and unhealthy," "overcrowded," and "dilapidated." The facilities were separate, but by no means equal.

In November 1950, at a pre-trial hearing, U.S. District Court Judge J. Waties Waring told them the real issue was public school segregation, not just the unequal school facilities. Judge Waring dismissed the case. That same year, the NAACP team of lawyers filed *Briggs et al. v. Elliott et al.* in the Federal District Court. They protested the *Plessy v. Ferguson* "separate but equal" ruling. Harry Briggs Sr. signed his name first to the petition. The case challenged Roderick W. Elliott, chairman of the board, as well as the Board of Trustees of School District 22 and several school administrators.

On May 28, 1951, U.S. District Court Judges John J. Parker, George B. Timmerman, and J. Waties Waring heard the Briggs case. The court ruled in June 1951 that the school facilities were indeed unequal, and they told the Clarendon County officials to equalize them. Judge Waring, however, gave a dissenting opinion: "Segregation in education can never produce equality and is an evil that must be eradicated," he stated. The NAACP appealed the case to the U.S. Supreme Court that same year. But in January 1952, the Court returned the case to the lower courts for reviews on the county's progress in equalizing the school facilities.

On December 9–11, 1952, the U.S. Supreme Court heard Briggs and three other cases. The following day, the Court heard the fifth case—all under the title *Brown et al. v. Board of Education.* The question presented to the Court was the following: "Does segregation of children in public schools solely on the basis of race, even though the physical facilities and other 'tangible' factors may be equal, deprive the children of the minority group of equal educational opportunities?"[6] In December 1953, NAACP attorneys presented additional arguments to the Court on all five cases.

The Landmark Decision

In 1953, seventeen states and the District of Columbia had mandatory public school segregation: Alabama, Arkansas, Florida, Georgia, Louisiana, Mississippi, North Carolina, South Carolina, Tennessee, Texas, Virginia, Kentucky, Maryland, Missouri, Oklahoma, West Virginia, and Delaware. Kansas permitted school segregation based on local option.

On May 17, 1954, the Supreme Court ruled that public school segregation violated the Fourteenth Amendment and that segregation in public school systems was illegal. Chief Justice Earl Warren said, "We conclude that the doctrine of 'separate but equal' has no place. Separate educational facilities are inherently unequal."

The Court found that

> segregation of white and colored children in public schools
> has a detrimental effect upon the colored children. The impact

is greater when it has the sanction of the law; for the policy of separating the races is usually interpreted as denoting the inferiority of the Negro group. A sense of inferiority affects the motivation of a child to learn. Segregation with the sanction of law, therefore, has a tendency to [retard] the educational and mental development of Negro children and to deprive them of some of the benefits they would receive in a racial[ly] integrated school system.[7]

The Court concluded that in the field of public education,

the doctrine of "separate but equal" has no place. They stated that separate educational facilities are inherently unequal. Therefore, we hold that the plaintiffs and others similarly situated for whom the actions have been brought are, by reason of the segregation complained of, deprived of the equal protection of the laws guaranteed by the Fourteenth Amendment. This disposition makes unnecessary any discussion whether such segregation also violates the Due Process Clause of the Fourteenth Amendment.... We have now announced that such segregation is a denial of the equal protection of the laws.[8]

The Second Ruling

The Court handed down a second ruling on the five *Brown v. Board of Education* cases, declaring that public schools should be desegregated "with all deliberate speed."

History has since shown that *Briggs v. Elliott* was the most important of the five 1952 cases collectively argued under *Brown v. Board of Education*. The Briggs case not only contributed major portions of the supporting arguments but changed the NAACP's strategy of attacking "separate but equal" laws. The NAACP had laid the groundwork for these cases as it worked to end public school segregation. And "none of the cases would have been possible without individuals who were courageous enough to take a stand against the segregated system."[9]

By law, the U.S. Supreme Court ordered all public schools in the nation to open their doors to both black and white students. But still Alabama didn't obey the Court's order. For the following nine years, our father stepped into crowded courtrooms and fought for the privileges of black children who wanted to embrace their American rights and get a good education.

CHAPTER 22

The Perfect Storm

Early 1950s, in Birmingham, Alabama

(Barbara remembers.)

It is difficult to imagine that any group has been more committed than black lawyers to trying to restore a nation's lost dignity. Throughout the country, black lawyers have overcome numerous personal and professional obstacles, joining a profession once closed to them and working alongside others to eliminate the scourge of color caste. Specifically in Alabama, between 1940 and 1980, the NAACP Legal Defense Fund ("LDF") and a few legal giants took the brutal beast of state-sanctioned, racial segregation by its awesome horns, wrestled it to the ground, and over time have been slowly destroying its capacity to generate misery and oppression of colored citizens.[1]

—FROM AN ARTICLE in the
Alabama Law Review 52 (2001)

By the early- and mid-1950s, our father was deep in the civil rights struggle, which was rapidly heading toward a "perfect storm." The NAACP kept him very busy on high profile cases. Newspaper headlines across the nation captured his every move. Death threats and promises of violence to our family became commonplace, and our move to Dynamite Hill significantly increased our risk. When Daddy ignored the threats, as he always did, white supremacists and Klan members often tried to bribe him to drop a case or to leave a case untried. But Daddy didn't back down.

Daddy had conversations with Uncle Hollins about the bribes and threats from the Klan, but he kept them a secret from

Mummee. He knew that if she found out, she would be upset. He never talked with his family about the Klan, and he always took extra precaution for our safety.

Dangerous Years

It is difficult to describe the threatened violence our father and our family encountered when Daddy represented a young black woman, Autherine Lucy, in 1953. We had just moved into our new house on Dynamite Hill when our father took the case. Because of frequent bombings of houses on the Hill, the builder had constructed the house on a strong foundation and reinforced it with commercial steel beams.

Our friends and neighbors on Center Street understood the extremely explosive nature of this case and trial. Voluntarily, the Smithfield community men organized a 5:00 p.m. to 8:00 a.m. "neighborhood watch" to protect our family from violence. Fully armed, they took turns guarding our house while Daddy and the other lawyers worked and slept there. We heard a lot of "Lord, have mercy!" comments from Mummee during that trial. She didn't want to move to "Dynamite Hill" in the first place because of the bombings and violence. The high-profile Lucy case just heightened her sense of fear. Even at our young ages, we too felt afraid of the violence happening all around us.

Armed with shotguns, the neighborhood men patrolled our house on all sides and in the basement. The churches in our area and neighborhood women's auxiliaries brought home-cooked food every day for the guards. They loaded our kitchen table with cakes, chicken salad sandwiches, fried chicken, and always fresh hot coffee. The guards came in shifts to the kitchen, picked up food, and delivered it to the guards all around the house. They used walkie-talkies to communicate with each other throughout the house and grounds.

Thurgood Marshall was staying at our house during the Lucy trial, and he slept in the guest bedroom. He thoroughly enjoyed the good Southern food, especially the chicken salad sandwiches! Constance Motley stayed at our home too. Motley was a big woman, quiet, stoic, strong, and courageous. I sensed no fear in her at all, just as I sensed no fear in our father. But Mummee's fear grew with each hour. She again begged Daddy to move us away from Dynamite Hill.

On a particularly quiet evening, when most of the guards were outside or in the garage, I went down to the basement in my pajamas to iron a blouse. We kept the iron and ironing board downstairs. When I reached the bottom of the stairs, I saw a huge man dressed in old overalls sitting in a chair with a double barrel shotgun across his lap. I think I scared him more than he scared me. When he saw me, he sprang from his seat and pointed that loaded shotgun at me. I jumped back and screamed, and so did he! I flew up the stairs and found Daddy.

"Daddy," I cried. "Why didn't you tell me there was a man downstairs with a shotgun?!"

The Arguments

Lying in bed at night, I could overhear Mummee and Daddy argue. They rarely spoke unkind words to each other, so I worried about them. At times I worried they might be getting a divorce. I heard Mummee repeatedly ask Daddy, "Shores! Why would you put our family through this? Why can't we pack up our family and move far away from Birmingham, Alabama, and all this violence?!"

Our Dad's softly spoken words to her were always the same: "Dodie, we're going to fight this and stick it out. We can't move away."

Early in the marriage, Mummee lived in fear. At first she didn't encourage him in his work because she was concerned for her family's safety. But as the years passed, she became his strongest supporter. She learned what it meant to fully put your trust in God to take care of Daddy. In fact, she once said, "I'm turning you over to the Lord, Shores. He will keep you safe."

Mummee was so proud of Daddy's work in the fight for justice. Years later we found a private scrapbook Mummee had kept on our father for years. In it she noted his fight for equal rights and recorded the various awards he received. Mummee may have been one to sometimes criticize Daddy, but she didn't want to hear of anybody else criticizing him. When someone said something negative about Daddy, she indirectly (and sometimes directly!) gave them "a piece of her mind." When Daddy ran for City Council reelection, she heard an opponent say something negative about him. She directly confronted the man and politely set him straight.

Mummee never flaunted or bragged that she was married to Attorney A. D. Shores. She was confident in who she was. When Daddy became a city councilman, a sales clerk told her she "needed to dress better now." Mummee told the woman she was "quite comfortable in dressing herself the way she wanted to."

Mummee was proud of Daddy, even though she may not have openly spoken those words. She stayed right by his side. She avoided publicity, but when unexpectedly thrust into the spotlight, she handled it well. Mummee was the silent warrior.

The guards stayed all night long, but they left in the morning when Daddy and the others went to the office and Helen and I were driven to school. For most of the day then, Mummee stayed in the house alone. She grew very frightened at home by herself, and during that time she began to get sick physically. Her chronic asthma spells became worse, and at times she could hardly breathe. On many days, Aunt Teddy stayed with Mummee during the day.

The Kidnapping Attempt

Our parents had been most careful to deliver both of us girls to school each day. At the end of the day, one of them always arrived on time to pick us up. We wanted to walk home with our friends, but they felt they just couldn't be too careful.

On one particular ordinary day, I sat in my classroom listening to my teacher. A strange unidentified man drove a white unmarked van onto the school grounds. Then he walked into my school and spoke with my teacher.

"Attorney Arthur Shores asked me to come to this school and pick up his daughter, Barbara, and take her home early today."

"Mr. Shores didn't mention anything about this to me," my teacher told him.

"This is what he asked me to do," the man insisted.

"Wait here one moment," the teacher said. "I must call Mr. Shores and have his permission to release Barbara to you."

As the teacher walked out of the room to the office telephone, the man ran out the school door, jumped in his van, gunned his engine, and sped away.

"No," Daddy told the teacher over the telephone. "No one should be picking up Barbara and taking her home. I'll be right there." Daddy rushed to the school and thanked my teacher for calling him.

Our parents didn't say much to us about the kidnapping attempt that day. Maybe they didn't want us to be any more scared than we already were. But security in our household became even tighter after that incident. We have often wondered what might have happened had the teacher not been suspicious of the strange man and had failed to call our father.

Lawyer Carries a Gun

The threats against our lives continued to come unexpectedly and often. We kept up our guard — at home, at school, at church, and in the Dynamite Hill neighborhood. Daddy strapped the loaded gun to his shoulder each morning before he left for the office.

Somehow a reporter with the *Black Chronicle* newspaper heard about the gun Daddy carried with him for protection. On November 1, 1956, the *Black Chronicle* carried a story about our father titled "Lawyer Carries a Gun": "Arthur D. Shores, the lawyer fighting for Autherine Lucy's reinstatement into the University of Alabama, was told today that he would be killed 'like Emmett Till,' unless he dropped proceedings in the case." The article told how Daddy had received an anonymous telephone call at his Birmingham office, and how the caller had threatened him with violence.

> The black lawyer is not intimated. He has been in civil rights legal battles for some time, and started carrying a gun in 1952, when many of his clients received bomb threats.... Once a caller told him that three men were waiting outside his office with guns, ready to shoot him the moment he stepped out to file his case [the Autherine Lucy case]. Shores told the caller exactly when he would leave and the route he would take to the courthouse.... At the appointed time ... Shores left his office building and proceeded as planned to the courthouse. Nothing happened.[2]

Why did Daddy take on these high-profile, dangerous cases? At least one popular author insinuated that he did it for the money. Obviously, she didn't know our father.

The NAACP sometimes sent our father unrequested checks for very small amounts of money for his work with them. In his own practice, our father represented clients for little or no money. Most often, he gave *them* the money they needed to feed and shelter their families. Our father had received a sort of "vocational calling" to represent the people still bound by segregation and cruel Jim Crow laws—and that "calling" went well beyond dollars and cents.

For example, when our church, the First Congregational Christian Church in Birmingham, mysteriously burned down when we were children, he paid the total rent on another nearby church building so the congregation could continue to meet on Sundays to worship God. He also gave away a lot of money to everyone around him who had a need, something he did secretly. People came to our house constantly, and our dad opened the front door, invited them inside, and talked with them about their problems.

They always left our house with enough money for their next meal and their family's needs.

Perhaps Daddy fought for equal rights because he had two little daughters that would one day want a good education. Perhaps he fought the legal roadblocks so his own children and so many others could freely choose where to go to school and realize their individual dreams—he didn't do it for the money!

CHAPTER 23

The Shortage of Black Schools

(Helen and Barbara remember.)

The U.S.'s 15 million Negroes are still denied the right to the pursuit of happiness on equal terms with whites.... This is true on both sides of the Mason-Dixon Line. While the Negro is generally better off, economically and socially, in the North (as is shown by the fact that thousands of Southern Negroes still move north every year), the North has no cause to feel superior. The chains of prejudice can be as heavy in New York's Harlem or on Chicago's South Side as anywhere in the South.

—*TIME*, May 11, 1953

When black youths in Alabama graduated from all-black high schools, if they chose to go to college, they had few options. The nation had established black colleges and universities because African American students weren't allowed in the all-white colleges and universities.

In Alabama, a black student could go to Talladega College, founded in the late 1800s by white members of the American Missionary Association (AMA) for the education of black students. Both our father and I (Barbara) attended and graduated from Talladega College. Students could also attend Tuskegee Normal and Industrial Institute, founded in 1881 in Tuskegee, Alabama. The original white founders could find no white person willing to become Tuskegee's principal, so they hired Booker T. Washington, an African American man trained at Hampton. With a black man as principal, the school had to hire all black teachers, since a white man was not allowed to work for a black man.

Another university for black students was Alabama A & M University in Huntsville, Alabama. Founded in 1875 by a former slave, William Hooper Councill, the school began as a land-grant institution for black students in 1890 under the name "The State Agricultural and Mechanical College for Negroes." (The name changed in 1969 to the "Alabama Agricultural and Mechanical University.")

Alabama State University had opened its doors to black students as the Lincoln School on November 13, 1867, in Marion, Alabama. Founded by nine newly freed African Americans (called the "Marion Nine"), and helped by Northern white missionaries and black churches, the all-black university provided education for Alabama's freedmen. The rest of Alabama's state universities maintained all-white student status, and, on threat of serious violence, they admitted no African American students.

Alabama black students could also attend Morehouse College, which opened its doors to all black students in Atlanta, Georgia, in 1878. Founded by a white church group in Augusta, Georgia, the school hired John Hope as its first black president in 1906. The Reverend Dr. Martin Luther King attended and graduated from Morehouse College.

Another out-of-state college opportunity for Alabama's black students was Fisk University in Nashville, Tennessee. A private all-black college, sponsored by the American Missionary Association, the college opened on January 9, 1866, right after the Civil War ended. Helen attended and graduated from Fisk.

Uncle Hollins' Request

In August 1950, our Uncle Hollins wrote to the University of Alabama Law School, asking for admittance. Inspired by our father, he too wanted to study law. He wrote a simple, straight-to-the-point letter:

> Dear Sir: this comes to inform that I am interested in studying
> Law at the University of Alabama. I was born in Birmingham,

Alabama, February 26, 1909. I graduated from Parker High School of this City in 1927, and from Alabama State Teachers College, which is now bearing the name of Alabama State College for Negroes, in 1931. I served as an instructor of Social Science in the Fairfield Industrial High School for six (6) years and for the past ten (10) years I have been engaged in the Real Estate and Insurance business. It is my desire to study in my home State where I have lived all of my life. I trust that this letter will be honored and treated as a part of my application for admission. Respectfully, W. H. Hollins.[1]

On August 17, 1950, Uncle Hollins received this reply from William F. Adams, Dean of Admissions:

Dear Sir: Your letter of August 14 to the Dean of the Law School has been referred to me for reply. The Dean of the Law School is ill at the present time and is away from his office; and, also, all requests for admission are generally referred to this office.

As you have requested, I am enclosing for you application forms. Applications must be supported by transcripts in duplicate from the colleges you have attended. In addition, an applicant to the School of Law must meet the requirements set up and announced by the Board of Commissioners of the Alabama State Bar.

Then the tone of Adams's letter changed unexpectedly.

I am venturing to write to you a friendly letter to tell you frankly that the problem posed by your application is one of which we have long been conscious and which we have from time to time been called upon in the past to meet. We recognize that it is entirely conceivable that the Supreme Court of the United States can say to the State of Alabama that it must either provide in a separate institution for colored people opportunities for the study of law equal to those being provided for white people or, as an alternative, admit colored people to the institution maintained by the State for white people, assuming that the applicant can in every case meet the entrance requirements in force at the institutions maintained by the State for white people.

As you may know, machinery is provided in this state through the State Department of Education to assist colored students who desire to engage in the study of law to obtain opportunities for entering high class institutions located elsewhere which accept colored students. It is hoped that you will see your way clear to avail yourself of the opportunities thus afforded which will enable you to obtain a law degree in a high class graduate institution comparable to the Law School of Alabama.

While this may be gratuitous, I am adding that we at the University of Alabama are convinced that relationships between the races, in this section of the country at least, are not likely to be improved by pressure on behalf of members of the colored race in an effort to gain admission to the institutions maintained by the State for members of the white race. On the contrary, we feel that inter-racial relationships would suffer if there is insistence that anything that the issue be joined at this time. The better elements of both races deplore anything that tends to retard or jeopardize the development of better relationships between the races. For these reasons, therefore, we hope that you can persuade yourself not to file your application for admission here.[2]

Perhaps our father stepped into the civil rights movement with both feet and endured the threats of violence and the demeaning letters because he shared the wisdom and insight expressed by Carter G. Woodson, editor of the *Journal of Negro History* and director of the *Association for the Study of Negro Life and History*. "A Negro child should be taught that he is black, beautifully black!" Woodson stated. "While others are trying to make him accept his color as a mark of inferiority, I would show by the achievements of his forebears that they measured up … to the levels of the greatest peoples of the world."[3]

CHAPTER 24

Miss Autherine Lucy
and the University of Alabama

1952–1956, in Tuscaloosa, Alabama

(Helen and Barbara remember.)

The Autherine Lucy case became a symbolic battlefield for those who were determined to maintain segregation and those who had resolved to eradicate it.
— HISTORIAN NORA SAYRE, *Previous Convictions*

Born in Shiloh, Alabama, in the year of the nation's devastating 1929 stock market crash, Autherine Juanita Lucy became the first African American to enroll at the segregated University of Alabama in Tuscaloosa. Autherine enjoyed school and worked hard to become a good student. A reserved, soft-spoken, and shy young woman, she attended the all-black Linden Academy in Linden, Alabama. She also received a two-year teaching degree from the all-black Selma University in Selma, Alabama. In 1949 Autherine entered another all-black college — Miles College in Fairfield, Alabama. She graduated three years later with a B.A. in English.

Some years before, while studying at Miles College, Autherine Lucy had met and befriended an African American woman, Pollie Anne Myers. While Autherine was shy, Pollie, three years younger, was an extrovert and actively involved in the NAACP's Youth Chapter. In 1952, after Miss Lucy's graduation from Miles College, Pollie Myers asked Autherine Lucy to enroll with her to study for a graduate degree at the University of Alabama. At that time, the all-white university remained strictly segregated. The U.S. Supreme Court, in *Brown v. Board of Education*, had not yet ruled that school segregation is illegal, a decision that would not come until three years later.

Reluctantly, Autherine Lucy agreed to enroll with Pollie Myers in the University of Alabama's Master of Education program. Both young women requested and received the university's application, filled in the necessary spaces, and mailed them back to the university.

Accepted

On September 13, 1952, the University of Alabama accepted both Myers and Lucy into their Master of Education program and asked each woman to send $5.00 to reserve dorm rooms on campus.

We still have the letters written by the University's President, John M. Gallalee, on September 13, 1952, individually welcoming each woman: "Dear Miss Lucy," his letter to Autherine began.

> Dean William F. Adams, Dean of Admissions and Records, has told me that you are coming to the University. Let me assure you that we shall be glad to welcome you to our campus. You will find it a delightful place in which to live and work. If there is anything we can do to help you in making your arrangements to come to the University, please let us know.

Both women sent the University the requested $5.00 to reserve a dorm room on campus, and Pollie Myers received another letter from the University:

> Dear Miss Myers: I am enclosing a receipt for your room reservation deposit. You should save this and show it when you pay your fees. You have been assigned to Adams-Parker. Please report to this dormitory when you arrive on the campus. Mrs. Green, the house director, will be expecting you and will show you your room. We are so glad that you are to be a member of our student body. Sincerely, Mrs. Shaler Houser, Director of Housing and Counselor to Women.[1]

Suspicious, however, that the University of Alabama might reject them on account of their race, they contacted our father to represent them if a rejection came.

Rejected

Their suspicions proved to be correct. On Saturday, September 20, 1952, the women showed up in Dean William F. Adam's office on the university campus. Seeing with his own eyes that Myers and Lucy were African Americans, he rejected the women's applications for enrollment—the same applications the university had accepted the week before and confirmed with enthusiastic letters of welcome. He gave the two women no reason for the rejection. And he tried, without success, to return their money to them.

On September 24, 1952, our father wrote a letter to President Gallalee:

> Dear Sir:
> I have been retained by Misses Pollie Anne Myers and Autherine J. Lucy, of this city, to represent them in the matter of obtaining admission to the University of Alabama. Both Misses Lucy and Myers have submitted their applications and transcripts, as well as having been assigned to one of the dormitories, having receipts for their room deposits. They applied to the Dean of Admissions, in person, on Saturday, September 20, to complete their registration, and pay the necessary fees, but were denied this privilege by Dean William F. Adams on basis of their race. As President of the University, again Misses Lucy and Myers apply to you for admission to the University of Alabama. Please let me hear from you by return mail, as to the action taken on these applications, in order that I might know what steps to take to protect my clients' interest.
> Yours very truly, Arthur D. Shores[2]

On June 6, 1953, in the midst of the *Brown v. Board of Education* case, Daddy received a reply from J. Rufus Bealle, secretary of the university's board of trustees:

Dear Sir, At the request of Governor Gordon Persons, President Ex-Officio of the Board of Trustees, the applications of Pollie Anne Myers and Autherine J. Lucy for admission to the University of Alabama were presented to the Board of Trustees at its annual meeting on June 1, 1953. Much careful consideration was given to this matter by the Board but no final action was taken. The Board directed me to advise you, as attorney for the applicants, of its consideration of this matter and of its action deferring final action pending receipt of a court decision concerning litigation now before the Supreme Court of the United States [*Brown v. Board of Education*]. The Board has also directed me to point out to you that there are courses in journalism and library science given at Alabama State College at Montgomery, or at Tuskegee Institute, [both all-black student schools] which are available to your clients and to suggest that they make application for admission to those institutions.

Alabama's Slow Court System

Three years passed while the women's cases journeyed through the slow court system. During those years, Lucy received offers of university scholarships from groups in Belgium, Denmark, and Norway. The *Birmingham Post-Herald* even reported that President Eisenhower said the U.S. Department of Justice was looking into the Lucy and Myers case.[3]

While she waited, Lucy taught English at the Conway Vocational High School in Carthage, Mississippi. During those years, NAACP lawyers (including our father) actively fought school segregation in the *Brown v. Board of Education* case. The decision on that case came on May 17, 1954, when the U.S. Supreme Court ruled that the nation's segregated schools must integrate.

With the new *Brown v. Board of Education* decision in hand, our father and Thurgood Marshall knew the right time had arrived to take the Lucy/Myers school segregation case to court.

Their case became the first test of the new *Brown v. Board of Education* ruling. Surely both lawyers knew a thunderous storm awaited them. On June 29, 1955, Judge Hobart Grooms ordered the University of Alabama's doors opened to both African American women for enrollment.

Storm Clouds Gather

Again, on October 18, 1955, our father wrote to the University of Alabama. He addressed the letter to Dean William F. Adams. On October 20, 1955, a reply came from O. C. Carmichael, the university's president at that time:

> Dear Sir, This letter is being written in answer to your letter of October 19 addressed to Dean William F. Adams. In the current University of Alabama bulletin October 6 is designated as the final day of registration during the current semester. It has been the uniform practice of the University of Alabama not to accept students after the final day of registration. In view of such fact it is now too late for your clients, Autherine J. Lucy and Pollie Anne Myers, to be registered as students during the present semester. There is no provision whereby students can be registered at the present time retroactive to September 1955 as requested in your letter. In my opinion the above position does not violate either Judge Grooms' judgment or the recent order of the United States Supreme Court.[4]

The university immediately hired private investigators to find anything negative on Lucy and Myers, and though they found nothing on Autherine Lucy, they discovered that Pollie Myers had been pregnant and not married at the time of her enrollment to the university. They claimed Myers ineligible for admittance due to the university's moral policy.

Feeling frightened, vulnerable, and quite alone without the companionship of her friend, Lucy decided to go ahead and enroll. On February 1, 1956, at the beginning of the school's new semester, Lucy officially enrolled at the University of Alabama. But university officials refused her a room on campus. They also forbade her to eat meals in the school's cafeteria.

An anonymous, typed letter from the university advised Lucy:

> The Authorities of the University are instructed to study each application for room and board with respect to welfare, safety and other effect upon the applicant and other students and other occupants of the dormitories and to deny such applications as might endanger the safety or result in sociological disadvantage of the student. The authorities are instructed that if Autherine Lucy is enrolled and if she applies for room in the dormitories and board that these accomodations [*sic*] be refused to her.

Our father, as well as Emory Jackson, editor of the black newspaper *The Birmingham World*, protested the university's order that required Lucy to live off campus. But that was a decision on which the university officials would not budge.

Arthur D. Shores (fourth from bottom left),
on graduation from Talladega College, 1927

Mummee, 1932

Daddy and Aunt Sylvia, 1944

Mummee and Daddy's wedding, August 5, 1938

Arthur D. Shores in court (Mitchell vs. Wright Case), 1946

Arthur D. Shores at his office, 1947

Helen, Daddy, and Barbara in the sitting room, 1948

Segregated café with "colored" and "white" signs, 1949

Segregated bus interior with passengers, 1949. Note the movable signs to distinguish where "coloreds" could sit.

Arthur D. Shores with U.S. Senator Glen Taylor and others, 1949

The Shores family, 1954

Arthur D. Shores with Autherine Lucy, 1956

Rev. Martin Luther King, Jr., shaking hands with his lawyer, Arthur D. Shores, as they stand in front of cheering followers after King's conviction for his part in the bus boycott in Montgomery, 1956

Arthur D. Shores, 1962

*Student demonstration against integration
at the University of Alabama, 1956*

First bombing of the Shores' home on Center Street, August 1963

Interior damage to the living room of the home on Center Street, August 1963

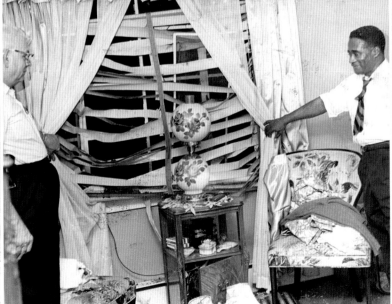

Second bombing of the Shores' home, September 1963

Police dogs breaking up the Children's March protest demonstrations in Birmingham as ordered by Eugene "Bull" Connor, 1963

Gov. George C. Wallace standing defiantly in the schoolhouse door, facing Deputy U.S. Attorney General Nicholas Katzenbach, 1963

Exterior damage from the 16th Street Church bombing, 1963

Autherine Lucy, Thurgood Marshall, and Arthur D. Shores leaving the Federal Courthouse in Birmingham, 1965

Swearing-in of the Birmingham City Council, 1969: (front row) Nina Miglionico and Arthur D. Shores, (back row) Overton, Cochran, and Yarbrough

Best wishes to Arthur Shores

Jimmy Carter

Arthur D. Shores and President Jimmy Carter, 1980

Arthur D. Shores, 1982

Daddy and Helen at her graduation from Cumberland Law School, 1987

Mummee and Daddy's 50th Anniversary, 1988

CHAPTER 25

Riots Break Out on Campus

(Helen remembers.)

"Well, we won! It took her [Lucy] four [*sic*] years and the Supreme Court to get her in and it took us only four days to get rid of her."

—UNIVERSITY STUDENT quoted in the
Birmingham News, February 7, 1956, front page

On February 3, 1956, Autherine Lucy entered the University of Alabama and, incredibly, completed her first day of class without event. Only one student left her geography class when Lucy entered. "For two cents I'd drop this class," the student muttered as he walked out.

But that evening trouble started to brew. Crowds formed. Some were disgruntled students who wanted to keep the university all white. But most were outside troublemakers, hard-core Klan members and racist agitators who used the occasion to stir up anger and cause rioting. Witnesses later noted that they saw Robert Chambliss—known as "Dynamite Bob" because of his many Birmingham bombings—in the crowds, handing out leaflets and inciting violence. (In 1977, courts convicted Chambliss of murder for his role in the 16th Street Baptist Church bombing in September 1963.) But Birmingham officials would later blame the NAACP for the mayhem—a "photo-shoot opportunity," they alleged. That accusation was false, of course, and never proven.

All Hades Breaks Loose

Lucy's second day of classes also proceeded without problem. But by the third class day, the situation became dangerous. Agitators had had the needed time to bring in outsiders, and the crowds that gathered on the campus grew large and violent. Outside her classroom window, rioters shouted out death threats. "Kill Lucy!" they chanted. The hostile crowds grew from hundreds to thousands. For her personal safety, university officials and police surrounded Lucy and sneaked her out of class to a waiting patrol car. As they delivered Lucy to her next class in another building on campus, rioters pelted them with rocks and rotten eggs, exploded firecrackers, shattered the patrol car's windows, and shouted more death threats. Later that day, police hid Lucy in the patrol car's backseat floorboard and took her to a "secret" place of safety. But while there, the young woman received two telephone death threats.[1]

The rioting went on for three days, and university officials talked about "disbanding the University for a time." Frightened administrators all agreed, "The Negro girl [is] in real danger during the demonstrations."[2]

The local press captured every violent image. One reporter wrote, "An uncontrollable outside mob would have killed University Negro Student Autherine Lucy if it could have gotten to her." Jeff Bennett, assistant to the university president, said "the demonstrators were making an attempt either to kidnap her or to kill her on the campus."[3]

On the night of February 7, the rioting grew even further out of control. Police tried without success to disperse the crowd of angry students and outside agitators. They shot tear gas and smoke bombs into the mob, but it did no good. Finally, the police gave up trying to control the riot and simply left the scene.[4]

The University "Excludes" Autherine Lucy

Claiming that they feared for Lucy's life and safety, the University of Alabama's Board of Trustees voted to exclude her from the university. The Western Union telegram, written in all capital letters, sent to our father from the university reads:

THIS IS TO NOTIFY YOU THAT THE FOLLOWING RESO-
LUTION WAS ADOPTED BY THE BOARD OF TRUSTEES
OF THE UNIVERSITY OF ALABAMA TODAY: IN VIEW OF
RECENT OCCURENCES ON THE CAMPUS OF THE UNI-
VERSITY OF ALABAMA AND THE ACTS AND THREATS OF
VIOLENCE PARTICIPATED IN BY OUTSIDERS, FOR THE
SAFETY OF AUTHERINE LUCY, A STUDENT RECENTLY
ADMITTED UNDER THE ORDER OF THE FEDERAL COURT,
AND FOR THE SAFETY OF OTHER STUDENTS, AND OF
FACULTY MEMBERS OF THE UNIVERSITY OF ALABAMA, AND
ONLY FOR THAT REASON, AND EXERCISING THE POLICE
POWER OF THE UNIVERSITY OF ALABAMA FOR THE SAFETY
OF THOSE ON THE CAMPUS, THE BOARD OF TRUSTEES OF
THE UNIVERSITY OF ALABAMA EXCLUDES AUTHERINE
LUCY UNTIL FURTHER NOTICE FROM ATTENDING CLASSES
AT THE UNIVERSITY. PLEASE INFORM AUTHERINE LUCY OF
THIS ACTION....[5]

That's when our father sent a telegram to the University of Alabama giving them an ultimatum to reinstate Lucy's student status
and allow her to go to classes. "It is regrettable that the University
of Alabama would submit to mob rule in excluding Miss Lucy," he
wrote. "It is the responsibility of the State of Alabama to insure
Miss Lucy's safety, and she expects the University to reinstate her
within the next 48 hours or we will be compelled to take further
legal action."[6]

President Eisenhower: "We Won't Get Involved!"

At a White House press conference in Washington, D.C., President
Eisenhower described the rioting as deplorable and announced
that the federal government should not get involved. The President "expressed confidence that the State of Alabama, from Gov.
Folsom on down, would do everything possible to work out a settlement" and said he "hoped to avoid any federal intervention."[7]

On the evening of February 10, 1955, more than 11,000 people from several Southern states filled Montgomery's Cow Coliseum to hear U.S. Senator James Eastland speak up for racial segregation. The Montgomery Shrine Band played "Dixie" from the American-and-Confederate-flag-draped balcony. One man in the crowd shouted, "Big Jim's [Governor of Alabama, Jim Folsom] gotta go."

"R. E. Chambliss of Birmingham received a hand when he stomped onto the stage, a cigaret [*sic*] dawdling from his mouth, and planted a Confederate flag," a newspaper reporter recorded.[8]

After the violence shown to Lucy, Allan Knight Chalmers, chairman of the NAACP's "Committee of 100" wrote an open letter on February 20, 1956, for all Alabamians to read.

> Dear Friend, Once again I come to you for assistance in a grave emergency—not in behalf of a helpless victim of racial bigotry —but in the name of a wonderful human being, Autherine Lucy, whose courage before a brutal mob at the University of Alabama will bring nearer the realization of the American dream of equality for all our people.
>
> In her hour of trial Autherine Lucy was almost alone. Today, she is determined to continue her struggle for an education, convinced as her enclosed brief statement says, that the white students who stoned her will next time choose the way of decency. We can help Autherine Lucy by standing behind the lawyers who champion her, Arthur D. Shores and Mrs. Constance Baker Motley of the NAACP Legal Defense and Educational Fund.

The letter closed with a direct appeal:

> With our help, Autherine Lucy will have her education. She will hold the door open to other serious young men and women, deprived by their color of a chance to prepare themselves to serve their country as teachers, scientists, engineers and better mothers and fathers. By her action, she will enable white students and their elders, in Alabama and elsewhere, to wipe out the shame of last week's mobs.[9]

A Complaint Filed

Our father and Thurgood Marshall immediately filed a complaint accusing the University of Alabama of "conspiring with the mob to prevent Autherine Lucy from attending classes."

The *Black Chronicle*, on November 1, 1956, published a "Letter to the Editor" that described the feelings of many white Alabamians at that time:

> Dear Editor: I don't believe there are very many colored people down here that want to do away with segregation any more than we white people do. I do know that we won't stand for colored children to go to our schools and ride un-segregated in the buses. We don't mind colored people prospering, but we don't want to mix with them. My advice to that Lucy wench is to stay put and not try to come back to the University of Alabama.

The letter was signed "(Mrs) I. V. Welch, Samantha, Alabama."[10]

During the heat of the controversy, a newspaper reporter interviewed Lucy's 69-year-old parents, Milton and Minnie Lucy. They said they were not happy about their daughter's decision to attend the University of Alabama.

> "We raised ten head of children," they said, "and every one of them was taught to stay their distance from white folks, but to give them all their respect. If Autherine has changed from this, she didn't get her new ideas from home."
>
> "She was born and raised right down here in these woods," her father continued, "and it looks like to me she ought to be the last one to get in a mess like this. Why, I keep asking myself, out of all the colored folks in Alabama, did this have to fall to my baby daughter's lot."[11]

On the last day of February, 1956, our father and Thurgood Marshall appeared with Miss Lucy in Federal Judge Hobart Grooms' courtroom. The *Birmingham Post-Herald's* Thursday, March 1, 1956, edition described what happened:

Federal Judge Hobart Grooms ruled here yesterday that the University of Alabama must readmit Negro student Autherine J. Lucy before 9 a.m. Monday.... In a short statement before his ruling, Judge Grooms said "there are some people who believe this court should serve out a province ... man the battlements ... and defy the U.S. Supreme Court. This court does not have that perogative [*sic*].... The Court is, therefore, of the opinion that the order or suspension or exclusion of the plaintiff Lucy should be lifted by 9 a.m., March 5, 1956."[12]

The University "Permanently" Expels Lucy

But within hours, the university's trustees met and voted to expel Lucy "permanently." "The basis for the permanent expulsion of Miss Lucy from the University," they noted, "was the petition she had filed several weeks before in Federal Court charging that the University trustees and other officials of the school had 'conspired' to cause demonstrations which resulted in her temporary suspension from classes Feb. 6."

After hearing that she had been "permanently" expelled from the school, she said, "I have done all that I can. I was looking forward to returning to school. At this point there is nothing more that I can say."[13]

By this time, Lucy felt mentally drained from all the court battles and the constant local, national, and international attention focused upon her and her cause. "God knows," Lucy had written earlier in the *Birmingham World*, "that I didn't intend to cause all this violence and agitation among my fellow citizens and fellow students. I merely wanted an education—the best education possible."[14]

Autherine Lucy Leaves Alabama

Feeling defeated and exhausted, she packed up and left the state of Alabama. Thurgood Marshall wrote Lucy an encouraging letter that reminded her that "whatever happens in the future, remember for all concerned, that your contribution has been made toward equal justice for all Americans and that you have done everything in your power to bring this about."[15]

Former state senator J. M. Bonner supported the university's decision to permanently expel Lucy. He urged university officials to continue to bar African American students, declaring that the school should continue as a "white man's university." "The admission of Lucy [should have] never be[en] tolerated," he suggested, and he asked that no student be punished "for any action heretofore taken in resisting her admission."[16]

But Daddy wasn't defeated. He was still determined to fight the South's school segregation practices. On Sunday, May 6, 1956, Louisville, Kentucky's Zion Baptist Church invited our father to address the congregation. Louisville's *Courier-Journal* covered the story in Monday's paper.

"Shores had a Biblical parallel for those who would slow the pace of integration," the reporter wrote. "He told how Moses (in chapter 13 of Numbers) sent spies into the land of Canaan. 'And even the spies had a majority and minority report,' Shores said. 'One group told Moses, "Surely it floweth with milk and honey and this is the fruit of it.... Let us go up at once, and possess it; for we are well able to overcome it."'

"But the 'gradualist' told Moses that the inhabitants of Canaan were giants and that the people of Israel were relative grasshoppers."

"We Negroes won't be grasshoppers before giants," Daddy told the congregation.[17]

For the next seven years, the University of Alabama remained a segregated, all-white university. At the end of those years, however, our father would once again involve himself deeply in the university's battle to resist forced integration. And the demonstrated bigotry that would occur in June of 1963 would prove no less violent than it had in 1956. Only this time, President John F.

Kennedy, the White House, and the United States National Guard would actively intervene.

In 1956, an exhausted Autherine Lucy married a fellow student she had met at Miles College, now a young minister. Hugh Lawrence Foster and Autherine Lucy Foster produced four children over the years that followed. For many years, the Foster family lived in Louisiana and Texas before they moved back home to Alabama in 1974.

In 1988 the University of Alabama publicly overturned her expulsion. The next year, they invited her to enroll as a student at the university. Four years later, she finally graduated with her master's degree in education. Two of her children also attended the University of Alabama, and her daughter Grazia graduated with her in 1992.

At their University of Alabama graduation commencement services, fellow students gave Autherine Lucy a standing ovation. The university surprised her with a $25,000 endowed scholarship in her name, and they also hung Lucy's portrait in one of the busiest places on campus. Below her portrait, a sign read, "Her initiative and courage won the right for students of all races to attend the University."

CHAPTER 26

Montgomery's Bus Boycott

1955–1956, in Montgomery, Alabama

(Helen remembers.)

Of these local NAACP leaders in the South … there isn't
a threat known to men that they do not receive. They're
never out from under pressure … I don't think I could
take it for a week. The possibility of violent death for
them and their families is something they've learned to
live with like a man learns to sleep with a sore arm.

—THURGOOD MARSHALL

On December 1, 1955, Montgomery Fair department store seamstress Rosa Parks, 42, refused to give up her seat to a white man
on the city bus. The city's code required that public buses be segregated. Whites entered the front of the bus, paid their fare, and
sat in the front seats. Blacks entered the front of the bus, paid
their fare, then had to get off the bus and re-enter it at the back
door whether in rain, sleet, or snow. Sometimes bus drivers drove
off before black passengers could enter through the back. Often
the white drivers treated African Americans with little respect,
intimidated them, and called them demeaning names. A movable sign "For Coloreds" at the middle back of the bus designated
where African Americans could sit. When the bus filled up with
white passengers, the driver moved the sign closer to the back of
the bus. Then he demanded that the black passengers move farther to the back so white passengers could sit in the front part of
the bus. In case of trouble or neglect of the segregation codes, the
city gave white bus drivers police authority.

When white passengers boarded and the driver moved the

"For Coloreds" sign closer to the back, Rosa Parks refused to move back a few seats. The bus driver called the police, and the police arrested her at the scene and charged her with violation of Chapter 6, Section 11 of the Montgomery City code. Police took her to their headquarters and fingerprinted and photographed her. Later, police released Parks on bail.

Some historians say that Rosa didn't move because "she had tired feet" from working all day. Others say Rosa was just tired of segregation on public city buses. For whatever reason, she stayed in her seat, and her actions caused worldwide attention and helped to change the South's segregation laws.

The years 1955 and 1956 were difficult and violent times in the civil rights battle. Our father, of course, stood right in the middle of those battles. And before things got better, they would get far worse.

The Montgomery Bus Boycott

E. D. Nixon, president of the Montgomery chapter of the NAACP, invited a group of black leaders to Montgomery, and asked newcomer Dr. Martin Luther King, Jr., 26, to lead the newly formed "Montgomery Improvement Association," of which Ralph Abernathy was the vice-president. King had just graduated from Boston University and had become pastor of Montgomery's Dexter Avenue Baptist Church.

The official bus boycott began on December 5, 1955. Throughout the city, Montgomery's African American population (some 40,000 people) stopped riding the city's buses in protest of unfair segregation bus codes. Some African Americans rode black-operated cabs to work or carpooled together, but most walked to work, some up to twenty miles one way. Day after day, public buses ran empty and lost money, greatly impacting the city's economy.

A year and half earlier, on July 11, 1954, a month after the U.S. Supreme Court ordered the integration of the nation's public schools, a group of white Mississippi doctors, lawyers, bankers,

plantation owners, and others came together to form a hate organization called the White Citizens Council. They sought to hinder
the Court-ordered integration of public schools. Unlike the Ku
Klux Klan, the White Citizens Council denounced violence. Yet
their actions actually caused and increased violence toward African Americans. The "philosopher" of the White Citizens Council,
Justice Tom P. Brady of the Mississippi Supreme Court, attacked
the U.S. Supreme Court's decision in *Brown v. Board of Education*,
calling it "Black Monday." He insisted that the decision was "not
the law of the land."

"The loveliest and the purest of God's creatures," he was quoted
in *Time* magazine as saying, "the nearest thing to an angelic being
that treads this terrestrial ball is a well-bred, cultured Southern
white woman, or her blue-eyed, golden-haired little girl." By contrast, he added, "The social, political, economic and religious
preferences of the Negro remain close to the caterpillar and the
cockroach.... proper food for a chimpanzee."[1]

Within a short time, across the South, the strong White Citizens Council grew to 80,000 white members. As a result, blacks
in favor of integration or seen trying to register black voters lost
their jobs, their homes, and even their lives. White businessmen
faced boycotts and politicians lost votes if they were believed to be
sympathetic to African Americans' efforts at integration.

The White Citizens Council worked together through state
governments and launched a state-by-state effort to destroy and
outlaw the NAACP. In 1956, Alabama, Arkansas, Florida, Georgia,
Louisiana, Mississippi, South Carolina, Tennessee, Texas, and Virginia all initiated court cases and/or passed laws aimed at elimi-
nating the NAACP.

Alabama Attorney General John Patterson blamed the Lucy
desegregation attempt as well as the Montgomery Bus Boycott
on the NAACP. A legal attack followed and effectively banned the
NAACP from Alabama for eight years.[2]

During the Montgomery Bus Boycott, violence in Montgomery
increased. White segregationists and supremacists were no doubt

to blame for firebombing Dr. King's home on January 30, 1956. They also bombed E. D. Nixon's home two days later. Fortunately, no one suffered any injuries.

Less than three months into the bus boycott, on February 22, 1956, Montgomery police arrested a group of African American ministers and charged them with "taking part in an organized unlawful boycott." One of those ministers was Dr. Martin Luther King, Jr.

Dr. King Arrested

On February 21, 1956, the Montgomery County Grand Jury indicted Dr. King, accusing him (and 89 others) of violating a 1921 statute that outlawed boycotting Montgomery's businesses. The trial began on March 19, and over the following four days of the trial, our father, representing the NAACP, along with several other lawyers, defended King.

The segregated courtroom was packed to its 230-seat capacity, and some five hundred additional people waited outside. Reporters came from England, France, India, and other countries, and the *New York Times* gave the trial front page coverage.

After Dr. King was sworn in, our father began King's questioning. He asked Dr. King to state his name and occupation. Then he questioned him about his involvement with the Montgomery Improvement Association (MIA) and the mass meetings that had taken place related to the bus boycott. When asked about instigating any violence, Dr. King told the court that he urged nonviolence. When cross-examined, King answered in simple, direct words.

The defense team told about all the abuse Montgomery blacks had suffered from white bus drivers. Thirty-one defense witnesses claimed to be victims of abuse by bus drivers. Many testified that the bus drivers called them names and refused to give them change after they paid their fare.

One woman, Georgia Gilmore, testified that after she paid her fare, the bus driver shouted, "Nigger, get out that door and go around to the back door!" Then, before she could board through the back door, the driver sped away.

Another woman, Martha Walker, told the court she was helping her blind husband off the bus when the driver slammed the door on her husband's right foot and drove away, dragging the man some distance before he managed to free his foot.

Unfortunately, our father and his defense team of lawyers lost the case. Judge Eugene W. Carter found Dr. King guilty of "conducting an illegal boycott against Montgomery City Lines."[3] The court fined him a total of $1000, which Dr. King refused to pay. Instead, he went to jail. But maintaining that King's lawyer had missed the 60-day deadline, the Court of Appeals rejected the young minister's appeal (April 30, 1957). That December, 1957, Dr. King paid the fine.

The Requests

During the boycott, Montgomery's African American population requested only four changes:

1. that bus drivers be courteous to them
2. that they be able to enter the front door of the bus, pay, and come aboard
3. that seating be first-come, first-served (with blacks sitting from the rear and whites sitting from the front)
4. that buses stop at every corner in black residential areas as they did in white neighborhoods

But the white power structure fought hard to resist these requests, causing the black boycotters to fight back even harder. The NAACP in Montgomery filed a case in the Federal Court in February 1956 that essentially said, "Forget our four requests. We demand that bus segregation be totally outlawed."

Finally, on November 13, 1956, the U.S. Supreme Court agreed with the NAACP and ruled the segregated system unconstitutional. By Thanksgiving 1956, the city of Montgomery had lost nearly $1 million because of the boycott. The boycott officially ended on December 21, 1956. To everyone's amazement, before it finally ended, the boycott had lasted 382 days, crippling the city's public transportation system.

Not wanting any sudden surprises, African Americans in Montgomery maintained the bus boycott until the court actually received the official documents on December 20, 1956. They returned to riding the now "integrated" buses the very next day.

To celebrate the boycott's victory, Dr. King and three ministerial colleagues tested the new law. They publically boarded a Montgomery city bus on December 21, 1956, and took seats throughout the bus.

The 1956 arrest and trial of Dr. King wouldn't be his last. Four years later, in February 1960, an Alabama grand jury would order Dr. King's arrest and charge him with two counts of felony perjury. The state would charge Dr. King with signing fraudulent tax returns for 1956 and 1958, but the court would find King not guilty.

And then, in 1963, our father would once again represent the famous civil rights leader when Birmingham police imprisoned Dr. King in the infamous Birmingham Jail.

CHAPTER 27

Growing Up
in Jim Crow Alabama

Late 1950s, in Birmingham, Alabama

(Barbara remembers.)

One day things will be different. I am working hard so
that when you grow up ... you'll be able to go anywhere
and not be turned away because of the color of your skin.

—ARTHUR SHORES speaking to Barbara

In May 1957, Helen celebrated her 16th birthday, and the following November, I turned 12. The bus boycott in Montgomery had
ended successfully, and the Autherine Lucy case was over. We took
a deep breath and exhaled slowly with relief. The neighborhood's
faithful volunteers took a rest from guarding our home on Dynamite Hill. It seemed the storm of violence had passed. "If our
home hasn't been bombed during this Lucy trial," Daddy told us,
"we can relax now. The worst of it is over."

And so we let down our guard a bit. Things were beginning to
change for African Americans in the South. Many of our father's
court victories had led to better conditions for African Americans
and their families. But change came slowly—much still needed
to be done.

For instance, as hard as he had worked for equal voting registration, in 1957 only 20 percent of African Americans had registered
to vote. Also, public all-white student schools had yet to admit a
single African American student. Violence erupted almost every
time a black school child crossed that Jim Crow boundary line.

Sadly, over the next few years, the violence would intensify.

Death Threats and Threats of Violence

Daddy mostly ignored the death threats that had become commonplace for our family. A building contractor, on a monthly retainer plan, routinely replaced our front picture window whenever gunshots "pinged" or cracked it. When our family sat on the front porch in the evenings, Daddy still laid the shotgun across his lap—just in case he needed it. Cars of white people continued to slow down in front of our house and shout profanities at us.

But Daddy promised us that "things will change," and we believed him. I remember one night, when I was a little girl, I sat in his lap on the front porch, and together we watched the sun go down. "One day things will be different," he told me, gently wrapping his loving arms around me. "I am working hard so that when you grow up, you as well as other boys and girls will be able to go anywhere and not be turned away because of the color of your skin."

The Jim Crow Laws That Shaped Our Lives

As a child, I never realized our father's importance in the civil rights struggle in the 1940s and 1950s. Thurgood Marshall, Constance Motley, and other lawyers and well-known civil rights leaders who would one day become household names came in and out of our home like family members. They often spent the night, ate at our kitchen table, and played with Helen and me. They worked hard to change the way things were when we were children.

For instance, before 1954, African Americans could not serve on juries, send their children to white public schools, drink from a "whites only" water fountain, or use a "whites only" restroom. They could not try on clothing in a store, eat at a white restaurant, or sit on the main floor of a movie theater, concert hall, or other public arena. We attended a one-room schoolhouse taught by one teacher, Mrs. Lawhorn. She taught kindergarten through eighth grade. While there were other schools we could have attended, our parents chose to send us to a private Christian school. At that time we could not attend the well-supplied and maintained white elementary school in our neighborhood. Moreover, the laws prevented black Americans from sitting in the front of the bus or visiting a public park or beach or swimming pool. Black men were routinely beaten or killed for "reckless eyeballing" (looking at), whistling at, or marrying a white female. Normal human social courtesies did not exist for black Americans. In courtrooms, black witnesses were referred to by their first names or called "uncle" or "gal." In some towns, blacks had to step off the sidewalk and into the street when a white person passed by. In some areas, police even warned black people to be out of town by sunset.

It is no wonder that Mummee seemed fearful throughout those years of living under strict, punishable Jim Crow laws. Our father had purposely entered a war zone by engaging in dangerous work in the segregated South. He challenged the system legally and usually won the law suits. We expected to hear Mummee exclaim, "Lord, have mercy!" whenever Daddy told her about another new civil rights case the NAACP had asked him to take. But surely Daddy understood the importance of the times, the struggle for civil rights and how his hard work and sacrifices, as well as those of others, would change the course of history.

As children, Helen and I had learned what was appropriate behavior for black girls in Jim Crow Alabama. When Mummee took us to a downtown Birmingham department store to buy new shoes, she walked through the store's front door and sat down on one of the padded benches. Store clerks accepted her there because they thought she was a white woman. The store clerks allowed us to try on shoes, but they refused to allow us to try on clothes. When we shopped at Birmingham's beautiful Loveman's Department Store, only white shoppers could eat in the beautifully decorated mezzanine restaurant.

Doctor's offices were also segregated. We could enter through the office's front door, but then had to wait our turn in the "colored waiting room" in the back. Mummee never complained. She just wanted to do what needed to be done, finish, and go home.

The Jack & Jill Club

Walt Disney's *Mickey Mouse Club* was all the rage among children in the mid- to late-1950s. The series ran from 1955 to 1959 and featured such stars as Jimmie Dodd, Tommy Cole, and Eileen Diamond. Like the actors on the show, the child "Mouseketeers" in our area wore the popular hats with large mouse ears and planned fun and educational activities. Helen and I wanted so much to be part of the exciting new Mickey Mouse Club sponsored by the Alabama Theatre, but only white children could belong to the club.

So the mothers in our neighborhood got together and started a Birmingham chapter of the Jack & Jill Club for children in the area. We met once a month, held meetings, elected officers, and decided the next month's activities. Moms and dads came together and planned cultural trips around the city and state as well as trips to regional and national Jack & Jill Club conferences. It was a family affair, and all the parents stayed involved and active.

Because everything in Birmingham was segregated, I rarely had an opportunity to be around white children. However, sometimes I traveled with Daddy to Talladega College where, as a trustee of the college, he attended various programs and meetings with other trustees and professors. Some of the white professors who taught there also brought their children, so we enjoyed talking and playing together.

Later in life I became friends with Kathy Brown, an African American from Chicago. Kathy told me about the many trips she had made as a child with her uncle to segregated Birmingham in the 1950s. Her uncle's skin was coal black, but Kathy's skin was so light that she could easily pass as a white child. Oftentimes, her uncle drove her to the popular, but segregated, KiddieLand. She walked in, ate cotton candy, and had a fun time on the rides.

Meanwhile, her uncle stood by the car, pretending to be her black chauffer.

During our childhood and youth, Helen and I participated in as many activities as possible. We especially enjoyed our Girl Scout activities. Helen attended the first Girl Scout Roundup in Milford, Michigan, in 1955. She told me that her troop and the white troops did not get on the train at the same time in Birmingham. The white troop got on the train farther down the tracks. But once on the train, several of the white girls came to them, introduced themselves, and they talked. Later, others joined in, and they sang songs together. Helen maintained her friendship with one of the girls from Birmingham. After the Roundup was over, they often met below the clock at Loveman's Department store and talked.

I attended the second Girl Scout Roundup held in Button Bay, Vermont. We were excited about going. Once we got to Button Bay, we met girls from all over the United States that were friendly and not afraid to form friendships. We had great times talking about everything from camping to curling our hair to the latest hot rock band or singing group.

It seemed that Scouts from other parts of the country had already experienced integration. There were no barriers. The girls in my troop found themselves reaching out to help others, pitching their tents or building their dinner table. Coming back to Birmingham, however, the same white Girl Scouts that were so friendly in Button Bay seemed to shy away from conversations as we traveled back South.

The Autograph Book

As a young teenager I had an autograph book, a cheap little book bought at one of the local five and dime stores. The blue plastic front cover had line-drawn teenagers in poodle skirts and bobby socks dancing around a portable record player. These books were popular at the time, and all my friends signed each other's books.

As a hobby, I began to collect autographs. Whenever people came to our house, I always asked for their signatures. I asked Daddy to carry the plastic book with him on trips and ask for autographs of people he worked with, met, and knew. I often think back now to our father, a well-known civil rights attorney, pulling the plastic autograph book out of his pocket and asking people, "Would you please sign my daughter Barbara's autograph book?" He took the book with him when he traveled and brought home all kinds of interesting personal signatures and notes written to me.

The autograph book lay buried in some dark, unused closet in my house for most of my adult life, and I didn't think much about it until recently. When I rediscovered it not long ago, I flipped through its yellowed pages and saw the notes and names of a variety of well-known people. In fact, it reads like a "who's who" list of the world's famous civil rights leaders, a member of Congress, a presidential associate press secretary, a U.S. attorney general, a governor, the State Attorney for Israel, a Secretary of War, and many others. Here are a few examples:

> *Dear Barbara, I have only known you for a short while and already I know you will be a success. Follow in your father's footsteps to success. Best of luck in all your endeavors.* **Vivian Malone, "UA" "'65."**

> *To Barbara, with best wishes and congratulations on being the daughter of a dedicated and courageous leader of our cause.* **Ralph Bunche.**

> *With warm regards,* **A. T. Hatcher.**

> *Best wishes,* **Willie Mays.**

> *Wishing Barbara health, happiness, prosperity, and freedom.* **Charles Diggs, Jr.**

> *For Arthur Shores and Barbara, with highest regards and best wishes,* **Robert Kennedy.**

Best wishes to my friend Barbara. **Mrs. Constance Baker Motley.**

Best wishes and warm regards, **Martin Luther King, Jr.**

Barbara, we fight so you and all Americans may be free someday. **Ralph D. Abernathy.**

Race Relations on Campus

After my experience of growing up in Birmingham, I decided to attend Talladega College, a historically black college with only a few of the white professors' children in the classes.

Daddy was so proud that I chose to go to Talladega College. It was, after all, his school, and I had heard many stories of his fond memories at "Dega." He wrote to me every week, and I received a special delivery letter every Sunday. He told me everything going on in Birmingham as well as about the cases he had. Mummee sent me special packages just about every week, which usually held new outfits, baked cookies, and other food items. Because I lived so close to home (only about sixty miles away), many times Mummee and Daddy rode down on Sundays and spent the day with me. On holidays, I invited classmates home with me.

After graduating from "Dega," I was accepted at the University of Illinois, the Champaign-Urbana Campus, where I studied social work. This was a complete change for me because, while African Americans were the majority at Talladega College, at the University of Illinois African Americans were definitely in the minority.

I really didn't know what to expect. Students were somewhat friendly, but oftentimes they were aloof, and I didn't make any friends with my white university counterparts. It sort of reminded me of what Vivian Malone may have felt when she attended the University of Alabama. One thing I learned was the difference between whites in the North as compared to whites in the South. In the South, I knew just where I stood with them. But in the North, I never quite knew for sure. If Southern whites didn't like me, they let me know. But Northern whites weren't so vocal. They often *pretended* to care. I did meet some genuinely kind white people, however, outside of my classes.

After receiving my master's degree in social work, I worked as a school social worker in Champaign, Illinois. I met some wonderful friends in that school system that happened to be white. We had a mutual respect for each other and became friends. During those years in Illinois, I learned to look at the person's character rather than a person's color. Today I enjoy a diverse group of friends where the person's skin color does not matter.

My birth city, Birmingham, Alabama, has made some great improvements in race relations since its early Jim Crow years — but it still has much to accomplish. The races are still somewhat divided in many pockets of the state. For instance, Alabama has one of the most prestigious medical centers in the country. Yet we still see health disparities in minority populations, particularly among African Americans. We are looking closely at this problem and trying to find ways to eliminate these inequalities.

Even though our public schools were integrated in the 1960s, we still see differences in the level of education provided African American students. And we are aware of racist behavior among many of the state's young white children. They reflect the attitudes of those who opposed integration during the civil rights era. We need more diversity training in our public schools to ease the tension that still exists between black and white students.

Alabama is also losing its much-needed young and well-trained college graduates, who too often leave the state to seek employment elsewhere. We need to offer greater incentives to encourage them to stay here and work. I have seen some growth in this area, but more needs to be done.

Perhaps as new generations are born, and as they continue coming together from diverse backgrounds, Birmingham will see even greater improvements for all her citizens.

I have hope that will happen.

CHAPTER 28

The Lillie Boman Case

October 20, 1958–1962,
in Birmingham, Alabama

(Helen remembers.)

White Passengers Seat from Front,
Colored Passengers from Rear
—NEW INSTRUCTIONS
painted in Birmingham buses

After Rosa Parks refused to give her seat to a white male passenger on December 1, 1955, the city's black population boycotted the Montgomery bus transit system and crippled it. But city leaders in Birmingham still strictly enforced the General City Code of Birmingham regarding public transportation and the separation of the races. Section 1413 demanded that "every owner or operator of any jitney, bus or taxicab in the city shall provide equal but separate accommodations for the white and colored races by providing separate vehicles, or by clearly indicating or designating by visible markers the area to be occupied by each race in any vehicle in which the two races are permitted to be carried together, and by confining each race to occupancy of the area of such vehicle so set apart for it."

Bus drivers who decided to disobey this city code risked punishment, fines, and jail time. "It shall be unlawful for any person to operate or cause or allow to be operated or to aid in operating for the carriage of white and colored passengers any vehicle not equipped as provided in this section [Sec. 1413 above]. And it shall be unlawful for any person, contrary to the provisions of this section providing for equal and separate accommodations for the white and colored races, to ride or attempt to ride in a vehicle or a division of a vehicle designated for the race to which such person does not belong."

The code ended with this warning: "Failure to comply with this section shall be deemed a misdemeanor."[1]

New City Buses, New Segregation Signs

On October 14, 1958, the commissioners of the City of Birmingham enacted ordinance No. 1486-F repealing Sections 1002 and 1413 of the General City Code, which required racial segregation of passengers in streetcars, buses, and taxicabs within the city, and made failure to comply therewith a misdemeanor. On the same date, ordinance No. 1487-F was enacted, challenging the repeal!

Prior to October 14, the Birmingham Transit Company used movable color boards attached to the tops of the seats to segregate the races on its buses. Upon the action of the commissioners, painted signs in the front and rear of its buses replaced the old movable color boards. The new statements read, "White Passengers Seat from Front, Colored Passengers from Rear." At the same time, notices were posted on the employees' bulletin boards advising them of the passage of the ordinance and instructing them in the proper loading of passengers:

BULLETIN ORDER

BIRMINGHAM TRANSIT COMPANY

Date Effective: Thursday, October 16, 1958
"Bulletin Order No. 176

Subject: ORDINANCE COVERING THE SEPARATION
OF RACES OF ALL CONCERNED:

As you have seen in the newspapers, the City Commission has unanimously repealed all bus segregation ordinances to become effective Thursday, October 16, 1958. Signs have been placed in front and rear of all our buses which read as follows:

WHITE PASSENGERS SEAT FROM FRONT
COLORED PASSENGERS FROM REAR

Every effort should be used to avoid conflicting problems. May we suggest that you use calmness and your very best judgment in handling any situation that might arise?

J. E. Crutchfield
Superintendent of Transportation

On October 20, 1958, a few days after the new signs were posted, a group of twenty-five black Americans boarded a city bus and purposely sat down in the front seats. The startled bus driver quickly shut the doors and allowed no one else to enter the bus.

"Move to the rear of the bus," he ordered the black passengers.

They refused and stayed in their front seats.

The bus driver refused to move the bus. He found a nearby telephone and called his supervisor.

The supervisor arrived at the scene.

"Move to the rear of the bus," the supervisor ordered the group.

Again they refused.

A police officer arrived. By this time, a crowd of several hundred onlookers gathered around the bus. The police officer telephoned his superior. When his superior came to the scene, he ordered the bus driver to take the bus to the barn. Two other police officers came, and they ordered the group to move to the back of the bus. Everyone obeyed the officers and moved back—except nine people, including Lillie Boman. Police arrested Boman and the other eight people, jailed them until 2:00 a.m., charged them with "disorderly conduct and conspiracy to commit a breach of the peace," and then released them on bond. The nine were tried and convicted of "breach of the peace" before the city recorder, and jailed for the next four or five days as they awaited sentences.

On November 11, 1958, the Alabama Christian Movement for Human Rights and our father signed an agreement for representation on behalf of Lillie Boman, Rev. F. L. Shuttlesworth, and others. The agreement engaged our father "to represent the above named parties and all Negroes, in the City of Birmingham in an action in the Federal Court, to have declared unconstitutional the application of Ordinance 1487-F and its application to the above named parties and all Negroes similarly situated, and have the City restrained from enforcing said Ordinance."[2] The agreement was signed by the Rev. F. L. Shuttlesworth, the Rev. N. H. Smith, and Arthur D. Shores.

The next day our father filed a class action suit against Eugene Connor, J. W. Morgan, and J. T. Waggoner (both individually and as members of the Board of City Commissioners and the Birmingham Transit Company). The suit was filed in the U.S. District Court for the Northern District of Alabama, and it alleged that the City of Birmingham had enacted an ordinance designated as No. 1487-F that granted Birmingham Transit Company and other carriers of passengers for hire operating in the City Authority to formulate and promulgate rules and regulations for the seating of passengers on public conveyances operated by them. They further alleged that the ordinance has been applied by the defendants so as to deny them the rights, privileges, and immunities of citizens of the United States, and to deny them the equal protection of the laws as secured by the Fourteenth Amendment to the Federal Constitution and the rights and privileges secured to them by Title 42, United States Code § 1981 and 1983. The Ordinance read as follows:

ORDINANCE No. 1487-F

AN ORDINANCE RELATING TO CARRIERS
OF PASSENGERS FOR HIRE.

BE IT ORDAINED BY the Commission of the City
of Birmingham as follows:

Section 1. That carriers of passengers for hire, operating in the City of Birmingham, are authorized to formulate and promulgate such rules and regulations for the seating of passengers on public conveyances in their charge as are reasonably necessary to assure the speedy, orderly, convenient, safe and peaceful handling of passengers.

Section 2. A willful refusal to obey a reasonable request of an operator or driver of such a public conveyance in relation to the seating of passengers thereon shall constitute a breach of the peace.

Judge Hobart Grooms heard the case. On November 23, 1959, he ordered the case dismissed as to the Birmingham Transit Company. He denied injunctive relief without prejudice, and he ordered the case be retained and remain pending for a reasonable time awaiting further and appropriate order of the Court.[3]

Not to be deterred, our father filed an appeal to the Fifth Circuit of the U.S. Court of Appeals. The U.S. Court of Appeals reversed the decision and remanded it back to Judge Grooms. In keeping with the mandate of the U.S. Court of Appeals for the Fifth Circuit, Judge Grooms finally issued an Order that read as follows:

IT IS ORDERED, ADJUDGED AND DECREED
by the Court as follows:

That the action of Birmingham Transit Company in posting and maintaining the signs: "White Passengers Seat From The Front, Colored Passengers Seat From The Rear," on the basis of color, is forbidden by the Fourteenth Amendment to the Constitution of the United States:

That the defendant Birmingham Transit Company, a Corporation, its agents, servants, employees and attorneys, and all persons in active concert and participation with them be, and they hereby are, restrained and enjoined from further or continued display or maintenance of the signs described in paragraph (1), and from promulgating and enforcing any rule or regulation on the basis of race or color requiring white passengers to seat themselves from the front and colored from the rear;

That jurisdiction of this cause is hereby retained as to the other defendants herein, pursuant to the original opinion and order of this Court; and

That the costs of court incurred herein be, and the same hereby are, taxed against the defendant Birmingham Transit Company.

DONE this the 8th day of November 1961.

s/s H. H. Grooms
United States District Judge

In plain everyday language, the ugly old boards on Birmingham's streetcars and buses used to separate the black race from the white race came "a tumbling down," and people—no matter what color their skin—could finally sit where they darn well pleased!

CHAPTER 29

The Year of Greatest Conflict: 1963, Birmingham

(Helen and Barbara remember.)

It is, therefore, no coincidence that since 1947, *"Bomb-ingham"* has known 50 bombings that can be ascribed to racial conflict—and not one of them has been solved.

—*TIME*, September 27, 1963

Several events led up to the year when Alabama would suffer its greatest racial conflicts. In an effort to stop Dr. King, in February 1960 the Alabama grand jury issued a warrant for his arrest, accusing him of two counts of felony perjury. The state charged that Dr. King had signed fraudulent tax returns for 1956 and 1958 regarding funds he had received on behalf of the Montgomery Improvement Association and the Southern Christian Leadership Conference. They claimed that Dr. King owed the state $1,700. Our father represented Dr. King in this suit and trial. Over the following few years, he would work closely with Dr. King as his attorney and friend.

To raise money and to support the young pastor, a group of like-minded people met in entertainer Harry Belafonte's New York home. Belafonte had long been a supporter of Dr. King and the civil rights movement. In her autobiography, Coretta Scott King said of Belafonte, "Whenever we got into trouble or when tragedy struck, Harry has always come to our aid, his generous heart wide open." Together they formed the "Committee to Defend Martin Luther King and the Struggle for Freedom in the South." A. Philip Randolph, whom Dr. King called "truly the Dean of Negro leaders," served as the committee's fundraising chairman.

Others on the committee included Gardner C. Taylor, a preacher; Mordecai Johnson, first black president of Howard University; clergyman Harry Emerson Fosdick; African American playwright Lorraine Hansberry; first black Major League Baseball player Jackie Robinson; and Ruth H. Bunche, a teacher. The former First Lady, Mrs. Eleanor Roosevelt, served as a member of the committee, as did actor Sidney Poitier and singer Nat King Cole. The committee ran a full-page ad in the *New York Times* on Saturday, March 19, 1960, urging men and women "of good will" to join in the fight in this "stormy history of Freedom."

"We urge you to join hands with our fellow Americans in the South by supporting, with your dollars, this Combined Appeal for all three needs—the defense of Martin Luther King—the support of the embattled students—and the struggle for the right to vote," the ad read, listing the names of the committee's supporters.

King's trial began in Montgomery on May 25, 1960, and ultimately Dr. King and our father won the case with the all-white jury returning a "not guilty" verdict.

Racial tension was increasing steadily in Alabama. George Wallace, a determined segregationist, became the state's governor in 1963. He had made a promise of strict segregation to the white people of Alabama, and as governor, Wallace knew he had to keep it.

There is an irony in that promise.

Wallace Becomes Alabama's New Governor

In 1958, George Corley Wallace had lost the Alabama governor's race to KKK-backed John Patterson. Patterson had accepted the Ku Klux Klan's offer of support and ran strong as a strict segregationist on the turbulent race issue in Alabama. Wallace had refused the Klan's support, but had accepted the NAACP's endorsement instead. After his loss, Wallace told friends that he had learned a lesson from the failed election: "They just out-segged me ... they're never going to do that again." After that

Wallace drastically changed his political statements and public views on the issue of race relations, running in the Alabama governor's primary of 1962 as a determined segregationist. And the white people of Alabama elected him governor.

On January 14, 1963, in his inaugural address as Alabama's new governor, George Wallace promised his fellow Alabamians that he would maintain segregation forever: "Each race," he declared,

> within its own framework has the freedom to teach ... to instruct ... to develop ... to ask for and receive deserved help from others of separate racial stations. This is the great freedom of our American founding fathers ... but if we amalgamate into the one unit as advocated by the communist philosophers ... then the enrichment of our lives ... the freedom for our development ... is gone forever. We become, therefore, a mongrel unit of one under a single all powerful government ... and we stand for everything ... and for nothing.

Racial tension and relationships grew worse under Wallace's leadership. In 1963 a reporter for *Time* called the state of Alabama "a state of deep superstitions, fierce prides, sudden violence and voiceless fears." (Alabama would soon earn that tragic description.)

Compared to other states in the nation, the *Time* reporter noted, "Alabama rates 47th among the states in per capita income ($1,538), leading only Arkansas, South Carolina and Mississippi. And, at a time when George Wallace is inveighing against the Federal Government in the name of states' rights, the extent to which Alabama depends on economic help from the Government is an immense irony."

Moving toward "Project Confrontation"

Birmingham's race battle was intensifying. Nine years before Wallace's inaugural day, the U.S. Supreme Court, in *Brown v. Board of Education* (1954), had ordered the nation's schools to integrate —but it had not yet happened in Alabama. In 1954, Autherine Lucy had almost been killed after she enrolled at the University of Alabama at Tuscaloosa, and school trustees ousted her from the campus and classes. Elementary schools, middle schools, and high schools in Alabama also remained segregated.

And still Wallace was telling the people of Alabama that "we will not sacrifice our children to any such type school system [integrated]—and you can write that down." He was determined that Alabama's schools would not integrate, regardless of the U.S. Supreme Court's decision in 1954. He wanted to keep the state's school system "separate but equal." It was separate, but it was certainly not equal—for black student schools had only a fraction of the resources white students enjoyed.

Something had to give.

Then, in the spring of 1963, at the peak of Birmingham's civil rights unrest, the young Dr. Martin Luther King, Jr. and the Southern Christian Leadership Conference answered pastor Fred Shuttlesworth's urgent and desperate plea to come to Birmingham. The city needed help. That April, a group of civil rights leaders, led by Dr. King and the SCLC, introduced "Project C," or "Project Confrontation."

During that turbulent year, our father, along with several other attorneys, became Dr. King's legal representatives in Birmingham. The eyes of the world, through newspapers and television reports, stayed on violent Birmingham that year. Even the President of the United States, John F. Kennedy, became involved in the fight for racial freedom. George Wallace and his promised Jim Crow laws didn't stand a chance of keeping Alabama segregated "today, tomorrow, or forever." But Birmingham would experience much violence in the quest for equal rights for African Americans, and Daddy would sacrifice his time and energy and suffer as he never had before. In fact, our entire family would be caught up in the intense racial struggle of 1963.

As pastor of the Dexter Avenue Baptist Church in Montgomery,

Alabama, Dr. Martin Luther King, Jr. had helped black people in the 382-day bus boycott in 1955–56. In 1957, the Southern Christian Leadership Conference had elected the young pastor as its president. Then, in the spring of 1963, King came to Birmingham.

He and the SCLC had just failed in their campaign in Albany, Georgia. The schools there remained segregated, and city parks had been closed to avoid integration. Pastor and active civil rights leader Andrew Young remembered later that King had been "very depressed" after the failed campaign.

"D Day" in Birmingham

The SCLC planned a number of boycotts throughout Birmingham, for the leaders knew that economic pressure on businesses would speak loudly to Birmingham's officials. Started in the fall of 1962, the "Selective Buying Campaign," as they called the boycott, encouraged black people to stop buying clothes, shoes, and other items at Birmingham's downtown stores.

"[Black people] were outside the [Pizitz] store saying 'don't come in,'" Mr. Richard "Dick" Pizitz remembered.

> And if black customers did come in and buy something … they would actually take the bags away from people and say "you shouldn't be buying here. Don't come back!" There were white [shoppers] that were intimidated [to shop at the store] because they feared violence.

The large downtown department stores such as Pizitz lost so much business it became a "sink or swim" issue for them. If they didn't agree to fully integrate their stores, they knew they couldn't stay in business. But if they did integrate their stores, hire black workers, and take down the Jim Crow signs as protest leaders called for them to do, they feared violent retaliation from Birmingham's strong Ku Klux Klan. The stores had already received numerous bomb threats as well as personal threats against storeowners.

It was a bad time for a store boycott in the Shores family. Helen's wedding was coming up, and she had many things to buy. Mummee and Helen decided to drive to Cain-Sloan's department store in Nashville to buy Helen's wedding dress and other necessities. The wedding gifts that friends bought for Helen and Bob also came from stores outside of Birmingham.

Easter 1963

The boycott gained new strength right before Easter 1963. Southern tradition held that every church member would buy a new outfit for Easter Sunday morning. Men bought new suits, ties, shirts, shoes, and hats. Women bought dresses, gloves, pumps, purses, and hats. Children chose lacy white dresses with matching pinafores, gloves, purses, and hats. Most of Birmingham's black population—some 40 percent—shopped at the big downtown department stores. They spent their money there, but stores refused to hire black clerks. They also refused to allow African Americans to try on clothes or eat in their department store restaurants. Racial signs above store water fountains pointed white people to one fountain and black people to another. Helen would often have me (Barbara) as a "lookout" as she drank from the white fountain.

Easter provided a good time to stress the Selective Buying Campaign. Weeks before Easter, pastors urged their congregations to forget buying new clothes for Easter Sunday. During that Easter season, instead of buying new clothes, Mummee remade Barbara's Easter outfit from the previous year, and Daddy had her previous year's Easter shoes polished to perfection. Both black and white people stopped shopping downtown, and the boycott severely hurt Birmingham's businesses.

"We had a little branch [Pizitz store] in Bessemer and a little branch in Roebuck," Mr. Pizitz said,

> but we had no other branch stores. [Pizitz Department Store] was a downtown structured business and we enjoyed a lot of

economic benefit from African American customers. When the boycott came in, it was extremely effective. Retailers went to the power structure ... the industrialists, the bankers, etc., and said "This is going to shut Birmingham down.... Something has got to be done. We got to change. This was the 'perfect storm.'"

The Arrest

On April 3, 1963, during the Selective Buying Campaign, the SCLC staged sit-ins inside several downtown whites-only lunch counters. Three days later, police arrested forty-five protesters as they marched from the Sixteenth Street Baptist Church to Birmingham's city jail. The next day, police arrested even more protesters, whom Daddy represented in court. The city charged $100 for each person's bail, and Daddy, Mr. Gaston, and others raised much of the bail money so these protesters could leave jail and go home.

In light of the protests, Judge W. A. Jenkins Jr. ordered that the civil rights leaders, including Dr. King, Ralph Abernathy, and Fred Shuttlesworth, organize no future protests in Birmingham.

On Good Friday, April 12, 1963, police arrested Dr. King and placed him in a Birmingham city jail cell in solitary confinement. The small cell held a metal-slatted cot with no mattress, a toilet and sink, and a mirror on the back wall. The cell had no overhead light or other light source. He spent most of his imprisonment in the dark. King later called those long hours and days in solitary confinement "the most frustrating and bewildering" he had ever lived.

On the second day of King's confinement, Bull Connor in City Hall granted three attorneys permission to visit Dr. King. They were Norman Amaker from the NAACP, Orzell Billingsley, and our father. Perhaps one of them took Dr. King the ad that ran in the *Birmingham News* where eight local white ministers referred to King as a troublemaker. In any event, King read the ad and felt that he had to somehow respond to it.

Letter from Birmingham Jail

Dr. King had no paper, so he wrote his response around the edges of the newspaper ad and on pieces of toilet paper in his cell. Later, Daddy or one of the other attorneys brought him a notepad. King could only work in the daytime when he had enough scant light to see. When he finished the response, our father and his other attorneys secretly slipped the assorted bits and pieces of the letter from King's cell and into the hands of NAACP's Wyatt Walker. Walker and his secretary, Willie Pearl Mackey, pieced together the scraps of paper, and Mackey typed out the rough draft of the letter.

Andrew Young recalled that Willie Pearl Mackey "had a terrible time reading Martin's handwriting. Most of the letter was brought in installments delivered from the jail by our attorneys, Clarence Jones, Ozell Billingsley, and Arthur Shores, during their trips to jail to visit Martin." When Mackey had finished typing the draft, one of King's lawyers smuggled it back to Dr. King to edit and make corrections. Then one of the lawyers carried it back to Walker.

In his response, on April 16, 1963, Dr. King addressed directly the eight white pastors ("My dear fellow clergymen") who had written the newspaper ad. Using passages and characters from the Bible, he eloquently explained his reasons for coming to Birmingham (because he found injustice in the city), and he outlined both the process and the goal of his visit and activities, carefully describing the four basic steps of his nonviolent campaign: collection of the facts to determine whether injustices exist; negotiation; self-purification; and direct action. He also called Birmingham the most segregated city in the United States and mentioned its ugly record of brutality, including the Negroes' unjust treatment by courts and the unsolved bombings. He told the clergymen: "The purpose of our direct-action program is to create a situation so crisis-packed that it will inevitably open the door to negotiation."

His response ran to more than 7,000 words in length. By May

13, 1963, the American Friends Service Committee (Quaker) had received permission from the SCLC to print the letter for wide dissemination and published 50,000 copies of the document in pamphlet form for national distribution. Other publications printed King's *Letter*, including the *Christian Century*, the *Saturday Evening Post*, the *Birmingham News*, and *Atlantic Monthly*, among others.

Half a Century Later

Almost a half-century later, theologians are still calling King's *Letter from Birmingham Jail* "towering" and "magnificent." In his letter,

> King clearly cataloged the injustices faced by African Americans. He called "white moderates" to task and forcefully reminded them that justice delayed was justice denied. And most famously, citing Augustine, he claimed that "an unjust law is no law at all...." King had reason, justice, facts, and conviction on his side—as well as the gospel. He did not need vitriol, and he did not employ it.

Police released Dr. King from his Birmingham jail cell on April 20, 1963, some eight long and dark days after they arrested him.

Daddy didn't talk to us about Dr. King or "Project C." Racial conflict wasn't a topic discussed around our dinner table. In those days, few black parents talked with their children about what was going on. The motto in that day seemed to be, *Children are to be seen and not heard when adults have adult conversations.* Maybe they thought they were protecting their children from the fear of it all—like putting up a protective wall to bring them some sense of extra security. Daddy and Uncle Hollins got together often and talked about such current issues, but they never talked in front of us children.

Yet, even though Daddy didn't tell us those things, he did share with us still another irony about Governor Wallace.

Our Father and George C. Wallace

While most of the nation's people knew Wallace as a stubborn racist, Daddy had special insight into the man. He had tried a case before him years before when Wallace was a circuit judge in Barbour County. The case lasted a week, and in this trial, Daddy attacked Alabama's legal system because blacks had been excluded from serving on court juries. Throughout the trial, when no restaurant in Barbour County would serve food to black people, Wallace sent out for food for him and Daddy. Then together they ate lunch in Wallace's court chambers.

Daddy understood the man and his reasons for his segregationist statements and actions. He knew that black people had little voting power in those days and that in order for any politician to be elected in Alabama, he had to appear racist and promise continued segregation.

Daddy often told us that George Wallace wasn't the segregationist people made him out to be. He was always cordial to Daddy, and later in his life, Daddy and Mummee attended a program where Wallace was present. Wallace sat in a wheelchair, the victim of a shooting, and a photographer snapped a picture of Daddy and Wallace shaking hands. I remember Mummee saying that Wallace didn't look like the man as she remembered from the 1960s. "He's not the same strong man who stood for segregation," she said. "He's broken."

CHAPTER 30

The Days the Children Marched

Early May 1963, in Birmingham, Alabama

(Barbara remembers.)

One of our cousins, Walter Horace, a student in Birmingham, got arrested by Bull Connor's police during the march. I saw him inside the crowded paddy wagon, his arm waving at us through the opened window.

"Mummee!" I cried and pointed at the wagon. "That's Walter Horace!"

—BARBARA SYLVIA SHORES

On May 2, 1963, directed by local radio disc jockey Shelley Stewart (called "Shelley the Playboy"), thousands of Birmingham's children and youth slipped out of school, joined together, and marched to the Kelly Ingram Park near the Sixteenth Street Baptist Church. Civil rights leader James Bevel had recruited the children to walk the downtown Birmingham streets in non-violent protest for their equal civil rights, primarily to challenge segregation in Birmingham. Dr. King worried that something might happen to the children and argued with Bevel about the plan. But he finally agreed to the children's march.

Birmingham school children and youth filled the church. In waves, large groups walked down the stairs of the Sixteenth Street Baptist Church and into the streets. Bull Connor, Birmingham's Public Safety Commissioner, and the city's police officers met the children with small white army tanks, billy clubs, police dogs, and fire hoses. Photographers snapped pictures of children rolling across the street after getting blasted by the high-powered water from the firemen's hoses. The photos appeared on television and in newspapers, triggering outrage throughout the world.

Connor arrested the protesting children, put them in paddy wagons, and took them to Birmingham's city jails. But they continued, wave after wave, group after group, to pour from the church and march, dance, and sing in the downtown streets.

The children's marches and protests continued the next day, May 3, 1963. Connor brought in big yellow school buses and hauled hundreds of children to the city's jails. When the jails filled up, he directed the school buses to Birmingham's Fairgrounds. He locked up the children and youth in open hog pens, exposed and vulnerable to all kinds of weather.

Many of the imprisoned children spent up to two weeks jailed. Bull Connor ordered that each child, even children as young as four years old, be individually interrogated before he or she could be released. Daddy filed appeals and worked hard on all the legal ends to have the children freed.

Remembering Bull Connor

I remember Daddy saying,

> The [white] power structure [of Birmingham] put Bull Connor in office. It finally came to the point where the power structure could not control [him]. And they were helpful in seeing that some change did take place, because of the image that this city portrayed throughout the country.... [Bull] was satisfying the people who put him in power. That's what he was doing. During the Birmingham demonstrations,* Daddy told us, Bull Connor acted like a "fireball," like a crazy "madman," as he got out and led his firemen and policemen.[1]

I had a personal and close encounter with Bull Connor. I was a majorette at my high school at the football games. Bull Connor usually brought in his policemen and German Shepherds to keep

---

*That year of greatest conflict, 1963, Daddy stayed busy representing the demonstrators that Connor arrested and jailed. In fact, more than 3,000 demonstrators were arrested during the 1963 Birmingham "Project C" Campaign.

down fighting between the challenging teams. We were getting ready to go out on the field, when my friend and fellow majorette, Carolyn Nolan, ran to get in line. All of a sudden, one of the police dogs lunged toward her and ripped off her skirt. Carolyn became hysterical. Bull Connor and the policemen did nothing to help her. We all ran to her aid.

Needless to say, we didn't perform well that night. I'll always remember that half grin on Connor's face as he watched the confusion. Not long after, Connor, the policemen, and the dog disappeared from the football field.

Connor's Impeachment?

Perhaps Birmingham's white populace had forgotten about the February 7, 1952, Jefferson County Grand Jury's report that called for Connor's impeachment from Birmingham's Department of Public Safety. The report described Connor as "a hard task master, explosive, vindictive against those employees under his authority who disagree with him, given to jumping at conclusions, dictatorial, immoral, autocratic, and a failure as an executive in his relationship with his subordinates...." The report added that "[Connor] cracks the whip of authority but uses no persuasion, logic or reason, if any he has."[2]

On May 3, 1963, David Vann and our father sat down in the conference room of the Birmingham Realty Company with a group of white and black people. Mr. Vann had called Daddy some time before and asked for his assistance in putting together a biracial committee.

The men went to work and pulled together the black and white representatives. It was this group that would meet and ultimately bring an end to the demonstrations.[3]

CHAPTER 31

George Wallace Stands in the Schoolhouse Door

June 11, 1963, in Tuscaloosa, Alabama

(Barbara remembers.)

> Wherever the revolt of the Negro may lead in the long run, one direct clash looms dead ahead. Alabama's Democratic Governor George Corley Wallace, 43, a fiery ex-Golden Gloves featherweight, is looking toward a showdown next week when two Negroes will attempt to enter the University of Alabama for the summer session.
>
> —*TIME*, June 7, 1963

When James Meredith had tried to enroll at Ole Miss in 1962, violence, bloodshed, and death followed. So when two black students, Vivian Malone and James Hood, enrolled at the University of Alabama in the summer of 1963, civil rights leaders, Birmingham officials, and Alabama's residents braced themselves for a replay in Tuscaloosa.

At the time, Alabama was the only state in the nation barring African Americans from attending a state-supported all-white school. When George Wallace ran for governor of Alabama in 1962, he promised the people who voted for him he would keep the state's school segregated. "As your Governor," he vowed, "I shall refuse to abide by illegal court orders to the point of standing at the schoolhouse door if necessary."[1]

And on June 11, 1963, that's exactly what he did.

Our Father and Vivian Malone

Vivian Malone and James Hood were as different as night from day. Hood was more outgoing and had ambitious ideas. He signed my autograph book as the future governor of Alabama: "Dear Barbara, Congratulations for being the daughter of a man whom I feel is Mr. Civil Rights of Birmingham. Be ever sweet and always wonderful as I know you can." James A. Hood, *Governor of Alabama 1980!*" (James had a sense of humor!)

I remember Vivian Malone as a quiet, sweet, and courageous young woman. She came to our home several times when our father represented her. She always had great ambitions of going to college. She applied to the University of Alabama in 1961, when she was 18 years old, but the university refused to enroll her because they said they had a "crowded enrollment situation." She knew, however, that the university was still strictly segregated. So she applied and was admitted to Alabama's black school, Alabama A & M. After two years there, she set her sights again on the University of Alabama. But once again, she was turned down. She then asked for help from the NAACP Legal Defense Fund, which then contacted our father.

Since Vivian was considered a minor, her mother, Bertha Malone, filed the suit. Octavia Hood, Jimmy Hood's father, filed the suit for him against Hubert E. Mate, Dean of Admissions of the University of Alabama. Attorneys for the plaintiffs were our father, Fred D. Gray, Constance Motley, and Leroy D. Clark.

The night before the university "showdown," for her safety, Daddy arranged for Vivian Malone to spend the night at the home of his secretary, Agnes Stoudmire. She couldn't stay at the A. G. Gaston Hotel because it had been bombed the week before, and it was the only hotel in Birmingham for blacks. Everyone kept her whereabouts a secret. She wasn't even allowed to telephone her parents because they feared a "leak," and they wanted no homes bombed. Vivian's family had already received death threats.

The next morning, June 11, 1963, Vivian came to our house.

"Are you afraid, Vivian?" I asked her.

"No," she told me. "I can't imagine it will be as dangerous now as when Autherine Lucy enrolled at the University of Alabama years ago."

"I'll be praying for you today, Vivian," I promised her.

The Showdown—
A Turning Point in Alabama's History

People around the world were still reeling from the news reports of dog attacks and fire hoses aimed at Birmingham's children the month before and remembering the violence that had accompanied James Meredith's enrollment at Ole Miss. So on the morning of June 11, 1963, they watched with great interest the events that prompted Alabama's governor to block the entrance of the University of Alabama in Tuscaloosa, praying that the University of Alabama wouldn't experience the same rioting James Meredith had endured on September 10, 1962.

The press crowded around the entrance of Foster Auditorium with their news cameras set up, waiting to film the live showdown. President Kennedy himself had federalized the Alabama National Guardsmen, who stood armed outside of the university. State troopers in patrol cars pulled up at the campus, and troopers on motorcycles drove up and down the streets ready to keep the peace in case of trouble. Some guards carried billy clubs and wore steel helmets.

In Washington, D.C., President Kennedy and Attorney General Robert Kennedy discussed how the situation would be handled if Wallace refused to allow the two black students into Foster Auditorium.

The Alabama heat index was almost unbearable on that June day as Governor Wallace drove up in a state trooper's car. Vivian Malone, dressed in a light-colored dress, and James Hood, dressed in suit, tie, and hat, sat together in a car with more than one hundred protective guards waiting to escort them into Foster

Auditorium. Governor George Wallace stood defiantly in the school's doorway, chin held high, jaw clenched, as he blocked the entrance with his body. Everyone waited to see what he would say and do. They knew he had made a campaign segregation promise to Alabama voters earlier that year, and that he was determined to keep it "today, tomorrow, and forever."

Wallace Makes His Stand

No one moved as cameras recorded the event. Wallace held the small microphone that hung on a cord around his neck close to his mouth, and tried to look strong and confident. Still, he seemed nervous.

"The unwelcomed, unwanted, unwarranted and force-induced intrusion," he said,

> upon the campus of the University of Alabama today of the might of the Central Government offers frightful example of the oppression of the rights, privileges and sovereignty of this State by officers of the Federal Government. This intrusion results solely from force, or threat of force, undignified by any reasonable application of the principle of law, reason and justice....[2]

The scene was tense. The crowd stood still and waited to see what the governor would do.

After Wallace spoke, Lieutenant General Henry Graham and Alabama National Guard soldiers walked to the podium, as planned, and handed a printed presidential order to Wallace. United States Deputy Attorney General Nicholas Katzenbach and federalized Alabama National Guardsmen then asked Governor Wallace to step aside. Daddy stood beside Katzenbach at the schoolhouse door.

Katzenbach told Wallace that he simply wanted him to abide by the federal court order, but Wallace refused and publicly cited the constitutional right of states to operate public schools, colleges, and universities. Then Katzenbach called President Kennedy.

Wallace Stands Down

Ultimately, Governor Wallace stepped aside, walked forward, and —looking straight ahead—he passed crowds of reporters, guards, and onlookers, and climbed into a waiting car. The car drove away quickly.

After Wallace left the scene, James Hood walked through the entrance of Foster Auditorium, escorted by soldiers and without incident. Vivian Malone, also escorted, followed him. Later Malone recalled, "I was never afraid. I did have some apprehensions in my mind, though, especially having gone to segregated ... schools. God was with me."

Daddy later told us that when Malone and Hood walked into the all-white University of Alabama, he considered that his greatest moment in Alabama's history.

The First African American Graduate

Vivian Malone became the first African American student to graduate from the University of Alabama, receiving a bachelor of arts in business management. After graduation, she joined the U.S. Department of Justice's Civil Rights Division. She later became director of Civil Rights and Urban Affairs and director of the U.S. Environmental Protection Agency before she retired in 1996. In 2000, the University of Alabama awarded Vivian Malone-Jones a doctorate of humane letters. Jones, 63, died in 2005 after suffering a stroke.

James Hood continued his education at Wayne State University and Michigan State University. He returned to the University of Alabama in 1995 and received a Ph.D. in interdisciplinary studies in 1997.

Years later, Professor of Communication Studies and History E. Culpepper Clark described Daddy in this way: "Arthur Shores's persistence and bulldog tenacity won victory after victory as the courts applied more systemically the principles of equality to his cases…. His practice continued to expand. He maintained the respect of the white community and became Birmingham's first black city councilman. In 1975, the University of Alabama awarded him an honorary doctorate."[3]

In his book, *The Schoolhouse Door: Segregation's Last Stand at the University of Alabama*, E. Culpepper Clark wrote of our father,

> Arthur Davis Shores occupied center stage in the legal battle to end segregation in Alabama. He looked something like a compact, dark-skinned Errol Flynn. A pencil mustache highlighted the crisp details of a wardrobe that always appeared to have been pressed against a straight edge. His manners were more relaxed than his appearance, but he displayed a quiet tenacity in the legal arena. He forced his way into the all-white Democratic Party. He was forever turning adversity into advantage…. Shores was supremely confident because he knew the law was on his side. He watched in bemused satisfaction as white lawyers squirmed in legal contortions trying to preserve tradition.[4]

When people come to Tuscaloosa's University of Alabama today, they can see the Autherine Lucy Clock Tower that honors our father's client, Autherine, the first black student accepted and enrolled at the university in 1956. They can also visit the Malone-Hood Plaza named in honor of Vivian and James, who, with our father's help in 1963, were also allowed to enroll at the University of Alabama during the days of segregation. Both the Tower and the Plaza have been placed outside the renovated Foster Auditorium where Governor Wallace blocked the entrance.

Who would have known in 1963 that my own son, Damien Larkin, would become a student today at the University of Alabama at Tuscaloosa, studying for a doctorate in communications. Damien is the only one in our family who is attending the University of Alabama.

"When days get hard here," he tells me, "I think about Granddaddy's courage. I know Granddaddy is smiling down on me."

CHAPTER 32

Frustration and Fury
in Washington

The White House, Washington, D.C.,
on the evening of June 11, 1963, and summer
and autumn 1963, in Birmingham, Alabama

(Helen remembers.)

I hope that every American, regardless of where he lives,
will stop and examine his conscience about this [the incident at the University of Alabama earlier that day] and
other related incidents.

—PRESIDENT JOHN F. KENNEDY
in a televised national address, June 11, 1963

Birmingham's residents breathed a sigh of relief that the University of Alabama had not experienced the riots and violence Ole
Miss had suffered with the enrollment of James Meredith the year
before. But that evening, a highly frustrated President John F.
Kennedy addressed the nation on live television:

This afternoon, following a series of threats and defiant statements, the presence of Alabama National Guard was required
on the University of Alabama to carry out the final and
unequivocal order of the United States District Court of the
Northern District of Alabama. That order called for the admission of two clearly qualified young Alabama residents who
happened to have been born Negro. That they were admitted
peacefully on the campus is due in good measure to the conduct of the students of the University of Alabama, who met
their responsibilities in a constructive way.

This nation was founded by men of many nations and

backgrounds. It was founded on the principle that all men are created equal, and that the rights of every man are diminished when the rights of one man are threatened.

Looking directly into the camera, he told the nation,

It ought to be possible for American students of any color to attend any public institution they select without having to be backed up by troops. It ought to be possible for American consumers of any color to receive equal service in places of public accommodation, such as hotels and restaurants and theaters and retail stores, without being forced to resort to demonstrations in the street. And it ought to be possible for American citizens of any color to register to vote in a free election without interference or fear of reprisal.[1]

In his speech, Kennedy characterized the civil rights struggle as a moral issue, and he told the nation he would submit a new bill to Congress regarding civil rights (later passed as the Civil Rights Act of 1964). Roughly two months later, on August 28, 1963, people from all over the nation, both black and white, gathered in Washington, D.C. at the request of civil rights leaders and participated in a peaceful march and demonstration. Dr. King told the thousands of participants from the steps of the Lincoln Memorial,

I have a dream, that one day, down in Alabama, with its vicious racists, with its governor having his lips dripping with the words of interposition and nullification; one day right there in Alabama, little black boys and black girls will be able to join hands with little white boys and white girls as sisters and brothers.[2]

Dr. King's dream was to become a reality, but very slowly.

The Desegregation of Birmingham's Schools

President Kennedy feared the outbreak of violence when public schools began that fall in Birmingham schools. The U.S. Fifth

Circuit Court of Appeals had demanded the city integrate schools, including Graymont Elementary School, Ramsay High School, and West End High School. On September 9, 1963, Kennedy reported:

> In 144 school districts in 11 Southern and border States, desegregation was carried out for the first time this month in an orderly and peaceful manner. Parents, students, citizens, school officials, and public officials of these areas met their responsibilities in a dignified, law-abiding way. It wasn't necessary for the Federal Government to become involved in any of those States.
>
> In the State of Alabama, however, where local authorities repeatedly stated they were prepared to carry out court directives and maintain public peace, Governor Wallace has refused to respect either the law or the authority of local officials.

Then the President made this promise:

> This Government will do whatever must be done to see that the orders of the court are implemented—but I am hopeful that Governor Wallace will enable the local officials and communities to meet their responsibilities in this regard, as they are willing to do.[3]

Retaliatory Bombings

As President Kennedy had feared, white people began rioting when all-white schools admitted their first black students. And on the evening of September 4, 1963, after schools had opened that morning to black students, our home on Center Street was dynamited. It was the blast described earlier that injured Mummee. Our home had been bombed twice in two weeks!

But the violence didn't stop there. After the four Klansmen planted dynamite on Sunday morning, September 15, 1963, outside the Sixteenth Street Baptist Church, killing the four Sunday school girls, *Time* magazine plastered Governor George Wallace's photograph on the cover of its September 27, 1963, issue with the damaged "Jesus" window in the background. In the article, Wallace was quoted as saying,

> I deplore violence, but who started all this violence? There's a lot of agitators and the Communist Party mixed up in this picture, and people pooh-poohing around sitting up in their ivory towers, a bunch of sissy britches. I don't believe just because somebody has a grievance that you should destroy the whole fabric of the Constitution, of private property. You don't burn the house down to destroy a rat. If they go ahead, they will destroy a lot more than they realize.[4]

Surely, Governor Wallace knew the days of segregation were coming to an end—that Jim Crow was dying in Alabama and elsewhere in the South. Wallace still believed that the communists were behind the civil rights movement, including all the social chaos and rapid changes in old Southern tradition. No doubt the governor feared that his state and country had become a part of a communist agenda, a forceful takeover of the U.S. government.

The Ad: A Public Declaration of Integration

On Sunday, October 20, 1963, a full-page ad appeared in the *Birmingham News*. One hundred and fourteen leaders and residents of Birmingham, including medical doctors, lawyers, ministers, business owners, and others wrote, signed, and ran the ad. Our father's name was the first signature listed.

The newspaper ad stated:

We, the undersigned Citizens of Birmingham, are convinced that the time has come for us to say these things clearly:

The Negro members of this community believe that we are now in a period of crisis as great as any we have known. The unhampered criminal acts that have been recently perpetrated against us cause us grave concern. Our churches and homes have been bombed, and no one has been charged with one act of bombing. Our children have been wounded and killed, and no murderer has been convicted. Therefore, we fear for our lives, and the lives of our families. We are forced to stand guard at our homes. Negro citizens find it extremely difficult to trust the agents of law enforcement—local, state or federal; and all too often they have come to feel that resort to the courts has resulted in justice delayed and, in many a case, justice denied.

At this urgent moment we believe that strong, fearless, immediate action on the part of our city government is absolutely necessary. The protection of its citizens and the allaying of their just fears is the responsibility of any government, and the government of Birmingham must not allow threats of reprisal nor unnecessary bureaucratic machinery to stand in the way of its clear and present duty.

Both the grave concerns and the firm convictions stated above are shared by the vast majority of Birmingham's Negro citizens. We are not satisfied with a life of constant intimidation, segregation and fear, nor have we ever been. No human being is. Therefore, we the undersigned, are all proud to endorse and support the leadership of our friends, Martin Luther King, Jr., and Fred Shuttlesworth, in our common struggle to make Birmingham a better place for all of its citizens. We do not consider these men outsiders to our cause. (Indeed, Rev. Shuttlesworth voted in the last municipal election, and pays taxes in this City and County.) So, we affirm that Dr. King and Rev. Shuttlesworth are our leaders; their goals are ours, our struggle is theirs.

Standing together with these men, in the present moment of crisis, we are convinced that there is one logical first step the city of Birmingham must take now: hire a substantial number of Negro policemen for duty in this city. If, in their assigned districts, these men are given the same authority as all other officers of their rank, their presence will make a great difference to us. It will bring to us a greater confidence in the local police force and a greater sense of safety. Indeed, we are certain that the presence of Negro officers will help convince many persons that they no longer need to depend on their own resources for protection nor turn to violence in search of justice. The morale of Birmingham's Negro citizens is at least as important as the morale of its police force.

We believe that such action by the city is a reasonable first step—but only a first step. For Birmingham has much unfinished business in the difficult undertaking of making basic constitutional rights available to all of its citizens, without regard to race. Therefore, we are still convinced that action must come in the immediate future on such issues as: removal of racial signs on city-owned premises; employment of Negroes in all tax-supported municipal offices; desegregation of all public facilities, including hospitals; and desegregation of those private facilities serving the public. These steps cover only the minimum distance that we must travel to a reign of justice in our city. Because Birmingham is our home, we pledge our lives and our fortunes to this cause, promising to persevere in this pilgrimage until we have reached the goal of liberty and justice for all![5]

Our father, the city's black leaders, and many others had had enough. Racial violence and strife had to come to an end, and so they bravely published their opinions for the city and world to read.

CHAPTER 33

Holidays after
a Long Hot Summer

Autumn/Winter 1963

(Barbara remembers.)

The rights of every man are diminished when
the rights of one man are threatened.

—JOHN F. KENNEDY

Our family felt heart-broken over the loss of those little Sunday
school girls, three of whose families were friends of ours. But the
heartache wasn't over yet. Right before Thanksgiving, on November 22, 1963, President, John F. Kennedy died, the victim of an
assassin's bullet in Dallas, Texas.

I was shocked by Kennedy's murder. I saw him as a president
for all the "real people"—for everyone—and he had given us so
much hope for the future. He had such potential, and he was still
so young. The students, faculty, and staff of Talladega College,
where I was living and studying at the time, gathered in the chapel
to pray. I felt devastated by his sudden death and feared that no
one could step in and take his place.

Helen said she cried when President Kennedy was killed. *What
is happening to our world?* she wondered at the time. She stayed
glued to the television all that day in her Los Angeles apartment.
"Kennedy had done so much good for so many people," she told
me. "Why was he taken so early in life?"

My birthday came on the day after President Kennedy died,
but I didn't feel much like celebrating. It was a somber occasion,
and no one said much. I was home for the Thanksgiving holiday,

and Mummee and Daddy were grieving too. "He had such great potential," they said. "We had so many hopes that Kennedy was going to make many good changes."

A Somber Christmas, 1963

The Christmas holidays that year weren't the same as in previous years. We usually brought lots of student friends home for Christmas holidays, but not that year. Helen and her husband, Bob, stayed in California, so she missed that Christmas's light snowfall. Snow at Christmas came rarely in Birmingham.

Previous Christmases were such special times with Mummee and Daddy. Our mother would cook ten to fifteen fruitcakes and nut cakes, wrap them in cheesecloth, and store them. Daddy would decorate the yard with elaborate ornaments such as life-sized sleighs, reindeer, and a Santa. He strung bright lights all around the house. By the front steps, he placed four-foot Christmas candles. Mummee made an outside church choir with painted faces and red robes, white capes, and green bows. She placed about ten of these wooden choir members in the front yard, and Daddy connected outside speakers that played Christmas music. People in Smithfield came to see our house each year and take photos. In addition to the extraordinary outdoor decorations, Mummee always decorated every room of our house with Christmas trees, ornaments, and other treasured trimmings.

But that year, 1963, I missed my dog Tasso, who had been killed in the house bombing a few months before. My parents gave me another dog, a small poodle I named Trixie.

In past years, we had a family get-together at our house on Christmas Eve. Everyone came—our parent's sisters and brothers, and lots of children. We exchanged gifts, sang carols, and ate dinner together. The ladies in the families prepared simple foods that reminded them of the old days when no one had much money. It became quite an experience trying to put together the menu. We served fallen cakes, in which someone baked a cake and then purposely let it fall. We placed a huge chicken on the table and told everyone to "pull off what you want to eat." Everyone brought a dish to our table, and Aunt Teddy made the same thing each year—potato salad. It was always such a fun time of the year.

But not that Christmas, 1963. After the trauma of that year, I hardly even remember celebrating the holidays.

(Helen remembers.)

That was the first Christmas I had spent away from home and my family, and I missed everyone terribly. No matter where I was, I had always made it back home to celebrate Christmas, but, pregnant with our first child, I had decided to stay in California.

I cried all day on Christmas. During the long days that followed, I thought about the warmth of our house on Center Street during the holidays, the friends and family members who gathered there, and the elaborate decorations and festivities. I could almost smell the live Christmas tree we placed in our den each year, and I could almost taste the delicious food Mummee made for all our guests. And every time there in California I heard the song "I'll Be Home for Christmas," our dad's favorite Christmas song, I cried even more.

That year, I made myself a promise never to miss another Christmas with my family and friends in Birmingham.

The New Year, 1964

The new year, 1964, would bring the black people of Alabama, as well as the nation, some good news for a change. The Civil Rights Act of 1964 was passed into law that summer. Some people said that the deaths of the children at the Sixteenth Street Baptist Church on September 15, 1963, followed by the loss of President Kennedy two months later, gave birth to a surge of emotional momentum that helped ensure the passage of the Civil Rights Act.

The weak and ineffective civil rights bills passed in 1957 and 1960 had amounted to little to attain the equal rights of African Americans. But the Civil Rights Act of 1964 proved to be different. It banned segregation in all public facilities and authorized the Department of Justice to bring legal action against those who still practiced or tried to enforce segregation. What our father had fought for, and what President Kennedy had begun, President Johnson finished. John F. Kennedy was right when he said, "A man may die, nations may rise and fall, but an idea lives on." The new president, Lyndon B. Johnson, made the Civil Rights Act of 1964 his primary goal—and on June 19, 1964, the United States Senate passed the landmark Civil Rights Act. Johnson signed the bill on July 2.

Earlier, when he was urging Congress to pass the bill, President Johnson had notably commented, "No memorial or eulogy could more eloquently honor President Kennedy's memory than the earliest possible passage of the civil rights bill for which he fought."[1]

CHAPTER 34

1965:
Marching toward Freedom

Spring 1965, in Selma
and Birmingham, Alabama

(Barbara remembers.)

But even if we pass this bill, the battle will not be over.
What happened in Selma is part of a larger movement
which reaches into every section and State of America.
It is the effort of American Negroes to secure for themselves the full blessings of American life. Their cause
must be our cause too. Because it is not just Negroes,
but really it is all of us, who must overcome the crippling
legacy of bigotry and injustice. And we shall overcome.

—PRESIDENT LYNDON B. JOHNSON,
March 15, 1965

Despite the passage of the 1964 Civil Rights Act, segregation
remained strong and unchanged in Selma, Alabama. The sheriff
of Dallas County, Jim Clark, had used violent tactics to intim-
idate African Americans in the late 1950s and early 1960s. He
beat a 54-year-old black woman with a billy club as she stood in
line to register to vote. Clark forced black youths at a civil rights
demonstration to march until some collapsed or vomited from
exhaustion. He claimed that "any attempt to gain voting rights by
African Americans was part of a plan for 'black supremacy.'" On
his jacket, he wore a button that read "Never." It symbolized his
opposition to equal rights for blacks. Like Wallace, Sheriff Clark
blamed "outside agitators" for the civil unrest of the 1960s.

In an effort to secure the vote for African Americans in Dallas

County, organizers scheduled several marches in January of 1965. Clark stopped them, harassing and arresting the demonstrators, including Dr. King. By the end of February 1965, little had happened in the area of voting rights for African Americans.

But on January 17, when a state trooper fatally wounded activist Jimmy Lee Jackson during a Perry County march, interest again grew strong. To honor Jackson's memory and to protest his murder, the SCLC organized a march from Selma, Alabama, to the State Capitol in Montgomery, Alabama—planned to begin on Sunday, March 7, 1965.

"Bloody Sunday"

Some six hundred people took part in the march from Selma to Montgomery. The marchers headed east on U.S. Route 80 out of Selma, and six blocks away, as they walked peacefully across the Edmund Pettus Bridge, Sheriff Clark's state troopers and a horse-mounted posse stopped them.

Without warning, the officials began savagely beating and tear-gassing the unarmed marchers: men, women, and youth of all ages. They knocked them down, hit them with clubs, and drove them back across the bridge. Clark's gang rode on horseback through the confusion, giving rebel yells and attacking protestors with bullwhips, ropes, and pieces of rubber tubing wrapped in barbed wire. Photographers and reporters captured the violence and cruelty, and shared it with the public over national television. The shocking event halted the marchers and turned them back —an event that became known as "Bloody Sunday."

As I watched the violence on the television news, I was astonished to see that the police weren't helping the victims but were actually causing the violence and injuries. John Lewis, a student at the time who participated in the march, tells about how brutal the assault was and how he, himself, was beaten. I don't think the marchers anticipated the violence before it happened. They acted with non-violence, but the police still beat them down.

LBJ and Civil Rights

In response to the violence in Selma on March 7, President Johnson addressed a national television audience and a joint session of Congress on March 15, 1965. There he proposed a law to strike down restrictions to voting in all elections: federal, state, and local. "Mr. Speaker, Members of the Congress," he began,

> I speak tonight for the dignity of man and the destiny of democracy. I urge every member of both parties, Americans of all religions and of all colors, from every section of this country, to join me in that cause. At times history and fate meet at a single time in a single place to shape a turning point in man's unending search for freedom. So it was at Lexington and Concord. So it was a century ago at Appomattox.
>
> So it was last week in Selma. There, long-suffering men and women peacefully protested the denial of their rights as Americans. Many were brutally assaulted. One good man, a man of God, was killed. There is no cause for pride in what has happened in Selma. There is no cause for self-satisfaction in the long denial of equal rights of millions of Americans. But there is cause for hope and for faith in our democracy in what is happening here tonight.
>
> For the cries of pain and the hymns and protests of oppressed people have summoned into convocation all the majesty of this great Government — the Government of the greatest Nation on earth.[1]

The President ordered the nation to "open your polling places to all your people. Allow men and women to register and vote whatever the color of their skin. Extend the rights of citizenship to every citizen of this land." And he promised "no delay, no hesitation and no compromise with our purpose" regarding the action of this new Voting Rights Bill.

Daddy had always said, "Justice in Alabama, as in most of the deep Southern states (to take a phrase from *Yick Wo v. Hopkins*) was 'administered with an evil eye and an unequal hand.'"[2]

In his speech, President Johnson promised to send to Congress a law designed to eliminate all illegal barriers to the right to vote. Our father's hard work with voter registration, starting back in 1937, had not been in vain. In fact, on that very day, his dream had finally come to fruition.

Many things hoped for in Alabama and the South would finally change.

Another March
from Selma to Montgomery

After the violent "Bloody Sunday" tragedy, Dr. King asked civil rights supporters from across the nation to come to Selma and help him organize another Selma-to-Montgomery march. A white Unitarian minister from Boston, James Reeb, came down with hundreds of others to participate in the rescheduled march. But shortly after arriving in Selma, as he was leaving a restaurant on the evening of March 9, four white men attacked Reeb, hitting him in the back of the head with a club. He died two days later, and his attackers were later acquitted in a jury trial.

President Johnson intervened in Alabama's politics to make possible a rescheduled and safe Selma-to-Montgomery March. After three weeks of legal battles, on March 17, a federal court ruling gave Dr. King and the marchers permission to proceed with the peaceful march. President Johnson invited Governor George Wallace to meet and talk with him at the White House, then Johnson federalized the Alabama National Guard, and sent 2,200 additional troops from the U.S. Army to help protect the marchers. The protesters planned to resume the Selma-to-Montgomery March on Sunday, March 21, 1965.

On that sunny Sunday morning, a crowd of 8,000 stood in front of Brown's A.M.E. Chapel in Selma and participated in an ecumenical service. Some 3,200 marchers then set their sights on Montgomery and began the fifty-mile journey. They planned to walk about twelve miles a day and to sleep in fields at night.

A Bombing Attempt Thwarted

On Sunday, March 21, 1965, as marchers in Selma, Alabama, gathered and readied themselves for their march across the Edmund Pettus Bridge, the residents on Center Street in Birmingham, Alabama, dressed and got ready for church services. Around 7 a.m., some members of the nearby Our Lady Queen of the Universe Catholic Church arrived for mass. Some of the celebrants noticed an unfamiliar green box on the street beside the curb of the brick church, but they paid no attention to it.

Green boxes loaded with powerful dynamite had also been placed at other locations: a funeral home, a high school, and at our house on Center Street.

At 9:20 a.m., the Reverend Edward Foster stopped the communion service when his usher discovered the box and told him about it. Father Foster told the congregation about the bomb and asked the 120 worshippers to leave the church.

About 9:30 a.m., our father left the house and headed across the street to the First Congregational Church. As he crossed the street, someone told him about the bomb found at the Catholic Church. He and some other members of the First Congregational Church began a neighborhood search. They found nothing and went on to Sunday school.

Police arrived around 9:45 a.m., and they evacuated people from their homes in the neighborhood. Demolition experts arrived from Anniston's Fort McClellan, some sixty miles away.

At about 10:45 a.m., Daddy came home from Sunday school.

"Shores," Mummee told him when he walked inside the house. "I noticed a green cardboard box at the edge of our yard."

Daddy walked down to the edge of the yard, found the green box, and immediately called the police. In the meantime, neighbors discovered more green boxes around the neighborhood. One resident saw a green box at the base of a utility pole between 15th and 16th Streets, North. He heard it ticking, raised the lid, and saw the dynamite and clock device. Someone else found a bomb beside the Smith and Gaston Funeral Home.

Two army demolition experts worked quickly to disable the bomb at the Catholic Church, which was one block from our house. They discovered the bomb had been set to go off at noon. They cut the wire and disabled it only three minutes before it would have exploded. One of the demolition experts then ran to our house. At 11:59 a.m.—a mere 60 seconds from detonation —he snipped the wire and disabled the bomb in our yard that was also set to go off at noon.

The bomb at the Smith and Gaston Funeral Home had also been set to explode at noon, but fortunately it malfunctioned. They disabled that bomb at 12:10 p.m. Army experts then sped to nearby Western High School, where two boys playing around the school's incinerator found another green box with a bomb inside. It was set to go off at 6 p.m.[3]

Fortunately, residents and police found all the green boxes with ticking bombs inside, and the army demolition experts disabled them before any exploded. Police later told us that the bombs were so powerful that they would have destroyed most of the neighborhood had they gone off.

When I Heard the News

On that Sunday, March 21, 1965, I was living in the dorms at Talladega College. I had just walked out of my dorm room and into a crowd of fellow students in the hall. Surprisingly, as I entered, the students moved to the sides of the hallways to let me pass. It reminded me of when the waters of the Red Sea divided to allow Moses and the Israelites to pass through.

"She doesn't know about it yet," I heard someone say.

Someone told me to go and watch the TV. Confused, I turned on the radio and heard about the bombing attempts on Center Street in Birmingham and other places. I tried to telephone my home, but no one answered. Then I called Aunt Teddy who lived up the street from my parents. Still there was no answer. I flipped through my address book and tried to find phone numbers of other people I knew who lived in that area around the Smithfield neighborhood. I imagined the worst. They had bombed our home twice before, and I could reach no one who could tell me that my parents were okay.

I finally reached Reverend McNair, the chaplain at Talladega College.

"Sir," I asked, "could someone please drive me home so I can see what's going on there?"

"No, Barbara," he told me. "You need to wait here."

I held my breath and prayed for Daddy's and Mummee's safety.

A short time later, Daddy called me. "Everything is okay here," he said. "They found all the bombs, and just to be safe, they evacu-ated the whole block on Center Street."

I was relieved at first. Then I felt downright angry that they had not called me. I had been filled with anxiety and fear. I can remember my tearful conversation with Daddy, pleading with him to promise me never to keep me waiting and not knowing that everything was okay. Daddy told me to calm down. He assured me that they were all right. When I talked with Mummee, she seemed calm. She also assured me that they were safe. I stayed upset for several hours before finally feeling calm. I thanked God that everyone was all right and that no one was hurt. Had the bombs gone off, lives could have been lost. I felt that angels' wings had surrounded our community and kept it safe. I knew God was in control.

The Marchers Arrive

Five days later, on March 25, 1965, the Selma-to-Montgomery marchers arrived on the steps of Alabama's State Capitol. Many had joined them on their way, and now they numbered more than 25,000 people. Dr. King delivered a powerful speech on freedom, justice, and equality. He encouraged his fellow African Americans not to defeat or humiliate the white man, but to strive to be friends. He announced that segregation was on its deathbed. He urged the society to be at peace. He ended his speech with a loud and repeated "Glory, Hallelujah!" The crowd clapped and cheered with thunderous response. The service lasted more than two hours. The rescheduled Selma-to-Montgomery March had finally been accomplished, and peacefully.

CHAPTER 35

Birmingham in 1968: Becoming a New City

1968, in Birmingham, Alabama

(Helen and Barbara remember.)

Mr. Shores' civil rights work on behalf of all Alabamians is his living legacy for our State. He not only was part of the Change during the civil rights era, but he made it happen.[1]

—FROM MARKER ON THE ARTHUR D. SHORES
LAW CENTER BUILDING, Birmingham, Alabama

Change came slowly to Birmingham over the next few years following the Selma-to-Montgomery March, the "green-box" bombing attempts, and the passing of the 1965 Voting Rights Bill. People and city leaders had come to trust our father and honor him with their printed words, awards, and honorary degrees, and he stayed busy with his legal work, helping as many people as he could, giving many of them free legal aid as well as gifts of money when they needed them. But our father had always wanted to serve the people of Alabama at a deeper political level.

"Well, the first time I ran for public office was in 1942," our father said in an interview in July 1974. "I ran for the legislature and at that time, of course, it was merely to encourage blacks to register because we had less than 1,000 voters in the county, entire county."[2]

He knew that in 1942 he could not win because he was an African American in a segregated state where mostly only white people voted. But he wanted to make a point and encourage black voters to register to vote. He filed the required paperwork to run for the Alabama State Legislature, but they told him he was ineligible for candidacy because he was a "Negro." They returned his filing fee and the papers of declaration he had filled out and filed.

His Second Attempt,
Alabama State Legislature, 1954

In 1954, Daddy again tested the world of Alabama politics. He decided to try to run again for a seat in the Alabama State Legislature. Even though a dozen years had passed, Alabama's black citizens still lived under restrictive Jim Crow Laws. He knew his chances of winning were slim, but when asked by a *Birmingham Post-Herald* reporter why he wanted to run, our father replied, "I feel, in view of the world situation as well as our domestic situation, now would be a good time to have someone in the Legislature who is acquainted with the problems of large segments of the county ... [and] there's nobody else acquainted to help the county and state to progress and solve the problems."

"Will the NAACP contribute to your campaign?" the reporter asked.

"No," Daddy answered. "Very definitely not. The NAACP is non-partisan. It can't contribute to my campaign." He also added that he was running "on no slates, with no alliances, not as an independent candidate but as a Democrat."[3]

Daddy knew the needs of Alabama's populace, both black and white, and his platform promised what he would do if elected:

- Curb juvenile delinquency
- More assistance for the aged and needy
- More money for public institutions caring for mental and health patients
- Better highway safety program
- Increased teacher salaries and adequate school resources

- Continued development of the roadway programs
- Harmonious labor-management relations

His campaign motto was "Be Sure With Shores!"

He would also seek to work for better education for Alabama's children and youth, push for compulsory inspection of automobiles at periodic intervals, and work toward strengthening Alabama's health laws—including compulsory testing for the highly contagious disease of tuberculosis.

Tuberculosis still infected people in the 1930s, 1940s, and 1950s, killing millions worldwide. Daddy's own brother had died of tuberculosis. In Alabama, in 1939, some 2,942 people suffered from the disease, and by 1949, the disease still affected 2,642 Alabamians. By 1954, antibiotics were becoming more sophisticated, finally offering hope to those Alabamians infected and dying of the disease. Researchers found that these new drugs, given to people before they contracted the disease, would prevent them from getting tuberculosis. So as part of his campaign platform, our father yearned for Alabama to make tuberculosis testing compulsory.

Another area that caused our father deep concern was the sudden rise in the nation's juvenile delinquency rate. In fact, the Federal Bureau of Investigation reported that juvenile delinquency rose 55 percent between 1952 and 1957. As a father himself, Daddy saw how the postwar economic boom of the 1950s had allowed U.S. teenagers more money, more time, and more freedom. He also noted how American's music and movies had changed and the negative impact they were making on the nation's youth. He wanted to do something about that too before the problem became worse.*

But again, the time was just not right for his bid for a seat in the Alabama State Legislature, and he lost the election.

---

*It would be years later, in 1961, that the passage of the Juvenile Delinquency and Youth Offenses Control Act by Congress would finally address the problem of juvenile delinquency, providing large-scale social action and research programs directed at it.

Alabama State Legislature, 1962

Almost a decade later, in 1962, our father ran again as a candidate for the Alabama legislature. He told Alabama voters that the greatest problem facing Alabama was race relations. He described communication between the races as practically nonexistent and called on citizens to get together and discuss the problems with all segments of the community. As part of his campaign platform, he promised voters no new taxation, legislation to control air and stream pollution in Jefferson County, and increased school revenues under the present tax structure. He also intended to organize new programs for treating mentally ill residents and to provide better health care for the elderly and indigent.

Once again, he lost. White Alabama was not yet ready for an integrated legislature.

Alabama Vacancies in 1965

On June 14, 1965, a vacancy opened for a judge in Birmingham's Recorders Court. Mr. A. G. Gaston, our father's friend and business associate, wrote a letter to Birmingham Councilwoman Miglionico on our father's behalf. The letter read in part as follows:

> Please permit me to compliment our Mayor and City Council for your dedicated and sincere effort in giving leadership that has greatly improved the image of the City of Birmingham. Much is still necessary to be done to give confidence and faith on the part of all our citizens in our City Government, including the Negro population of the community, which I understand is approximately 40% of the total.
>
> The recent death of one of our respected citizens and Judge of our Juvenile Court, and the appointment of the Honorable Judge Bell to fill the Juvenile Court position leaves a vacancy in Recorders Court.
>
> With no other motive than as a responsible citizen, representing no group or organization, I am making a personal

appeal to you as I recommend that you consider a most important step in demonstrating faith and confidence in the Negro
community by recommending namely, Arthur D. Shores. He
is not only qualified and a responsible citizen of Birmingham,
having received his education in Alabama, but has practiced
law in our community for twenty-eight (28) years. He is married and has reared a family in our community. He is highly
respected by both white and colored.

I feel that the appointment of Atty. Shores (who is well
qualified by training and experience), as Judge of Recorders
Court will not only be recognized as the recognition of the
most capable legal talent, but I am sure such an appointment
will boost the spirit of the Negro community and provide the
local Negro citizens of this community a symbol of leadership
on the local level, and increase our faith and confidence in our
local government.

I have been informed that the City of Atlanta has recently
appointed Atty. A. T. Walden as Recorders Court Judge. I
understand the appointment of Atty. Walden has met with
the approval of the white and colored community of Atlanta,
where he is highly respected by both races. Also, in Memphis,
Tennessee, Atty. Hooks, a Negro lawyer, was recently made
Judge of Recorders Court of Memphis, Tennessee.

Mr. Gaston ended his letter with the following paragraph:

I have faith in Birmingham and feel that we have capable,
loyal and dedicated Negroes in Birmingham comparable to
any other community. I feel in time we will be given more
opportunities to contribute our talent and worth to the cher-
ished goal of developing Birmingham to its fullest potential. I
think the appointment of Atty. Shores as Judge of Recorders
Court at this time would be most timely and appropriate, and
to the best interest of our community.

A. G. Gaston.

Sadly, our father wasn't chosen for this position. Again, the
time was still not right for an African American Recorders Court
Judge.

On October 1, 1965, a newly created Circuit Court judgeship in Birmingham became available. When the vacancy was created, attorney Orzell Billingsley sent a letter recommending our father to the Jefferson County Judicial Commission chairman Judge Whit Windham. Judge Windham was supposed to forward the letter to Governor Wallace for a final decision, but somehow the nominating letter for our father mysteriously went to the federal building rather than to Judge Windham, causing it to miss the vacancy's deadline. After discovering the "mistake," our father was finally ruled eligible for consideration, along with nine other persons, all of them white.

But once again, he was not appointed by Wallace to the Birmingham judgeship.

CHAPTER 36

Our Father's Political Dreams Finally Come True

October 1968,
in Birmingham, Alabama

(Helen and Barbara remember.)

Although many of my associates, who went north, east, and west, obtained high positions, I have chosen to remain in Birmingham where I have always felt that eventually Alabama and Birmingham would offer to its black citizens an opportunity to become a part of the main stream. I have kept the faith. I have had an exciting, challenging, rewarding career. And my election to the City Council of this city has justified my faith.

—ARTHUR DAVIS SHORES,
in a speech upon appointment to the
Birmingham Bar Association, 1968

On October 24, 1968, white City Councilman R. W. Douglas died while still in office. Our father, then 64 years old and very active in Alabama's Democratic Party, was appointed by unanimous vote of the city's all-white governing body to fill Douglas's seat on the Birmingham City Council. With that appointment, Daddy became the first African American ever to sit on the City Council. It was another dream come true for Daddy.

In an interview with the *New York Times*, our father said he thought his appointment would make "members of the black community feel the city is sincere in its efforts to change its image and the image portrayed by Birmingham to the rest of the country."[1]

The Public Responds

The appointment made headlines in the nation's newspapers. People from all over the world wrote him letters of congratulations and sent telegrams celebrating Birmingham's decision. However, he also received some letters from people who threatened him and wrote ugly remarks.

"Dear Nigger," one letter from Tampa, Florida, began. "See by the papers where you were selected to be on the city council. We do not need a darkie, and especially we do not need you. Suggest you resign to devote your time to other fields. Yours truly, C. M. J____, Birmingham." Another letter read, "Get out of B'ham you Trashey Nigger!" "Arthur Shores a Black Son of a Bitch." In the middle of the white paper, the author of the letter had drawn a stick figure with a dagger in its heart and blood dripping to the ground.

Daddy promised to continue to push for new industry and business to provide new jobs and additional revenue to the city and boost its economy. "I will continue my efforts to speed up our program of public improvements in streets and provide decent housing for the disadvantaged," he said. He also said the city must have more and better-paid firemen and policemen for the protection of people and property.

"I am at present making a study of the financing of some forty cities in an effort to discover new sources of revenue that will provide the necessary funds for new and expanded services, including our schools," he announced.[2] Later, from this study, our father wrote up the Occupational Tax Bill for Birmingham, which increased the revenues for the city by taxing those people who worked in Birmingham but lived outside the city boundaries. It proved to be a good idea at the time.

Daddy Takes the Oath of Office

On Thursday, December 12, 1968, at 9:00 a.m., Daddy took the oath of office. I (Barbara) was completing my second year of graduate school at the University of Illinois, and I flew home to be with our father on this wonderful occasion. I was so proud of him. He was committed and dedicated to the citizens of Alabama, and now he was in a place where he could make necessary changes for the better.

Daddy filled the Council seat until the following fall, 1969, when his predecessor R. W. Douglas's term was scheduled to end. He worked hard in his appointment, and in October of 1969, he ran for re-election and won the seat. A reporter with the *Birmingham News* wrote, "Arthur Shores ... pledged his best efforts in the continued service of the city and its people." He quoted him as saying, "I think my election is just another indication that Birmingham has really embarked on a course destined to bring about a fulfillment of the aspirations of all her citizens."[3]

The Encyclopedia of Alabama would also later comment upon Daddy's appointment: "The appointment garnered national attention, coming as it did in a city that only a few years earlier was known as one of the most segregated in the nation."[4]

My father was the first African American appointed to the Birmingham City Council, a position he took very seriously and faithfully held until 1978. Daddy believed in Birmingham and felt strongly that change could and would be made in this city. And change did come to Birmingham, albeit slowly. At the time he retired from the Council, he felt he had paid his civic "rent" and that now it was time for the younger generation to take the lead there.

CHAPTER 37

Arthur Davis Shores and the Chaotic 1968 Democratic Convention

August 1968, in Chicago, Illinois

(Helen and Barbara remember.)

> It is fitting that a man who has been defending Negro rights in Alabama for more than two decades should emerge as the race's most effective spokesman at this 1968 National Democratic Convention. He is Arthur Shores, Birmingham attorney, and one of the state's two members of the Credentials Committee for this convention.
>
> —JAMES FREE in the
> *Birmingham News*, August 26, 1968

While twenty-four states in the nation had no African Americans listed in their delegations in 1968, Alabama had two that year. Robert Vance, the Alabama delegation's chairman, had appointed our father as an Alabama delegate to the Democratic National Convention Credentials Committee. The other African American delegate was Joe L. Reed, executive secretary of the all-Negro Alabama State Teachers Association at Montgomery. Progress was slowly being made.

James Free, in the *Birmingham News*, reported that

> Shores' assignment was a crucial link in the complex plan aimed at giving Alabama Democrats who wanted to do so a chance to participate fully in this national convention and then to cast an unadulterated vote for the Democratic nominees if

they choose to in November. Shores was a key organizer and the first president of this statewide conference.... Earlier he had played an important part in establishing the Alabama Progressive Democratic Council.[1]

Not only did Daddy attend the Democratic National Convention and represent Alabama, but he was invited to address a plenary session. Once again, our father had made history.

The 1968 Democratic National Convention

It was the best of times, and it was the worst of times in our nation. Jim Crow laws no longer choked the necks of African Americans in Alabama and the other Southern states, and Daddy had successfully entered into Alabama politics and was admired and appreciated by both white and black people.

But the United States suffered because of the continuing war in Vietnam, for American troops in Vietnam peaked during 1968, reaching 542,000. Anti-Vietnam War protesters sparked violence in many of the nation's cities, including Chicago, Illinois, the chosen location of the 1968 Democratic Convention. As early as March 1968, young peace activists began planning demonstrations (which unfortunately resulted in riots) to take place during the August 26–29 convention. Our nation was sharply divided over the war.

On March 31, 1968, President Johnson announced he would not seek reelection. His presidency had suffered from low ratings due to his Vietnam War policies. Vice President Hubert Humphrey officially entered the presidential race on April 27 of that year, and Alabama Governor George Wallace entered the presidential race as an Independent.

The mood leading up to the convention was one of great uneasiness. Dr. King's assassination earlier that year, on April 4, 1968, caused riots throughout the country. And on June 5, Robert Kennedy had been assassinated after winning the California primary. Needless to say, the nation had suffered tremendously from the violence, and everyone was tense.

A Dangerous Place to Hold a Convention

At the time, Chicago seemed the worst place in the entire nation to hold the 1968 Democratic National Convention, and most Democrats strongly suggested moving the convention to Miami, Florida, where Republicans would be holding their event. Democrats feared violent protests and anti-war demonstrations taking place in Chicago that August. Chicago was also in the middle of a telephone strike that would cause numerous problems during the convention. Taxi drivers also threatened to strike during the convention, and the August heat in the city was almost unbearable.

Both President Johnson and Chicago's mayor, Richard J. Daley, wanted to keep the convention in Chicago, hosted at the International Amphitheatre. But those who planned to host and attend the convention feared the worst possible outcome even though Mayor Daley promised and prepared to enforce the peace. Daley organized almost 12,000 Chicago police, 7,500 Army troops, 7,500 Illinois National Guardsmen, and 1,000 Secret Service agents to handle the possible violence and clashes outside during the convention proceedings. He personally gave the order to "shoot to kill, if necessary!"

Radicals, Hippies, and Yippies Demonstrate

During the convention, riots broke out among radicals, hippies, yippies, and moderates. Delegations marched around the convention floor shouting and protesting while television cameras recorded all the mayhem and violence. Chicago police used billy clubs and tear gas bombs against protesters. Many were injured, including seventeen news reporters, innocent bystanders, and doctors who tried to treat the wounded. Chicago police arrested almost six hundred protesters.

Haynes Johnson, who covered the convention for the *Washington Star*, remembers that "the violence that rent the convention throughout that week ... confirmed both the Democrats' pessimism and the country's judgment of a political party torn by dissension and disunity. In November the party would lose the White House to Nixon's law-and-order campaign."[2]

At that Democratic National Convention, Mayor Joseph Alioto of San Francisco nominated Hubert Humphrey, and Senator Abraham Ribicoff nominated George McGovern. Humphrey easily won the nomination.

The Day I Rode Into Chicago

(Barbara remembers.)

I was attending the University of Illinois in Champaign, and I wanted to meet Daddy as he stepped off the plane in Chicago. My boyfriend at that time was 6'4", rode a motorcycle, and sported a beard. The rain fell in hard sheets that day. I threw on a stylish poncho and high boots, and we hopped on his motorcycle and headed for Chicago's airport. I had long hair in those days, and wore it very straight. By the time we arrived in Chicago, we were both soaking wet. My long straight hair, wet from the rain, had blown up into a huge, wild-looking Afro. We pushed our way through the crowds and chaotic mobs of hippies, yippies, musicians, and demonstrators.

"Hello!" I said to Daddy.

He looked at me, responded politely, and kept walking.

"Daddy!" I called after him. "It's *me*, Barbara!"

He turned around, took a hard look at me and my wild hair, and exclaimed, "Puchie?! Oh my goodness! What's happened to you?!"

Daddy went on to stand right in the middle of the 1968 Democratic National Convention, and he became the first of his race to speak at a national political convention. Not long after he returned home, he received a personal letter of gratitude from Hubert Humphrey.

Daddy also served as a delegate to the National Democratic Convention in 1972 and 1976. That year, President Jimmy Carter invited him to the White House and asked him to serve as a member of the Judicial Commission for the U.S. Fifth Circuit of Appeals. He accepted.[3]

Elected to the State Democratic Executive Committee

In 1974 our father was elected as a member of the State Democratic Executive Committee. From Governor George Wallace, on June 6, 1974, he received the following letter:

> Dear Arthur: My sincere congratulations to you on your election as a member of the State Democratic Executive Committee. Your election is especially significant since you were elected directly by the people. Never before in the history of the Democratic Party have we had the opportunity to build the party as we do today. There are bold challenges before us but I know we will meet them with people of your caliber serving on the state committee. I look forward to working with you and if I can be of service to you in any way, please do not hesitate to call. With kind personal regards, I am sincerely, George C. Wallace.

By 1976, Birmingham had changed significantly. The police dogs, bombings, racial beatings, the "Whites Only" signs, the segregated waiting rooms and restaurants, were only bad memories of an embarrassing and bygone time.

"The voice of segregation is almost nonexistent in Birmingham," wrote a *Time* magazine reporter in a 1976 article. "Not even in private conversation is it any longer acceptable to say such things." The black vote in Alabama, by 1979, had increased from 15 percent to 40 percent. "Black and white children together go peacefully to Birmingham's once segregated schools," *Time* reported.

Birmingham: The "Magic City"

By 1979, old steel companies closed and Birmingham stepped away from most of its steel-making past and smoky skies. The University of Alabama Medical Center became the city's principal employer, and over the next three decades, Birmingham continued to move in the right direction, with the two races working hand in hand to make Birmingham truly the "magic city."

When it came to civil rights, Daddy saw the beginning struggles in Birmingham and the South, and he lived long enough to see the final victories. In a June 2011 interview, Richard "Dick" Pizitz had this to say about our father:

> Arthur Shores was probably more admired than any other black in the [Birmingham] community. [He was certainly admired] by the whites because Arthur Shores was seen as an extremely gutsy man that wasn't scared of anything. [Shores] was a statesman, and a lot of other black leaders in the community were not viewed by the white community as statesmen, but soldiers. [Shores] bridged that gap. He was an extremely brilliant Civil Rights Lawyer that got a lot of laws changed, but he could also work between the communities. The white people respected Arthur Shores. They trusted him. In Arthur Shores, they saw a steadier hand, and that was going to keep the communities together ... [Shores] was the glue that held a lot of this stuff together.[4]

Throughout his long career, Daddy never gave up on the law. "He lived a consistent life on the side of the Constitution and what was to become the Constitution," said Alabama lawyer Charles Morgan Jr. "I can't think of another lawyer who was more alone in a hundred different ways than Arthur Shores."[5]

When Daddy was inducted into the Alabama Lawyers' Hall of

Fame in 2004, members of the Alabama Bar Association and the Hall of Fame said of him:

> Arthur Shores can be described in many ways. He was a courageous battler for civil rights. He was considered Alabama's "drum major for justice." However, the most affectionate title which I heard referring to him was "Daddy Shores." This title was not limited to his own children—Helen and Barbara—but to generations of young lawyers who sought his advice and received his mentorship. Arthur Shores was a strong and brave advocate, a gentleman at the law, but a lawyer who got results for his clients.

Daddy could have decided to practice law in another state, and thus avoided the Klan's threats, violence, and bombings. But he chose to stay in Birmingham, Alabama, the nation's most segregated city. He envisioned a "new Birmingham," and worked hard to help accomplish it. And by the grace of God, he lived to see his dream come true.

CHAPTER 38

Final Days

(Helen and Barbara remember.)

The old warrior died peacefully and well honored in Birmingham by white and black alike. The mantle of national fame has justly settled on the shoulders of Martin Luther King Jr., who brought in the harvest. But Arthur Shores's death is a reminder that all across the South, in towns small and large, there was a generation of obscure black heroes who prepared the ground and planted the seeds and never minded the peril.

—"A PIONEER PASSES,"
New York Times, December 21, 1996

I have come a long way from that little girl standing on the front porch wanting to shoot somebody. The anger I felt that evening and throughout my childhood is gone now. I have learned anger can destroy you and being angry does nothing to change the person or situation you're angry with. If you let it control you, it destroys everything you love and care about. Instead of being angry, I turned that energy into a determination to succeed and accomplish those things I wanted in life. No longer would I have to be conflicted about what I could do and what I could not do. I learned that I can do all things through Christ who strengthens me, and I prayed hard to God to strengthen me and help take away the anger. The years have been kind to me, and God continues to shower blessings upon me every day.

I've also learned that one should *never* say "never." I swore I would *never* return to Birmingham, and that I would *never* go into law. Life has since taught me that you can't run from God's ultimate plan for you.

After graduate school, I was a practicing clinician in psychology for fifteen years before finally going to law school. A lot of people think it was our Dad's influence that caused me to go to law school. But the man who really encouraged me to go to law school was Chris McNair, the father of Denise, one of the girls killed in the September 15, 1963 bombing of the Sixteenth Street Baptist Church. I had grown disenchanted with mental health, working with kids and adolescents. There was a time when I could leave my work at the office, but there came a point when I couldn't get rid of thoughts I had about the children I had worked with. I worried about their safety. I felt their despair and their pain. I cared about them and their family, but that wasn't enough. I couldn't change their environment, their poverty, their dysfunctional families.

The day came when I felt I just couldn't do it anymore. So I went to see Chris McNair to ask if he knew where I could apply for another kind of job. He looked me straight in the eye and said, "I *don't* feel sorry for you. I *don't* know where you could apply for another job." I was rather stunned by his comments—I'd never known Chris to be so blunt. He went on to talk to me for hours about how and why I should be practicing law with our Dad.

Over the next several weeks, I thought about what he had said. I told myself, *this isn't what I really want to do.* But the more I thought about it, the more the idea appealed to me. I mentioned to my son that I was thinking about going to law school, and he, in turn, mentioned it to my dad. I have never seen Daddy so excited, and he promised to help me since I would have to quit my job.

I went to law school at the age of 43, some twenty-two years after I had finished college. Law school was tough, but I kept reminding myself that "I can do all things through Christ who strengthens me." I held on tight to that Scriptural promise.

I finished law school in 1987 and joined my Dad's practice. My only regret is that I only had five years to be with him before he retired. I missed him coming to work every day and the two of us eating hot dogs from Lyric's for lunch.

I'll never forget the first week at work in his law practice. He handed me a file and told me to go and try the case, a breach of construction contract case. When I told him I didn't know what to do, he said, "Chickadee, what did I send you to law school for? Go try the case, you'll do just fine."

I remember how he would introduce me as his "new partner" to all of his clients and explain to them that I would be taking care of their cases. Everything went well until I introduced the new fee schedules. Our Dad by this time was 84 years old and was still charging fees from the 1950s: $50.00 for a will and $100.00 for a divorce. I told him those fees were a little low. When I told him what the going rate was for deeds, divorces, and wills, he was in shock—and so were his older clients. If I told them the current fee, they didn't like it and would ask to see Mr. Shores. My first few years of practice were very lean years because our father would often change the fee schedule back to the old one if his clients asked him to. I enjoyed those years, but I often wished I had been with him in some of those earlier years of his practice.

After he left the practice, his health and his memory started to decline. I know he missed practicing law. It had been his dream, his life. It had also been his dream that one of his daughters would follow him in the practice of law—and he lived to see that dream become a reality. What pleased him even more was his grandson and namesake, Arthur D. Shores Lee, who had finished law school. He would often reminisce about his cases and the early years, and he told me that if God took him that day he had no regrets about his life. He was pleased with his life and his family. He would sing, "It is well with my soul," his favorite hymn. And during his last months he sang it a lot.

I decided to buy a building in downtown Birmingham and dedicate it to him, naming it the *Arthur D. Shores Law Center*. He attended the ribbon-cutting ceremony in the summer of 1996, and after that dedication, his health and memory continued to decline, and he became bedridden. It depressed me to see this once strong man now so frail and his memory fading. A marker on the building says this:

During the first 30 years of his 54-year-old practice, Attorney Shores practiced all over the State of Alabama—from the Tennessee line to the Gulf of Mexico at Mobile Bay, and from the Mississippi borders to the Georgia limits. During the period roughly between 1940 and 1950 he was the only lone voice in the wilderness defending the civil rights of black people. Mr. Shores practiced civil rights law all over the state of Alabama during an era in which his life was in constant jeopardy. He represented such civil rights pioneers as Martin Luther King, Jr., Autherine Lucy, Fred Shuttlesworth and Vivian Malone. Attorney Shores was responsible for successfully filing a case for voting rights in 1938. In 1942, he fought for and won pay equity for black teachers in Jefferson County, Alabama. Mr. Shores' civil rights work on behalf of all Alabamians is his living legacy for our State. He not only was part of the Change during the civil rights era, but he made it happen.[1]

I shall never forget, as long as I live, the look he gave me the night before he died. Our dad loved classical music throughout his life, and growing up, my sister and I recall him lifting his hands in the air and pretending to conduct the orchestra or play the piano as he listened to his favorite songs. As Tchaikovsky's *Symphony No. 6 in B Minor* played softly in the background, he stared at me and smiled. It wasn't an ordinary look. It was a look of good-bye. I smiled back and told him, "Everything will be all right; we will take care of Mummee." He closed his eyes, and the next day, December 15, 1996, he died. With his dreams realized, his promises kept, the "old warrior left us."

After our Dad died, we convinced our mother to come live with me. She reluctantly agreed, although she didn't want to leave her home. But every Sunday we would take her back to the home on Center Street on Dynamite Hill for dessert. She seemed to enjoy that.

I think what helped her make the transition were her great-grandchildren. They were her joy. At the time she came to live with me, she was 98 years old and I was raising my four grandchildren.

They were quite young at the time. The twins, Trenton and Trevon were one year old, Ashlee was three, and Vincent was five. She dearly loved and doted on them. She would slip them candy after they came home from day care and tell them stories every night. Ashlee would often slip out of her bed at night, and get in bed with her "Nana," as she affectionately called her. "Nana" enjoyed rocking them to sleep. During those years, we had four generations living under our roof. What a joy!

We often sat and talked about the past, about the days when I was a child. Mummee continued her various social and civic activities, always wearing stockings and high-heeled shoes. I could tell she missed my Dad though. When she moved to my house, besides a few clothes, the only thing she brought with her was a bag of pictures and her own personal scrapbook of my Dad's accomplishments.

At age 100, she got up every morning, dressed herself, put on her earrings, and came downstairs for breakfast. She was a proud woman and never wanted assistance. I was blessed to have had an angel of a caretaker—Augusta Cunningham, who had been with our family for over thirty-five years—who looked after her every day. She took good care of my mama while my husband and I went to work. She was truly God sent.

My mama never liked being alone at night, for she was afraid of dying in the middle of the night without anybody knowing it. Every morning at 2:00 a.m., she would start calling me. Even now, I still wake up at 2:00 a.m. Sometimes I think I still hear her calling me. She wouldn't want anything except to talk. I knew she was just afraid. One night as I was lying on her bed watching TV with her, she said, "You know I'm dying."

"I know, Mummee," I answered, "and everything will be all right."

I never thought I would acknowledge to our mother that I knew she was dying.

Three nights later, she died at the age of 101, surrounded by those she loved: Barbara and me, and her great-grandchildren.

Just when she took her last breath, Ashlee, who was four years old, and Vincent who was six, walked into the room. I told them Nana had just died. Ashlee spontaneously got up on her bed, kissed her Nana on the cheek and turned to Vincent.

"Nana has died," she told her brother. "Now she can go to heaven to be with granddaddy."

(Barbara remembers.)

Later in his life, and for many years, Daddy battled cancer. Even in great pain, he remained a joy to be around. He was always pleasant, kind, and thankful. Mummee proved to be a good caregiver for Daddy. We wanted Daddy home with us rather than in a hospital or nursing home during this time. His doctor, Dr. Jeroan Allison, came to our house every week to check on him and usually brought his nurses and his companion, John. When Dr. Allison came, he took his time with Daddy. He would spend two to three hours with him per visit. Sometimes he would just sit in the room with him. John sat at my mother's feet while she was teaching him some new craft she had learned. It was usually so late when they left that Mummee began preparing dinner for them each week. They become close personal friends, and Helen and I consider them "our brothers."

We knew the end was near, and we provided the best care we could for him at home. Caregiving was rewarding for me. I had facilitated many caregiver support groups over the years, and had heard the many stories the other caregivers had told me about problems they had with siblings once they entered the caregiving role. As sisters, Helen and I were fortunate that we did not have the usual disagreements that many families have. I knew the resources and the services we needed and what was available to us. I also knew how we could divide up our roles.

One morning, I received a telephone call from our father's sitter, Sherman Smith. He called to tell me that I needed to come home right away because our father was passing. As I raced out the door to my car, tears streamed down my face, my heart raced, and I prayed, "Lord, just let me be there to say my final goodbye." It had been only weeks before that I had prayed to God to take him home. I hated to see him suffering, and I didn't want to see him in pain. I never thought I'd pray such a prayer. I often prayed for strength to face the next day. It had been so difficult to see the once strong man, so full of life, dying.

When I arrived home, I found Mummee in the living room crying softly. At first, I thought I was too late. I ran into Daddy's room, held his hand, kissed, and hugged him. His breathing was labored. I could tell he was slipping away. I told him I loved him, and that he had been the best father, husband, and grandfather anyone could have been. I told him Jesus was waiting for him, that he had labored long and hard, and it was time for him to rest. "God's waiting for you with opened arms," I told him. "We will be okay."

Daddy was a gentle giant, the "Gentle Giant of Dynamite Hill." The expression on his face changed, and he seemed peaceful. I sensed he wasn't in pain anymore.

"Puchie," he said. "It is well with my soul. I'm ready to go."

I started singing some of his favorite hymns. Finally, Daddy took his last breath and died. Minutes later, Helen walked into the bedroom.

"He's gone," I told her.

We cried and hugged each other for a while. Then we told our mother. When she heard that Daddy was gone, she cried uncontrollably.

I had wanted our father with me forever. When he died I lost my best friend—my very best friend who was always there for me.

Mummee didn't want to stay in the house alone, so she went to live with Helen. She remained alert, and her mind was sharp. She continued her arts and crafts projects, and one time, when I thought she seemed a little depressed, I bought some yarn and asked her to make a bedspread for my bed. She took the colorful yarn and crocheted a beautiful bedspread.

We enjoyed so many good conversations about my children, Damien and Danielle. By this time Daddy's doctor, Dr. Allison, was also Mummee's doctor. He would come by and check on Mummee every week. Mummee made sure Helen had dinner ready for him, just like she did when he visited Daddy.

Then one night, Mummee's breathing became labored just like Daddy's breathing had before he died. Dr. Allison made Mummee as comfortable as he could. I remember Mummee's eyes becoming fixed in one corner of the room. I talked with her. I told her I loved her, and that we all loved her. I told her it would be all right to "let go" and that Daddy was waiting for her, that God was ready to take her home. I kissed her and said my goodbyes.

Then, just as Daddy had done, Mummee straightened her mouth as if talking quietly to someone, took her last breath, and died. I felt empty, but I also had joy knowing she was with God.

While Daddy was the gentle giant, Mummee was the silent warrior. Daddy was a fair man who showed a concern for his fellow man. He was respected for the way he carried himself, and for the life he lived. Daddy lived his life upholding his religious beliefs. He was a truthful and honest man. When he ran for office, his opponents could find no hidden secrets that would dishonor him in any way. He carried himself with dignity.

Daddy allowed my spirit to thrive. He taught me that when one door closes, another one always opens. He always said, "Don't get stuck on that door closing so that you can't see the blessing awaiting you." With his strong faith, he knew that things would get better. He worked to make them better. My parents are gone, but never gone from my heart. They left me with a rich legacy that money could never buy.

A Personal Memory

by Judge Helen Shores Lee

Our father *always* had time for us. He was never too busy or absorbed in his work that he didn't have time for family. I recall as a child, if he took a case out of town, he would always be back by nightfall or in time to take my sister and me to the movies on Saturdays. I remember the Sunday rides through Birmingham after dinner. Nothing was as important to him as love for his family.

I never doubted he loved me. He shared all my joys, and in sharing my joys, he doubled them. You see, Daddy understood me. He seemed to sense how I felt, my disappointments and my dreams. From him on more than one occasion, I sensed that loving understanding.

When I think of my Dad, I think of strength and deep conviction. I think of common decency. When I think of my mama, I'm reminded of a woman who lived in joyful service to those closest to her—her family. She too always put family first as she saw motherhood as God's call on her life. The only thing I regret is that I never got a chance to tell them that they were indeed "the wind beneath my wings."

I was fortunate to grow up in a time when married women stayed home to raise their children and devote themselves full time to the family. Time and conversation with my mama were plentiful whether she was at the sewing machine making our dresses or in the kitchen preparing dinner or just straightening my hair.

I remember the church activities, and often going with her to Miles Chapel, CME Church, where at the age of three, I stood up in church—to the embarrassment of my mama—and sang in my loudest voice, "Pistol packing mama lay your pistol down." She quickly removed me from church, took me outside, and spanked me. I never sang that song again.

She carried Barbara and me to many activities we enjoyed. She listened to us, encouraged us, and taught us life lessons. She also lovingly challenged my rebellion. I never remember Barbara ever rebelling against anything.

All of my life, I remember, our dad had been a humble man whose happiness in life was doing his work well. His belief and conviction led him to take on many cases and causes which were unpopular at the time. But because of his deep belief and conviction that certain laws affecting our people were blatantly wrong and a miscarriage of justice, he stepped out to correct these wrongs—often alone and in dangerous situations.

Our father taught me the value of having a good work ethic. "If anything is worth doing, it's worth doing well. Do it well, don't just half do it to get by," he said. He instilled in us the lesson that doing your work well would open new doors and that as we worked and humbled ourselves before others, as we practice the Bible's Golden Rule, we would receive a sense of satisfaction magnified tenfold.

Our mother told us that to enjoy the fruits of your labor, you had to work hard. She taught me to take care of myself and my things, and to do the necessary house chores.

My mama and our dad had giving hearts and a giving spirit. They taught me the importance of giving back to the community and of reaching out to others whose station in life may not be what it should be. Mama taught us to value those who were different from us and to have compassion for those in need. They set an example for us by volunteering in the community and by unselfishly giving of their time and service.

I remember my mama putting together and distributing Thanksgiving and Christmas baskets to needy families. When she heard of someone's illness or birthday, she would get a card, sew lace around its borders, and add a few pearls or glitter to make it extra special. She loved sharing her arts and crafts with others. No one else I know could string as many watermelon seeds and cantaloupe seeds into necklaces as she, and she delighted in giving them to others. Both my parents taught me that giving can be one of the most rewarding experiences in life.

They taught me that to ensure the future of our children, a future that includes respect, dignity, freedom, and longevity of our people, we must always continue to be involved. Sometimes I feel the most frightening part of being involved is being responsible. My parents taught me that to meet that responsibility and to make this city and this world a better place means living for your fellow man, giving your time and part of yourself to him or her. In that way, I can help promote the welfare of our community.

My parents didn't leave me a goldmine of money, but they gave me a living endorsement of a godly heritage and a model of faithfulness. My parent's most precious legacy to me was their spiritual legacy. I learned from them the value of courage, the power of prayer, and the strength of will. They taught me that despondency and despair can be overcome with determination and prayer.

It never occurred to me to wonder if our mother was enjoying this life because she was so wrapped up in her family and community—and I don't wonder about it now. I can still hear her walking through the house singing "Precious Lord Take My Hand" or "Just a Closer Walk with Thee." Her everyday life radiated such contentment and joy. She lived a genuinely fulfilled life. I watched her live a long life of dedicated service to which Jesus calls each of us.

My parents also taught me how to be strong and to cope with disappointment and hard times. They gave me the courage to be brave enough to do what I believe is right, to understand that fear is natural, but that fear should never stop me from doing what is right.

They also taught me the value of knowledge and prepared me to make decisions, big and small. They showed me that everyone makes mistakes, and how we should learn from them and move on.

I remember Daddy's forgiving spirit and close connection with God. I experience our father's special kind of peace when I sit on the judge's bench and face something that reminds me of society's racial prejudice during my childhood years. Daddy always told Barbara and me that we were equal to all other people, white and black. He said we could do anything we wanted to do and be anything we wanted to be.

Our father knew that society would change from its prejudiced past. He was a strong believer that one must fight through the court system to make things better. Sometimes, especially during the most visible years of the civil rights movement, people criticized him for not being a "hollering soapbox rabble-rouser-revolter." But he paid them no mind, and he continued working hard through the courts, as well as sitting down with people and negotiating differences and problems through reason. He was good at bringing the different races to the table and talking about ways they were alike. He usually dwelt on what blacks and whites had in common instead of dwelling on their differences.

Most of all, my parents taught me about life by setting an example with their own gentleness and openness and warmth.

I never ever doubted that they loved me. I could go to our father and know he would give me loving and sound advice. He never stopped loving his fellow man, in spite of the bombings and threats on his life. He knew the power of simple goodness. He allowed God to completely sustain him in all things.

These many lessons he taught me have stood me well and have influenced every aspect of my being. They have made me the person I am today. I am reminded every moment of every day that God gave me a special gift when he made me their daughter. I plan to honor Him and them with my life.

A Personal Memory

by Barbara Sylvia Shores

I was Daddy's girl from the start. When I was young, people told me I resembled our Dad and even walked like him. My childhood memories are so rich and colorful, even though they were sometimes tempered with the bitter realities of life.

My family life was filled with so much love. I received that *unconditional love* that all people desperately want, but some people never find. I witnessed my parent's love and commitment for each other, and for us, and I have loved my own children and others in my life with that same *unconditional love.* Looking back over my life, I realize more and more the impact they had on helping me form my values and beliefs that helped shape my life. I was truly blessed and grateful to have the parents I did.

Although our father was busy, he always had time for me. Whether reading me a story or sharing my prayers at night before bed, he was always there. No matter where he went, to meetings or out of town, he always tried to come home at night to be with his family. He also took time out each summer to take his family on great vacations.

Our mother and father always took an interest in what activities I was involved in and who my friends were. I totally respected them. They were my friends, my confidants. I felt secure and safe to tell them everything. They listened without judging and gave me sound advice. They taught me early on that my actions had consequences and that I needed to think before I spoke or acted. With my parents, I knew I was loved and I felt secure. They gave so much of their time and energy to me.

Our mother was the cement that held our family together. She was such a courageous, silent warrior. She endured hard, frightful, and trying times, but she survived and grew in strength and valor. She was a beautiful, sensitive, and nurturing mother.

In our family, there was always a sense of pride. Mummee prepared weekly family dinners, and she invited our extended family to share our meals. We often had fifteen or more family members, both young and old, around our table. These family dinners taught us a lot about communication and relationship.

It was a family tradition that we all ate together four times a week. Our Aunt Teddy always hosted dinner on Sundays, Mummee on Thursdays, Helen on Fridays, and I hosted dinner on Tuesdays. Helen still cooks and hosts dinner on Fridays.

Mummee had to learn to deal with her fears, and she became stronger each day, a strength she passed on to me. She truly loved everyone, and she gave others her love and her practical help. Whether through her creative arts and crafts, or taking in a neighborhood child to live with us, or providing her own version of "Meals on Wheels" to hungry people, she lived to help her fellow neighbor.

Through the years of living in Birmingham, Alabama, I observed the many threats, ill treatment, hate, and disrespect my parents often endured from other people. Sometimes as a child, I felt like because of our father's work we were the most hated black family in Alabama. Whenever an incident happened, our father would always tell me, "We have to forgive them, Puchie. We can't expect our Heavenly Father to forgive us if we can't forgive others."

He told me that *hate* was such a strong word that it was wrong to say you hated somebody. I felt those first stirrings of hate when my dog, Tasso, was killed by the Klan's bomb. I felt so angry, and I hated the person that killed him.

Our father understood my feelings, but told me, "Puchie, you shouldn't hold on to hate because it will eventually destroy you."

I learned to let go. I didn't want to hate white people, so I learned to release the ill feelings, to forgive, and to keep moving forward. As an adult, whenever I felt someone had wronged me, I didn't feel hate for them. Instead, I forgave them and I prayed for them. And then I moved on, just like Daddy told me to. I can remember our father telling me to "just let it go." My children have learned the same values taught to me by our father.

My parents also taught me to have a spirit of thanksgiving, to be grateful for God's good gifts. I never saw my parents envious of others. They lived in a state of gratitude, always expressing their thanksgiving for their family and good friends. They often thanked God throughout the day for His wonderful blessings.

"Puchie," our dad often said, "Mummee, Helen, and you are my 'jewels,' and you all make me very rich." Every night, together we listed all the things we were grateful to God for. I have also found that when I give my time and service unselfishly to others, I too feel rich. I also seem to receive more than double of what I give.

Mummee and Daddy stressed the importance of hard work and self-discipline. If they gave me a job to do, they expected it to be done right. Mummee would always say, "Regardless of what job or task you have to do, do it well, Barbara. Do it to the best of your ability, or don't do it at all." I tried to practice Mummee's advice throughout my school and work years. I watch with delight as my own children work hard at achieving their goals and do their best work.

Their strong faith in God kept us grounded. Daddy always said that he could feel God's presence with him all the time. I think this gave him the courage to keep fighting to right the many injustices he saw all around him. When he felt upset, he said aloud the words of the Twenty-third Psalm. It always calmed him. Mummee continually sang her favorite church hymns throughout the day. Both my parents were committed to God and to the church. They taught me to seek God's mercy when I faced tough times. I have passed on the importance of having a strong connection to God to my children. We often pray together by phone when we are away from each other.

Education was important for my parents, and they often stressed the importance of a good education. Our dad told me, "Education is something that no one could take away from you. Puchie. Do your very best work and accomplish what you need to accomplish."

Whenever he said that, I remembered how he had worked so hard to go to school and never gave up on his education. That memory motivated me to stay in school and work toward my educational goals.

After my divorce, Daddy provided a wonderful male role model to my son and daughter. Our mother could always give me solid advice in child rearing and often planned and gave special occasion parties for the children. When my energy was low, she would come through with all the plans, homemade decorations, and food for the special events. My parents loved my children with the same unconditional love they showed me. They were ever present, loving, caring grandparents in my children's lives.

Both my children have enjoyed the fruits of our father's labors, both attending integrated elementary schools. Damien, my son, graduated from Ramsay High School in Birmingham, and my daughter, Danielle, graduated from Cushing Academy in Ashburn- ham, Massachusetts. Both are pursuing advanced degrees. They each enjoy a diverse group of friends from all walks of life, and I'm so proud of who they are and who they are becoming.

While Helen eventually followed in our father's legal tracks, I followed a different path. When he ran for the Alabama Leg- islature in 1954, he promised Alabamians better services for the aged, the disabled, and children of the state. His compassionate influence led me to become a trained social worker. Through my professional career, I have worked in just about all of the areas where he had concerns. I worked with socially maladjusted chil- dren as a school social worker, as Director of Social Services in a rehabilitation hospital, and as Social Work Coordinator for clients released from mental institutions. For the past twenty-five years, I have been employed at the Jefferson County Office of Senior Citizens Services, where I am presently the Executive Director. I have found great joy in my life when I can serve others. Each day I pray for strength that God will continue to use me in empowering and helping others. I know my parents would be proud.

My life has been a journey, one that I would not change even if I could. I have experienced some bitterness in life, but then I have enjoyed the sweetness of life that always comes. The early events in my life and the love from my parents helped shape me into the person I am today. I was blessed to have such wonderful parents. As I continue my journey in life, I do so with confidence, courage, and strength to do good and make my parents and family proud. It is my prayer that I can continue to be a blessing to others.

Two Congressional Records Citing the Work of Arthur D. Shores

United States of America Congressional Record, Proceedings and Debates of the 97th Congress, Second Session, Washington, Tuesday, May 18, 1982, Vol. 128, No. 60.

Senate: "National Bar Association Honors Attorney Arthur D. Shores, Alabama's Black Pioneer in Civil Rights Litigation."

"Mr. Heflin, Mr. President. I rise today to commend the National Bar Association for its decision to honor Alabama's black pioneer civil rights attorney, the Honorable Arthur D. Shores.... Mr. President, Attorney Shores has been called affectionately by one of his legal protégés, 'the dean of black lawyers in the State of Alabama.' I would guess that he is so called by them because he taught all black lawyers admitted to practice in Alabama during the 1950s and early 1960s how to practice law. According to Attorney Shores, himself, during the period roughly between 1940 and 1950 he was the only black practicing attorney in the State of Alabama. He was the lone voice in the wilderness defending the civil rights of black people.

"During the first 20 years of his now 45-year-old law practice, Attorney Shores practiced all over the State of Alabama—from the Tennessee line to the Gulf of Mexico at Mobile Bay, and from the Mississippi borders to the Georgia limits. As I saw previously, he was and is a champion of blacks and their civil rights.

"Mr. President, there is one thing about Attorney Shores that a fellow lawyer might find perplexing. That is, how can a lawyer who has a wife and family not worry about collecting his share of an attorney's fee from another lawyer who has associated him on a case that requires countless hours of work? Also, how can he never refuse to help a younger lawyer try case after case, year in and year out and never worry about a fee?

"Mr. President, such was the nature of Attorney Shores during the training period in the lives of all the young black lawyers who sought the technical assistance and expertise of Attorney Shores.

"Now, Mr. President, there is one extremely commendable attribute of Attorney Shores from which we legislators ought to take heed. It is my understanding that no matter where in the State that Attorney Shores would travel—from coast to coast or wherever, he always would find the courage and stamina to drive back to his home in Birmingham, Alabama, to be with his family at night.

"You see, Mr. President, Attorney Shores practiced civil rights law all over the State of Alabama during an era in which his life was in constant jeopardy. His home in Birmingham, Alabama, was bombed so many times [*sic*] [only bombed twice] during the civil rights movement that the hill on which it sat came to be known as Dynamite Hill.

"Attorney Shores was counsel for all civil rights cases in the State of Alabama for approximately 19 or 20 years. He represented U.S. Senator Glen Taylor of Idaho in City of Birmingham against Taylor. He was chief counsel in the case of Autherine Lucy against University of Alabama, and counsel in the following famous cases: Dr. Martin Luther King, Jr., and others, in the Montgomery bus boycott prosecutions; State of Alabama against NAACP; F. L. Shuttlesworth and others against City of Birmingham, and Birmingham Transit Co.; Vivian J. Malone against University of Alabama; equalization of Negro teachers' salaries in Jefferson County, Alabama, and Columbia, S.C.; and United States Steele against L&N Railroad, and others.

"Attorney Shores is a deeply religious family man. He is married to the former Theodora Helen Warren. They have two lovely daughters: Helen Shores Lee and Barbara Shores Larkin.

"Mr. President I ask unanimous consent that a more in-depth biographical sketch of Attorney Shores be printed in full in the Record.

"Mr. President, as we can see, Attorney Shores, still practicing law in his seventies, is truly an outstanding lawyer. He is held in very high esteem not only in the State of Alabama, but also in this country as well. I salute him and congratulate him on his very fine and distinguished accomplishments."[1]

[The Congressional Record also included a biographical sketch of Arthur Davis Shores, A.B., L.L.B., L.L.D., L.H.D.]

United States of America Congressional Record, Proceedings and Debates of the 100th Congress, Second Session, Washington, Friday, September 30, 1988, Vol. 134, No. 137.

"Arthur D. Shores—Living Legacy Award Recipient."

"Mr. Shelby. Mr. President, it is with a great deal of pleasure that I ask my colleagues in the Senate to recognize with me not only an exceptional Alabamian, but an outstanding American as well.

"Arthur D. Shores of Birmingham has been selected as a 1988 recipient of the 'Living Legacy Award' by the National Caucus and Center on Black Aged. Mr. Shores will be honored at a banquet here in Washington on October 13, 1988.

"The Living Legacy Program was established in 1979 by the National Caucus and Center on Black Aged to honor older black Americans who have made important contributions to their communities.

"Arthur Shores more than meets those qualifications. For over 50 years, Arthur D. Shores has used his knowledge of the law, his skill and legal expertise as an advocate for blacks in Alabama. Working as a legal advocate during the early period in the civil rights movement, Shores made his mark as the only black practicing attorney in the State of Alabama and the only attorney defending the civil rights of black people.

"Arthur Shores has left a remarkable legacy in the many cases he was involved in — cases that helped pave the way for real changes under the law. He was responsible for successfully filing a case for voting rights in Birmingham; he fought for and won pay equity for black teachers in Jefferson County, Alabama.

"Arthur Shores worked on behalf of many people. Vivian Malone, F. L. Shuttlesworth, Autherine Lucy, and the Reverend Dr. Martin Luther King, Jr., were some of the clients he helped achieve victory for in their fight for equal rights.

"Mr. Shores' civil rights work on behalf of all Alabamians is his living legacy for our State. This award is a tribute to the change that he was not only a part of, but made happen.

"In addition to his unparalleled legal career, Mr. Shores' commitment to his community extended into the realm of civic and charitable endeavors. The Salvation Army, the Birmingham Urban League, and the YMCA, are just a few organizations that have benefitted by his participation.

Arthur Shores embodies the very characteristics that identify the American spirit — faith, courage, and determination. He is a most fitting and worthy recipient of the Living Legacy Award and a source of great pride for the entire State of Alabama. It is my pleasure to serve as his Senator in Washington."[2]

Lifetime Awards, Honors, Services, and Accomplishments of Arthur D. Shores

Memberships in Professional Organizations

American Bar Association (1937)

National Bar Association

Alabama Bar Association

Birmingham Bar Association

United States Supreme Court Bar Association (1943)

Presidents Club of Alabama

Alpha Phi Alpha Fraternity

Delta Phi Theta Legal Fraternity

Sigma Pi Phi (Boule)

Thirty-third degree Mason, Knight of Phythias

Awards and Honors

Southern Beauty Congress, Inc. Award for Eminent Leadership in Field of Civil Rights (1940)

Omega Psi Phi Fraternity Award for outstanding achievement in the field of Civil Rights (1948)

Omega Psi Phi Fraternity Award for Outstanding Lawyer in the Fight for Civil Rights (1954)

Most Ordinary Distinguished and Meritorious Alpha Medal of Honor

C. Francis Stradford Award of the National Bar Association for Inspiration to Fellow Lawyers and Rich Contributions to the Legal Profession (1960)

Cook County, Illinois Bar Association; For Twenty-Five Years of Outstanding Service in Legal Profession (1965)

National Newspaper Publishing Association's Russwurm Award for recognition of outstanding achievement and making possible a richer concept of Democratic Principles and Contributions for upholding those highest traditions considered as the ideal of the American Way of Life (1969).

Pioneer's Success Award from Jefferson State Junior College (1971)

Distinguished Service Award from the Black Lawyers Association (1977)

United Church Board for Homeland Ministries Award for Service (1977)

Humanitarian Award by the National and Research Center

Eddie Fisher Award by the Alabama Association of Colleges and Universities

Alabama Academy of Honor (1980)

Alabama Lawyers' Hall of Fame

Honors and Listings in Professional Journals

Who's Who in Commerce and Industry

Who's Who in American Politics

Who's Who in South and Southland

Who's Who in Negro America

Library of Alabama Lives

International Year Book & Statesman's Who's Who

Offices and Active Memberships

Vice President and General Counsel for Citizens Federal Savings and Loan Association

Secretary-Treasurer of the United Service Association

Housing Commission of the City of Birmingham

Birmingham City Council

Birmingham Chamber of Commerce

Commissioner, Birmingham Housing Authority (1965–1969)

Jefferson County and State Democratic Committees

Chairman of the Board of Trustees, Talladega College

Board of Directors, A. G. Gaston Boys Club

Board of Directors, Operation New Birmingham

Birmingham Urban League (Chairman of the Board and President)

Lawyers' Committee for Civil Rights (formed by President John F. Kennedy)[1]

Honorary Staff of Attorney General of Alabama (appointed by Attorney General Bill Baxley)

Board of Directors, Birmingham Festival of Art

The National Council of Christians and Jews

The Advisory Board of the Salvation Army

Delegate to the National Democratic Convention in 1968, 1972, and 1976

Member of the Judicial Commission for the U.S. Fifth Circuit Court of Appeals (appointed by President Jimmy Carter)

General Counsel, Miles College

General Counsel, Talladega College

General Counsel, Free and Accepted Masons of Alabama

Board member, National Bank of Commerce

Sunday school teacher and moderator, First Congregational Church

Board of Homeland Ministries, United Church of Christ

International Conference on Religion, Art, and Architecture in Jerusalem (1973)

Member, State Democratic Committee

Member, Executive Committee of Charter Commission of the National Democratic Committee

Honorary Degrees

Doctor of Law, Daniel Payne College, Birmingham, AL (1956)

Doctor of Law, Miles College (1971)

Doctor of Humane Letters, University of Alabama (1975)

Talladega College (1980)

Special Remembrances

Arthur D. Shores Hall constructed at Talladega College (1974)

Arthur D. Shores Law Center in Birmingham, AL (1996)

Arthur Shores Drive (a street in Birmingham named after Shores)

Arthur D. Shores Park (a park in Birmingham named after Shores)

Copies of Important Letters to or from Arthur D. Shores

The following pages contain some of the many letters that Arthur D. Shores received or wrote over the course of his illustrious career.

NATIONAL ASSOCIATION FOR THE ADVANCEMENT OF COLORED PEOPLE

69 FIFTH AVENUE, NEW YORK
TELEPHONE: ALgonquin 4-3551

Official Organ: The Crisis

May 12, 1942

Arthur D. Shores, Esquire
1630 Fourth Avenue North
Birmingham, Alabama

Dear Shores:

In reply to your letter of May 11, I will be busy the week of May 18 in Washington and in Little Rock, Arkansas, on our teachers' salary case there which is set for argument on Motion to Dismiss on May 20. I will be at the Annual Meeting of the Maryland State Conference of Branches in Baltimore on May 23. These are the only definite dates I have at the present time.

Please let me know your date as soon as you get it, in order that there may be no conflict with other cases.

Sincerely,

Thurgood Marshall

TM/gj

BY AIR MAIL

33rd ANNUAL CONFERENCE, LOS ANGELES, CALIF., July 14-19, 1942

NATIONAL ASSOCIATION FOR THE ADVANCEMENT OF COLORED PEOPLE

69 FIFTH AVENUE, NEW YORK

TELEPHONE: ALGONQUIN 4-3551

Official Organ: The Crisis

June 10, 1942

Arthur D. Shores, Esquire
1630 Fourth Avenue North
Birmingham, Alabama

Dear Shores:

I have just returned to the office and find your letter of May 30 concerning Bolden's induction into the Army.

I think you should exhaust the appeal, and then if the rules permit, appeal to the President. In other words, Bolden's case should be appealed just as far as possible.

Enclosed herewith is copy of my letter to Walter S. Smith re the Frank Johnson case, for your information.

Sincerely,

Thurgood Marshall
Special Counsel

TM/gj
enclosure

BY AIR MAIL

33rd ANNUAL CONFERENCE, LOS ANGELES, CALIF., July 14-19, 1942

N. A. A. C. P. LEGAL DEFENSE AND EDUCATIONAL FUND, INC.

69 FIFTH AVENUE, NEW YORK 3, N. Y.

June 20, 1944

Arthur D. Shores, Esq.
1630 Fourth Avenue North
Birmingham, Alabama

Dear Shores:

Please let me know what is happening in the registration cases being set for trial.

If the judge is not of a mind to set the cases for trial, I still think you should apply for a <u>writ of mandamus</u>.

Sincerely yours,

Thurgood

Thurgood Marshall
Special Counsel

TM:AG
uopwa-19
cio

N. A. A. C. P. LEGAL DEFENSE AND EDUCATIONAL FUND. INC.

69 FIFTH AVENUE, NEW YORK 3, N. Y.

April 4, 1945

Arthur D. Shores, Esq.
1630 Fourth Avenue, No.
Birmingham, Ala.

Dear Shores:

The date on the Charleston, S. C., Teachers case has been changed to May 9th. I am giving you this information because I told you before that the date was April 23rd.

Incidentally, the Susie Morris Teachers Salary Case in Little Rock will be argued in the Circuit Court of Appeals in St. Paul, Minnesota May 7th.

We are arranging to argue the LeFlore case on the 16th.

Sincerely yours,

Thurgood Marshall
Special Counsel

TM:GS
uopwa-19-CIO

STATE OF ALABAMA
JEFFERSON COUNTY

This Agreement made and entered into on this _11th_ day of November, 1958, by and between the ALABAMA CHRISTIAN MOVEMENT FOR HUMAN RIGHTS, hereinafter known as Party of the First Part, and ARTHUR D. SHORES, hereinafter known as party of the Second Part,

WITNESSETH:

1. Party of the First Part hereby retains and employs Party of the Second Part, as Attorney for and in behalf of the following persons, namely: Lillie Boman, James C. Suttles, Joe Hendricks, Jim Hendricks, Roberta Brinson, Rev. J. S. Phifer, Johnny C. Collins, Annie Burkley, Doris J. Burrell, Alfred Thomas and Rev. F. L. Shuttlesworth, to represent the abovenamed parties and all Negroes in the City of Birmingham, in an action in the Federal Court, to have declared unconstitutional the application of Ordinance 1487-F, and its application to the abovenamed parties and all Negroes similarly situated, and have the City restrained from enforcing said Ordinance.

2. It is further agreed that Party of the Second Part accepts the employment of party of the First part on the following terms and conditions: Party of the First Part agrees to pay to the Party of the Second Part the sum of Fifteen Hundred ($1500.00) Dollars for representing Parties of the First Part, and the abovenamed persons in a class action in the United States District Court.

3. It is further agreed that Party of the First Part will make payments as follows: On execution of this Contract the sum of Seven Hundred Fifty ($750.00) Dollars; the balance of Seven Hundred Fifty ($750.00) Dollars to be paid on or before ~~sixty (60) days~~ a hearing on the Merits of said Cause ~~from the date of the execution of this Contract.~~

4. It is further agreed that in the event the City of Birmingham repeals said Ordinance, prior to the first hearing of this matter, and no further litigation is required; Party of the Second Part agrees to cancel the remaining fee of Seven Hundred Fifty ($750.00) Dollars.

5. It is further agreed that Party of the First Part will pay the expense of the proceedings.

IN WITNESS WHEREOF, We have hereunto set our hands and seals this _____ day of November, 1958.

ALABAMA CHRISTIAN MOVEMENT FOR HUMAN RIGHTS

By: _____
        F. L. Shuttlesworth, President

_____
        N. H. SMITH, SECRETARY

PARTY OF THE FIRST PART

_____
        ARTHUR D. SHORES
PARTY OF THE SECOND PART.

April 9, 1959

Rev. F. L. Shuttlesworth, President
A.C.M. H. R.
3191 North 29th Street
Birmingham, Alabama

Dear Rev. Shuttlesworth:

I wish to acknowledge receipt of your letter of April 7, in which you make inquiry relative to certain cases, for which I am Legal Counsel. I regret that I will not be able to meet with your Board to discuss these matters, however, I shall take this means to give you the information.

The first Bus case known as: Viola Cherry, et al, vs. J. W. Morgan, et al; this case, as you know, is on appeal in the United States Circuit Court of Appeals. The Transcript of Record and Briefs have been filed, and the case is set for submission before the Court on Tuesday, May 19. I herewith enclose a copy of the Brief in the case.

As to the second Bus Case known as, Lillie Boman, et al vs. James W. Morgan, et al, is at issue in the United States Federal District Court, and awaiting a date for trial. It is my hope that it may be set down on the next civil docket. Within the next week or ten days, I may have further information on this case.

As to the fourteen cases known as, Doris Burrell, et al, vs. City of Birmingham; an appeal has been perfected in the Alabama Court of Appeals and the Transcript has been prepared.

Page 2
Rev. F. L. Shuttlesworth
April 9, 1959

Mr. Billingsley, with whom I am associated in this case, and I are in the process of preparing Assignments of Error, which will be attached to the Transcript, after which the Transcript will be sent down to the Court of Appeals, and we will have thirty (30) days in which to prepare a Brief.

From the standpoint of finally obtaining the hearing in the Court of Appeals, there is a possibility that it will not be heard before November of this year.

I trust this is the information you desire. I will be happy to answer any further questions.

Yours very truly,

Arthur D. Shores

ADS/ans

Enclosure.

March 5, 1960

Attorney Hubert T. Delany
Attorney Fred D. Gray
Attorney W. R. Ming
Attorney Arthur D. Shores
Attorney S. S. Seay, Jr.

Gentlemen:

In further reference to our conversations and under-
standings of the past two weeks, I desire to formally
confirm the fact that I have retained each of you to
jointly represent me in connection with the case of
the State of Alabama against Martin Luther King, Jr.,
and any other actions you think it wise to take in my
behalf relating to income tax matters as they may affect
me or the State of Alabama.

Very sincerely yours,

Martin Luther King, Jr.

MLK:mlb

Committee to Defend Martin Luther King, Jr.
and the Struggle for Freedom in the South

312 WEST 125th STREET ● NEW YORK 27, NEW YORK ● UNIVERSITY 6-1700

CHAIRMEN
A. PHILIP RANDOLPH
Rev. GARDNER TAYLOR

TREASURER
NAT KING COLE

CHAIRMEN, CULTURAL DIVISION
HARRY BELAFONTE
SIDNEY POITIER

CHAIRMEN, CHURCH DIVISION
Father GEORGE B. FORD
Rev. THOMAS KILGORE, Jr.
Rabbi EDWARD E. KLEIN

CHAIRMAN, LABOR DIVISION
MORRIS IUSHEWITZ

CHAIRMAN, STUDENT DIVISION
BERNARD LEE
*President, Montgomery
Student Protest Committee*

Rev. Ralph Abernathy
Willoughby Abner
Stella Adler
Hon. Raymond Pace Alexander
Orris Austin
Daisy Bates
Rev. John Bennett
Algernon Black
Marlon Brando
Councilman Earl Brown
Mrs. Ralph Bunche
Rev. Allan Knight Chalmers
Dorothy Dandridge
Sammy Davie, Jr.
Rev. Philip P. Elliott
Rev. Harry Emerson Fosdick
Anthony Franciosa
Lorraine Hansberry
Rev. Donald Harrington
Van Heflin
Rev. Richard Hildebrand
Mahalia Jackson
Rev. T. J. Jemison
Rev. Mordecai Johnson
Eartha Kitt
Rabbi Edward E. Klein
Russell Lasley
Rev. J. Oscar Lee
Viveca Lindfors
David Livingston
Rev. O. Clay Maxwell, Sr.
Rev. Matthew D. McCollom
William Michelson
Carl Murphy
A. J. Muste
Shad Polier
C. B. Powell, M.D.
John Raitt
Rev. Sandy Ray
Elmer Rice
Cleveland Robinson
Jackie Robinson
Mrs. Ray Robinson
Robert Ryan
Rev. F. L. Shuttlesworth
Rev. C. K. Steele
Hope Stevens
Norman Thomas
Harry Van Arsdale
Max Youngstein
Committee Incomplete

BAYARD RUSTIN
EXECUTIVE DIRECTOR

STANLEY D. LEVISON
ASSISTANT EXECUTIVE DIRECTOR

May 13, 1960

Mr. Arthur D. Shores
c/o Attorney Fred D. Gray
34 North Perry Street
Montgomery, Alabama

Dear Mr. Shores:

I trust that you have received by now the memorandum which Gardner Taylor and I sent you a few days ago. I sincerely hope that you will give every consideration to the proposals therein outlined and let me know what your decision is at your earliest convenience.

I want to thank you for the consideration I am sure each of you, individually and collectively, will give to this request made on behalf of our Committee.

Sincerely,

A. PHILIP RANDOLPH

APR/tk

Judge Helen Shores Lee

Judge Helen Shores Lee serves as Circuit Judge in the Tenth Judicial Circuit of Alabama. She graduated from Fisk University (1962), Pepperdine University (1971), and Cumberland School of Law (1987). From 1987 to 1995 she worked with the law firm Shores, Lee, Sparks, Atha & Choy. From 1995 to 2002 she worked in the Birmingham law firm Shores and Lee. She became an Alabama Circuit Judge in 2003.

Before she became a lawyer, Helen Shores Lee worked as a Director of Consultation and Education (1977-80) and Director of Clinical Outreach Services (1980-84) with Birmingham's Jefferson County Department of Health, Western Mental Health Center. From 1972 to 1977, Lee was an Instructor of Clinical Psychology in the Department of Psychiatry at the University of Alabama in Birmingham. She has also served as a counselor with T. A. Lawson State Junior College in Birmingham; a resident advisor with a Los Angeles (CA) Job Corps Center for Women; a field director with the Los Angeles Girl Scouts Council; and a teacher and counselor at the Institute of Child Study in Los Angeles.

Judge Lee is a member of numerous organizations, including the American Bar Association, the Alabama Bar Association, the Birmingham Bar Association, the Magic City Bar Association, Phi Alpha Delta International Law Fraternity, and the National Bar Association.

Her current community activities include Board of Trustees, Leadership Birmingham; Chair of Minority Health Research Center Advisory Counsel at the University of Alabama Medical Center; Cumberland School of Law Advisory Board; Board of Directors,

Blue Cross Blue Shield; Board of Trustees, First Congregational Christian Church; and Board of Directors, Campfire, Inc.

Her past memberships include National Board of Governors of the American Red Cross; Chairperson of Alabama Ethics Commission; Birmingham Airport Authority Director; and a member of the Board of Directors for the Birmingham Museum of Art, AmSouth Bank, the Civil Rights Institute, Blue Cross Blue Shield, United Way, United Cerebral Palsy, Young Women's Christian Association, American Red Cross (Birmingham Chapter), and the A. G. Gaston Boys Club.

She has been married to Bob Lee for fifty years. They have three children and five grandchildren.

Barbara Sylvia Shores

Barbara Sylvia Shores graduated from Talladega College (BA, 1966) and the University of Illinois (MSW, 1968). She is the Executive Director for the Jefferson County Office of Senior Citizens Services, Birmingham, Alabama. She served as Assistant Director for the Office of Senior Citizens Services from 1995 to 2011. She was Nutrition Project Coordinator from 1986 to 1995.

Other positions include Director of Social Services, Lakeshore Rehabilitation Complex, Birmingham (1980–86); Coordinator of Aftercare Services, Jefferson County Health Department–Western Mental Health Center, Birmingham (1977–80); Project Director for Homemaker Services for Children, Children's Aid Society, Birmingham (1976–77); Social Worker, Champaign Community School System, Champaign, Illinois (1970–76); and a Medical Social Worker with Spain Rehabilitation Center, Birmingham.

Barbara co-authored "A Second Look at Educating the Disadvantaged Youth" (*Illinois School Journal*) and "A Value Clarification Group in the Junior High School" (National Association of School Psychologists). Her current board memberships include Children's Aid Society, Birmingham Historical Society, OASIS, Alabama Health Quality Network, and Resource Center for Minority Aging Research. Barbara's past organizations include National Association of the Advancement of Colored People (NAACP), Metro Chapter; Les June Dames; Alpha Kappa Alpha Sorority; Birmingham Chapter of Links, Inc., Alabama; Gerontology Society; and the Greater Birmingham Humane Society.

Barbara's speaking engagements on civil rights history and aging problems have included elementary, middle, and high schools; universities; churches; women's and men's conferences; Civil Rights Institute; and social and civic organizations.

Barbara is the proud mother of twins, Danielle Renee Shores Larkin and Damien Laurent Shores Larkin.

Sources

CHAPTER 1: "Why, Daddy?"

1. J. Clay Smith Jr., *Emancipation: The Making of the Black Lawyer 1844–1944* (Philadelphia: University of Pennsylvania Press, 1999), 274.

2. Quoted from Shores's handwritten papers.

CHAPTER 4: The Public Reacts to the Bombing

1. Diane McWhorter, *Carry Me Home* (New York: Simon & Schuster, 2001), 482.

2. Quoted from an actual letter intended to be a news release.

CHAPTER 5: Lightning Strikes Twice

1. Governor George Wallace's press secretary, Bill Jones, in a statement authorized by the chief executive. "School Desegregation Continues Here Today," *Birmingham News*, 5 September 1963, 2.

2. "Two Negro Students Register Quietly at Graymont," *Birmingham Post-Herald*, 5 September 1963, 1.

CHAPTER 7: Our Father's Early Years

1. Found at http://www.jsums.edu/history/Voices/Voices_From_A_Shared_Past_-_Sustaining%20the%20Infrastructure%20of%20Public%20Education.html.

CHAPTER 8: The Early Practice

1. Houston, a Harvard Law School graduate, in the 1920s researched the entire South and found "fewer than 100 black lawyers serving nine million black people" (http://newsreel.org/transcripts/roadtob.htm).

2. From the *Weekly Review 66-Year Exposition Editor*, "Pass Alabama Bar," no newspaper name or date. Believed 1937, the year Shores passed the Bar.

3. Mr. Karl Friedman in a personal interview with Judge Lee, 2011.

CHAPTER 9: Standing Up to Be Counted

1. *The Revised Statute of the United States, Second Edition.* Chapter 7, of section 5507.

2. Found at http://www.nytimes.com/1997/02/03/us/w-c-patton-84-alabama-voice-for-black-voters.html.

3. From notes for a speech dated September 18, 1985.

4. Quoted from "Negroes Ask Adequate Education, Privileges," *Birmingham Post*, 22 September 1942, n.p.

5. "Judge Turns Down Writ of Mandamus: Shores Begins Attack On Voting Discrimination," *Birmingham World*, 20 June 1939, n.p.

6. Quoted from "Two Vote Cases To Be Reviewed," *Birmingham Herald*, 28 January 1947, n.p.

7. Quoted from "Negro Charges Racial Bias by Registrars," *Birmingham Post*, 22 August 1944, n.p.

8. Letter by Alonzo G. Moron, president of the Eta Lambda Chapter, to A. R. Shores, April 29, 1942.

CHAPTER 10: The Communist "Red" Scare

1. James R. Bennett, *Historic Birmingham & Jefferson County: An Illustrated History* (San Antonio, TX: Historical Publishing Network, 2008), 120–21.

CHAPTER 11: The Case That Changed Everything

1. Glenn T. Eskew, *But for Birmingham* (Chapel Hill: University of North Carolina Press, 1997), 92.

CHAPTER 12: The Rape

1. Eskew, *But for Birmingham*, 61–62.

CHAPTER 14: The Fight to Equalize Salaries for Black Teachers

1. From Negro Year Book (1941–1946) found at www.archive.org/stream/negro yearbookrev00guzmrich/negroyearbookrev00guzmrich_djvu.txt.

2. From information found at http://www.nber.org/chapters/c8794.pdf.

3. *Gainer v. School Board of Jefferson County*, 135 F. Supp 559, 566 (No. District of Al. 1955).

4. The NAACP Legal Defense Fund and the Development of Civil Rights Law in Alabama 1940–1980. Judge U. W. Clemons, U.S. District Court, N. D. of Alabama.

CHAPTER 15: Working on the Railroad

1. Found at http://newsreel.org/transcripts/roadtob.htm.

2. For more information, see http://www.lnrr.org/.

3. For this and other information about this case, see http://www.brownat50 .org/brownCases/PreBrownCases/SteelevLouisvilleRY1944.html.

4. "Railroad Fireman Seeks $50,000 Over Seniority Rights," *Pittsburg Courier*, 6 September 1941, n.p.

5. Found at http://www.brownat50.org/brownCases/PreBrownCases/Steelev LouisvilleRY1944.html.

6. Found at http://scholar.google.com/scholar_case?case=2085483146830516389 &q=Steele+v.+Louisville+%26+N.+R.+Co.,+323+U.S.+192+(1944)&hl=en&as_sdt =2,1&as_vis=1.

7. Found at http://aclu.procon.org/view.resource.php?resourceID=338.

8. Found at http://www.law.ua.edu/pubs/lrarticles/Volume52/Issue4/Clemon.pdf.

9. *Steele v. Louisville & Nashville Railroad*, 323 U.S. 192 (1944).

CHAPTER 16: The Continuing Voting Rights Battle: Mitchell v. Wright

1. "Vote Denial Because of Race Denied by Former Registrars," *Montgomery Advertiser*, 7 December 1946, n.p.

2. The case was *Mitchell v. Wright*, 154 F>2d 924 (1946).

3. Information about this case can be found at http://www.washburnlaw.edu/ wlj/50-1/articles/entin-jonathan.pdf.

4. See http://www.washburnlaw.edu/wlj/50-1/articles/entin-jonathan.pdf.

5. *Gomillion v. Lightfoot*, 364 U.S. 339 (1960).

CHAPTER 17: Unfair Zoning Laws

1. *Buchanan v. Warley*, 245 U.S. 60, 38 S. Ct. 16, 62 L. Ed. 149.

2. Eskew, *But for Birmingham*, 53.

3. *City Birmingham v. Monk*, 185 F2d859 (1950), U.S. Court of Appeals 5th Circuit.

4. Found at http://openjurist.org/185/f2d/859/city-of-birmingham-v-monk.

5. Eskew, *But for Birmingham*, 79.

CHAPTER 20: Bull Connor Arrests Senator Taylor

1. As quoted by the *Birmingham Herald* in "Editorial Round-Up," 15 May 1948, n.p.

2. Ibid.

3. Ibid.

4. John J. Abt to Shores, December 8, 1948.

5. "Taylor Loses Non-Jury Trial Plea—Judge Rules Segregation Test Is Out," *Birmingham Post*, 30 March 1949, front page.

CHAPTER 21: The Problem with Segregated Schools—
   Brown v. Board of Education

1. *Plessy v. Ferguson*, U.S. Supreme Court (1986): quoted from www.lawnix.com/cases/plessy-ferguson.html.

2. See http://caselaw.lp.findlaw.com/cgi-bin/getcase.pl?court=US&vol=347&invol=483.

3. *Brown v. Board of Education*, 347 U.S. 483 (1954), plus *Briggs et al. v. Elliott et al., Members of Board of Trustees of School District #22; Davis et al. v. County School Board of Prince Edward County, Virginia et al.; Bolling et al. v. Sharpe et al.; Belton et al. v. Gebhart et al.; Bulah et al. v. Gebhart et al.* See www.archives.gov/education/lessons/brown-v-board/bios.html.

4. See www.civilrights.org/education/brown/briggs.html.

5. Attorneys for Briggs were Thurgood Marshall, Chief Counsel, NAACP/LDF; Robert L. Carter, NAACP/LDF; Harold R. Boulware, SC NAACP; Spottswood W. Robinson III, VA NAACP; Arthur Shores, AL NAACP; A.T. Walden, GA NAACP.

6. Found at http://caselaw.lp.findlaw.com/cgi-bin/getcase.pl?court=US&vol=347&invol=483.

7. Ibid.

8. Ibid.

9. Quoted from http://www.nps.gov/brvb/historyculture/index.htm.

CHAPTER 22: The Perfect Storm

1. Found at http://www.law.ua.edu/pubs/lrarticles/Volume52/Issue4/Clemon.pdf.

2. "Lawyer Carries A Gun," *Black Chronicle*, 1 November 1956, 3.

CHAPTER 23: The Shortage of Black Schools

1. W. H. Hollins to University of Alabama Law School, August 14, 1950. Original letter in scrapbook.

2. William F. Adams to W. H. Hollins, August 17, 1950. Original letter.

3. Carter G. Woodson in *Black Chronicle*, 1 November 1956, 4.

CHAPTER 24: Miss Autherine Lucy and the University of Alabama

1. Both of these letters are found in a scrapbook in the authors' possession.
2. Arthur Shores to John M. Gallalee, September 24, 1952.
3. "University Plans Appeal to Top Court," *Birmingham Post-Herald*, n.d. (assumed to be 1955), 2.
4. O. C. Carmichael to Arthur Shores, October 20, 1955.

CHAPTER 25: Riots Break Out on Campus

1. "Get-Out-Of-Town Warnings Reported By Negro Co-Ed," *Birmingham News*, 7 February 1956, front page. See also www.encyclopediaofalabama.org/face/Article .jsp?id=h-2489.
2. "Faculty Hears Protection Plea for University," *Birmingham Post-Herald*, 8 February 1956, front page.
3. "Mob Was Deadly, Bennett Declares — Kill Or Kidnap Was Evident Aim," *Birmingham Post-Herald*, 8 February 1956, front page.
4. "Tear Gas, Smoke Bombs Fail to Disperse Crowds," *Birmingham News*, 7 February 1956, 3.
5. Western Union telegram dated Feb. 6, 1956 in scrapbook.
6. "Shores Gives U of A 48 Hours to Reinstate Negro Student," *Birmingham News*, 7 February 1956, front page.
7. "Ike Hopes State Acts, Wants U.S. to Stay Out," *New York Post*, 8 February 1956, 3.
8. "Crowd Fills Capital Coliseum," *Birmingham Post-Herald*, 11 February 1956, front page.
9. "Three Exhibits Filed With Lucy-Hudson Suits," *Birmingham Post-Herald*, n.d., n.p.
10. "Letters to the Editor," *Black Chronicle*, 1 November 1956, 2.
11. "Negro's Fight to Attend U of A Violates Home Training, Say Parents," *Birmingham News*, 26 February 1956, n.p.
12. "Co-Ed Ordered Readmitted Monday," *Birmingham Post-Herald*, 1 March 1956, front page.
13. "Move Made After Court Orders Her Return to Classes," *Birmingham News*, 1 March 1956.
14. Quoted from "Miss Autherine Lucy Tells Of Hectic Alabama U. Crusade," *Birmingham World*, 10 February 1956, front page.
15. Found at www.answers.com/topic/autherine-lucy-foster.
16. Quoted from a letter received from Mr. Bonner by the *Tuscaloosa News*, 22 February 1956.
17. "Autherine Lucy's Attorney Assails 'Gradual' Integration In Talk Here," *Courier-Journal*, Louisville, KY, 7 May 1956, n.p.

CHAPTER 26: Montgomery's Bus Boycott

1. "Judges: The Education of Tom Brady," *Time*, 22 October 1965.
2. Eskew, *But for Birmingham*, 22.
3. See http://mlk-kpp01.stanford.edu/primarydocuments/Vol3/22-Mar-1956_ TestimonyinStateofAlabama.pdf.

CHAPTER 28: The Lillie Boman Case

1. Code quoted from the U.S. Court of Appeals for the Fifth Circuit, No. 18,187, *Lillie Boman, et al., v. Birmingham Transit Company*, appellants' brief, pp. 2a and 3a.

2. Original agreement in the files of Arthur Shores.

3. Judge Groom's actual order, found in files of Arthur D. Shores.

CHAPTER 30: The Days the Children Marched

1. Interview at http://digital.wustl.edu/eyesontheprize/browse.html.

2. Eskew, *But for Birmingham*, 100.

3. W. Edward Harris, *Miracle in Birmingham: A Civil Rights Memoir, 1954–1965* (Indianapolis: Stonework Press, 2004), 123.

CHAPTER 31: George Wallace Stands in the Schoolhouse Door

1. See www.archives.alabama.gov/govs_list/inauguralspeech.html.

2. Governor Wallace's statement and proclamation at the University of Alabama, June 11, 1963, can be found at www.archives.alabama.gov/govs_list/school door.html.

3. E. Culpepper Clark, *The Schoolhouse Door: Segregation's Last Stand at the University of Alabama* (Tuscaloosa: University of Alabama Press, 2007), 255.

4. Ibid., 18.

CHAPTER 32: Frustration and Fury in Washington

1. John F. Kennedy, "Speech on Civil Rights," in American Rhetoric, http://www .americanrhetoric.com/speeches/jfkcivilrights.htm.

2. Found at http://www.americanrhetoric.com/speeches/mlkihaveadream.html.

3. "Report on Desegregation in the Schools of Alabama," in *American Experience: The Presidents*, at http://www.pbs.org/wgbh/amex/presidents/35_kennedy/ psources/ps_deseg.html.

4. Found at http://www.time.com/time/magazine/article/0,9171,875153,00 .html.

5. "Birmingham's Moment of Crisis: A Statement of Concern and Conviction," *Birmingham News*, Sunday, 20 October 1963, A–9.

CHAPTER 33: Holidays after a Long Hot Summer

1. Found at http://faculty.smu.edu/dsimon/Change-CivRts2b.html.

CHAPTER 34: 1965: Marching toward Freedom

1. Lyndon B. Johnson, "Voting Rights Bill Address, March 15, 1965," can be found at http://www.hpol.org/lbj/voting/.

2. Quoting *Yick Wo v. Hopkins*, 118 U.S. 356 (1886), at http://www.thefree library.com/Trials+Without+Truth.-a063503422.

3. Joe Campbell, "Disaster Lurked inside Little Green Boxes," *Birmingham News*, Monday, 22 March 1965, 4.

CHAPTER 35: Birmingham in 1968: Becoming a New City

1. Arthur D. Shores, "Dean of Black Lawyers in the State of Alabama," inscribed on the Marker on 5th Avenue North, Birmingham, Alabama, on the Arthur D. Shores Law Center Building.

2. From an Arthur Shores interview on July 17, 1974, found at http://docsouth .unc.edu/sohp/A-0021/A-0021.html.

3. Gene Wortsman, "Arthur Shores Says He's Out To Win Seat In Legislature Of Alabama," *Birmingham Post-Herald*, 10 February 1954.

CHAPTER 36: Our Father's Political Dreams Finally Come True

1. "Birmingham Puts Negro on Council," *New York Times*, 5 December 1968, 34.

2. "Shores to Seek Election," *Birmingham News*, 9 September 1969, n.p.

3. "Four Council Incumbents Re-elected," *Birmingham News*, 15 October 1969, 66.

4. Found at http://www.encyclopediaofalabama.org/face/Article.jsp?id=h–1644.

CHAPTER 37: Arthur Davis Shores and the Chaotic
1968 Democratic Convention

1. James Free, "Shores Stands Tall Among Loyal Demos," *Birmingham New Convention and Political Special*, 26 August 1968, 21.

2. Found at http://www.smithsonianmag.com/history-archaeology/1968-democratic-convention.html.

3. Found at http://encyclopedia.jrank.org/articles/pages/4458/Shores-Arthur-Davis-1904-1996.html.

4. Richard "Dick" Pizitz, in a personal interview with Judge Helen Shores Lee, June 2011.

5. "A Pioneer Passes," *New York Times*, 21 December 1996. See http://www .nytimes.com/1996/12/21/opinion/a-pioneer-passes.html.

CHAPTER 38: Final Days

1. Arthur D. Shores, "Dean of Black Lawyers in the State of Alabama," inscribed on the Marker on 5th Avenue North, Birmingham, Alabama, on the Arthur D. Shores Law Center Building.

APPENDIX 1: Two Congressional Records Citing
the Work of Arthur Shores

1. Congressional Record, Proceedings and Debates of the 97th Congress, Second Session, Washington, Tuesday, 18 May 1982, Vol. 128, No. 60.

2. Congressional Record, Proceedings and Debates of the 100th Congress, Second Session, Washington, Friday, 30 September 1988, Vol. 134, No. 137.

APPENDIX 2: Lifetime Awards, Honors, Services, and
Accomplishments of Arthur Davis Shores

1. William G. Weart, "100 Lawyers Join New Rights Group," *New York Times*, 11 July 1963, 17.

Share Your Thoughts

With the Author: Your comments will be forwarded to the author when you send them to *zauthor@zondervan.com*.

With Zondervan: Submit your review of this book by writing to *zreview@zondervan.com*.

Free Online Resources at

www.zondervan.com

Zondervan AuthorTracker: Be notified whenever your favorite authors publish new books, go on tour, or post an update about what's happening in their lives at www.zondervan.com/authortracker.

Daily Bible Verses and Devotions: Enrich your life with daily Bible verses or devotions that help you start every morning focused on God. Visit www.zondervan.com/newsletters.

Free Email Publications: Sign up for newsletters on Christian living, academic resources, church ministry, fiction, children's resources, and more. Visit www.zondervan.com/newsletters.

Zondervan Bible Search: Find and compare Bible passages in a variety of translations at www.zondervanbiblesearch.com.

Other Benefits: Register to receive online benefits like coupons and special offers, or to participate in research.

ZONDERVAN.com/
AUTHORTRACKER
follow your favorite authors